For Gold and Glory

INDIANA
University Press

Bloomington & Indianapolis

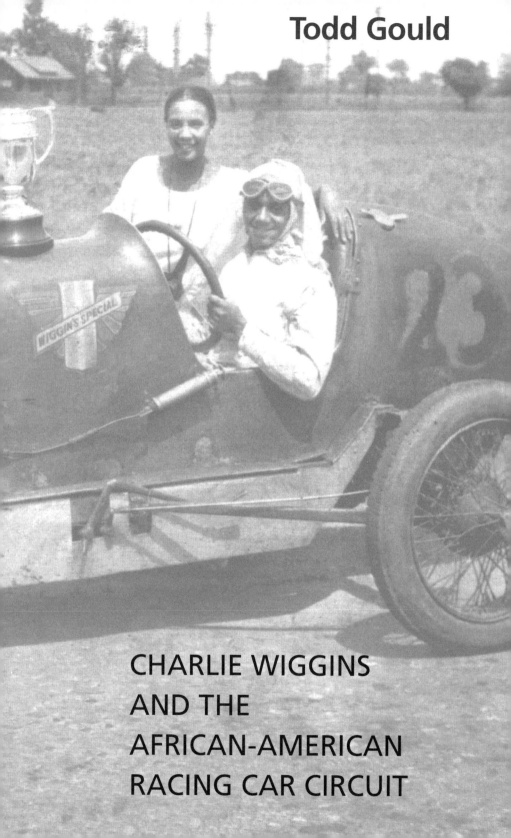

Todd Gould

CHARLIE WIGGINS
AND THE
AFRICAN-AMERICAN
RACING CAR CIRCUIT

GV
1033.5
.G65
G68
2002

This book is a publication of

Indiana University Press
601 North Morton Street
Bloomington, Indiana 47404-3797 USA

http://iupress.indiana.edu

Telephone orders   800-842-6796
Fax orders   812-855-7931
Orders by e-mail   iuporder@indiana.edu

The paper used in this publication meets the minimum
requirements of American National Standard for Information
Sciences—Permanence of Paper for Printed Library
Materials, ANSI Z39.48-1984.

Printed in Canada

Library of Congress Cataloging-in-Publication Data

Gould, Todd, date
   For gold and glory : Charlie Wiggins and the African-American
racing car circuit / Todd Gould.
      p.   cm.
   Includes bibliographical references (p.   ) and index.
      ISBN 0-253-34133-7 (alk. paper)
      1. Gold and Glory Sweepstakes (Automobile race)   2. Wiggins,
Charlie.   3. Automobile racing drivers—United States—Biography.
4. African American automobile racing drivers—United States—
Biography.   I. For gold and glory (Television program)   II. Title.
   GV1033.5.G65 G68 2002
   796.72'092—dc21
                                                                2002004211

1   2   3   4   5   07   06   05   04   03   02

148984522

To **Melissa** and **Nathan**
My joy. My strength. My inspiration.
Thank you!

and

To Mrs. Mildred Overton and Mrs. Betty Smith-Beecher
Thank you for graciously sharing your family's
wonderful story with me.

May the legacy of Charlie and Roberta Wiggins
live on to inspire others as it has me.

Contents

Acknowledgments

It was a clear, warm day in May 1996 when I stepped out of my car and headed to a strange house on Indianapolis Avenue in Indianapolis, Indiana. For two years I had been tracking down information for a television documentary segment that was to be featured on an upcoming episode of a weekly PBS magazine series. The program I was researching and producing highlighted a fascinating and little-known piece of American history: the Gold and Glory Sweepstakes, part of a professional auto racing circuit for African-American drivers and mechanics, held throughout the midwestern United States during the 1920s and '30s.

During my initial research one name kept popping up—Charlie Wiggins, a talented African-American mechanic from Indianapolis and a four-time champion of the Gold and Glory Sweepstakes. The few people still alive who had worked and raced with Charlie remembered him as a hero in the black community, and as a champion for civil rights in the same way Jesse Owens or Jackie Robinson would later become. I knew that Charlie had long since passed away, but I had an address for his wife, Roberta, on Indianapolis Avenue on the city's near west side.

Numerous phone calls and letters to the address went unanswered. Still, none of my letters were returned. The phone was still in service. My deadline for completing the program was drawing near. So, when the traditional approaches failed, I tried an unorthodox one. I decided to hop in the car, drive there, and snoop around to talk with family, neighbors, or anybody else in the area who might know anything about this talented, yet forgotten, sports hero.

When I arrived at the house, I walked up to the front door just as a man was stepping out with a box under his arm. By the look on his face, I knew I had startled him. I began quickly to explain the reason for my unexpected visit. Surprisingly (and to my relief), my questions and enthusiasm for the topic seemed to soothe his initial trepidation. The man, James Beecher, said that he knew Charles Wiggins as "Uncle Charlie," his wife's great-uncle. For the next fifteen minutes, he shared with me some incredible stories of Uncle Charlie's racing exploits. I learned that, indeed, the house on Indianapolis Avenue was Roberta Wiggins's home, though the hundred-year-old family matriarch, known as "Aunt Roberta," had recently been moved to a nursing home on the opposite side of town. In fact, James was at Aunt Roberta's home that day to help the family move many of her personal belongings out of the house. They were preparing to sell it. He then took me to his car, which was filled to the roof with clothes, lamps, and other personal effects. In it as well was a box of old photos featuring Charlie Wiggins and the drivers, mechanics, and promoters of the Gold and Glory Sweepstakes. There was a large silver trophy from one of Charlie's championship races. There were old entry forms for "coloreds only" events in many midwestern cities. From a research standpoint, I had finally hit the jackpot.

My initial conversation with James Beecher led to subsequent interviews with his wife, Betty, and her mother, Mildred Overton, one of the most warm-hearted women I have ever met. Mildred spent hours with me, telling of her experiences attending the Gold and Glory races as a little girl and rooting for Uncle Charlie. Charlie and Roberta Wiggins had no surviving children, and treated Mildred like an adopted daughter. Over the next two years, as I expanded my research to create this book and a one-hour national PBS documentary project, Mildred opened her heart and her family's history to me. Crystal-clear details of people and events brought the past to life. She even accompanied me on two occasions to the nursing home to talk with Aunt Roberta. In periods of lucid insight, Roberta Wiggins revealed both her feisty personality and her internal strength to overcome personal loss, social turmoil, and sudden tragedy.

Roberta died during the final research phase of the project. She was 102 years old. I went to visit Mildred to deliver my condolences. As we had grown accustomed to doing, Mildred and I spent much of that afternoon talking about Aunt Roberta, Uncle Charlie, and the life they shared. That would be one of the last times I would speak to her. A few months after that conversation came the unexpected news that Mildred herself had passed away. Her death was a sad loss for me. I felt as though I'd lost both a grandmother figure and a friend. Mildred's daughter, Betty, and I have since renewed our conversations about her family's rich

Mildred Overton was a young girl when she attended the Gold and Glory Sweepstakes and cheered for her uncle, Charlie Wiggins. "He treated me like the daughter he never had," she remembered. Courtesy Mrs. Mildred Overton

legacy. It is a legacy I am proud to share with all of you. You will notice as you read through the book that nearly half of the featured photographs are from Mildred's collection, with Betty's blessing. These photos preserve a valuable piece of the past and reveal to all of us a once-secret heritage. I have dedicated this book in part to Betty and Mildred for their kindness and generosity. It is because of them that I have enjoyed this incredible historical odyssey.

Acknowledgments

Throughout a seven-year research process, I have enjoyed working with the families of other Gold and Glory drivers, mechanics, promoters, and friends. In particular I would like to thank the families of Leon "Al" Warren, Sumner "Red" Oliver, and Bobby Wallace, three extremely talented African-American drivers who once raced and worked alongside Charlie Wiggins. Important contributions also came from Jack Schilling, the son of white racing promoter and Colored Speedway Association member Oscar Schilling; Paul Bateman, grandson of CSA founder William "Pres" Rucker; and Joie Ray, who became known as the "Jackie Robinson of auto racing" when he broke the motor sports color line in 1946. Though he raced a decade after the original Gold and Glory competitors, Ray attributed much of his success to the groundwork they had laid.

Though few surviving official records document this racing circuit and its participants, a handful of precious public and private resources were available to help me put together some of the missing pieces of this historical jigsaw puzzle. Key among them was some initial research by Father Boniface Hardin, historian, civil rights activist, and president of Martin University in Indianapolis. He was also a friend of Charlie and Roberta Wiggins. During the 1970s Hardin was the editor of the bimonthly *Afro-American Journal.* In the May–June 1975 issue, he featured an article on the Gold and Glory Sweepstakes, based on interviews with Charlie Wiggins and several other drivers and mechanics. Father Hardin agreed to share his notes and memories to help tell this story. I did additional historical research in photo collections and archives at the Indiana Historical Society, the Indiana State Museum, the Indiana State Fair, the Indianapolis Motor Speedway Hall of Fame and Museum, Crown Hill Cemetery, the Indianapolis–Marion County Public Library, and the Indiana State Archives. A special word of thanks to Susan Sutton, head of photographic collections at the Indiana Historical Society, Deb Taylor in the photographic collections department of the Indianapolis Motor Speedway Hall of Fame and Museum, and Judy Mac-Geath at the Indianapolis–Marion County Public Library for their continued patience and support of my work throughout the years. They have always gone above and beyond the call for me.

A group of highly respected historians and college professors kindly agreed to give me time from their busy schedules to delve into this subject and provide rich, colorful historical context. Chief among them was Dr. Richard Pierce, associate professor of history at the University of Notre Dame, who has spent years researching the social and cultural life of African Americans along Indiana Avenue in the heart of Indianapolis's black district during the early twentieth century. Joe Freeman, a motor sports historian and member of the board of a breathtaking automotive museum in Boston, also offered fabulous insights into early racing pioneers. Dr. James Madison, distinguished professor of history at Indiana University and author of numerous works on Indiana's rich heritage, painted a vivid portrait of the racial tensions in the midwestern United States during the 1920s and '30s. A Chicago union representative and official historian, Gary Niederkorn of IBEW Local #134 provided critical information on the Windy City's connections to auto racing and the Gold and Glory circuit. As well, Donald Davidson, curator of the Indianapolis Motor Speedway Museum, dove into the seemingly endless well of information stored in his mind to bring forth stories of America's first motor sports champions and their daring heroics during the early twentieth century. I am deeply indebted to each of these gentlemen for sharing their time and knowledge with me.

Dr. David Baker, noted jazz historian and professor of music at Indiana University, as well as a Pulitzer and Grammy nominee, also shared his immense talents with me in creating an original and unforgettably authentic jazz score to accompany the one-hour PBS documentary. Throughout several special sessions with Dr. Baker at his home and in the recording studio, I learned that history and music really go hand in hand. Each helps us come to a greater understanding of the other, which ultimately brings us to a greater understanding of ourselves. Dr. Baker also shared with me great insights into poetry and the arts and their influence within the black community in the 1920s, during Indiana's African-American renaissance. The heritage that surrounded this project simply came to life after I witnessed the birth of Baker's soundtrack.

Documenting a topic with few available sources is much like sailing uncharted waters. It is difficult to tell which clues or events will cause the boat to stall and which will sweep it along in new and unpredictable ways. When exploring such unknown territory, it helps to have a brilliant navigator beside you on the journey. Luckily for me, my research associate, Tim Altom, faced each new challenge with eagerness and joy. When obstacles presented themselves (which they did on many occasions), Tim discovered new ways to find the most obscure pieces of information, which often later proved to be critical to the telling of the story. I deeply value his instincts, his enthusiasm for the project, and his friendship.

I would also like to express a special word of thanks to the countless folks who have helped me create a very special documentary for PBS, which was the impetus for this book. My heartfelt gratitude goes out to general manager Lloyd Wright and the management and staff at WFYI-TV in Indianapolis. They allowed me to chase my dreams and develop this project into a national public broadcasting offering. As well, I could not have seen this project through to its completion without the support of some incredibly talented broadcast professionals who gave generously of their time and expertise. Among them are Tony Williams, a good friend and the most insightful, enthusiastic director of photography I've ever worked with, and David Tarr, an editor with WFYI who spent countless hours completing the initial rough cut of the program with me. Additional thanks go out to Conrad Piccirillo and Eric Maloney of Innovative, Inc., a communications design firm in Indianapolis that crafted an attractive print portfolio for the early stages of the project and completed the post-production of the video, and Brice Bowman of Earshot Productions, who did the sound design and audio mixing of the television program and its soundtrack CD.

Others in the community who have also lent their support to this project include Dr. Scott Massey of the Indiana Humanities Council, Charles Blair of the Madam Walker Theatre Center, Congresswoman Julia Carson of Indiana's Tenth District, and Indiana State Representative Bill Crawford. Their phone calls and letters of support have helped turn this project from a dream into a reality. As well, I would like to thank the editors and publishers at Indiana University Press for their continued interest in my work. It is through their vision, dedication, and professionalism that this exciting story can now be shared with each of you.

Finally, I would like to thank my family for helping me see this project through to its completion. More than seven years of research has been poured into this book. Throughout that period, there were many frustrating and difficult times in which I wanted to walk away from the entire subject. My family gave me the strength I needed to keep going, infusing me with passion in the moments when I lost heart, and vision in the moments when I lacked fortitude. My parents and my in-laws have always been great fans of and believers in my work, and for that I will be forever grateful. My wife, Melissa, is truly a blessing in my life. Throughout this writing process, as throughout my life, she has been my source of vision and strength, my alter ego and my devil's advocate, my cheerleader and the love of my life. She and my son, Nathan, are my greatest sources of inspiration and joy. These two special people continue to mold me into the best writer—and the best person—I can be.

What follows is the result of a vision shared by these and many other wonderful individuals. My hope is that this project will shed some long-overdue light on a talented group of sportsmen whose story has been lost to time. In 1903, the great black activist W. E. B. Du Bois noted, "[T]he problem of the Twentieth Century is the problem of the color line." Du Bois's prophesy certainly played out in dramatic form in the story of the drivers and mechanics of the Gold and Glory Sweepstakes. The colorful and often poignant saga of these intrepid sportsmen tells about far more than skilled racing techniques and automotive engineering expertise. By looking back at the social struggles and victories of these athletes, we can examine how far we've come as a society . . . and how far we still need to go.

Introduction: Racing "For Gold and Glory"

In 1991 Willie T. Ribbs became the first African American to qualify for the Indianapolis 500-Mile Race. His accomplishment was historic. And yet it was the pinnacle of a remarkably rich racing legacy that preceded Ribbs by nearly seven decades.

During the 1920s the Ku Klux Klan cast a dark shadow over the social and political landscape in Indiana and throughout the Midwest. Popular parks, clubs, and sports venues such as the Indianapolis Motor Speedway were rigidly segregated. It was during this era of racial turbulence that a dedicated group of individuals, both black and white, came together to create a sporting event for African Americans—an auto racing spectacle so grand it attracted the attention of national newspaper and newsreel agencies, as well as thousands of spectators from coast to coast. The event was the Gold and Glory Sweepstakes, a freewheeling, dust-raising, hundred-mile grind around the one-mile dirt track at the Indiana State Fairgrounds in Indianapolis.

"The Gold and Glory Sweepstakes was the race that belonged to the colored people," remarked historian Boniface Hardin. "It was something we could take joy in. And there was truly glory attached to winning it." Mildred Overton remembered that in her days as a spectator at the annual event, "The Gold and Glory race was the only race blacks could be a part of, because we could not be a part of the 500-Mile Race . . . and the top black drivers from the whole country would come when they had those races. It was so exciting to see all those people come out, sometimes ten to twelve thousand, all decked out in their Sunday best, to see those drivers in action."

Frank A. "Fay" Young, sports editor for the *Chicago Defender,* captured the color and pageantry of the inaugural event, which was held on August 2, 1924. "This auto race will be recognized throughout the length and breadth of the land as the single greatest sports event to be staged annually by colored people. Soon, chocolate jockeys will mount their gas-snorting, rubber-shod speedway monsters as they race at death-defying speeds. The largest purses will be posted here, and the greatest array of driving talent will be in attendance in hopes of winning gold for themselves and glory for their Race." Young's report inspired promoters to christen the event "the Gold and Glory Sweepstakes."

From the moment an official dropped the green flag to signal the start of the first Gold and Glory event in 1924, black drivers, mechanics, and spectators in many cities throughout the Midwest embraced the sport. Promoters formed a Gold and Glory circuit that featured events in cities such as Chicago, Dayton, and Detroit. Within five years, the popularity of the circuit had exploded, and black racing events were held on dirt tracks in places such as Atlanta, Langhorne (Pennsylvania), Fort Worth, and Los Angeles.

The top drivers all received invitations to "coloreds only" events. Most of these entry blanks promised "guaranteed purses" and a "square deal to all." Al Warren was one of the drivers who competed in these early affairs. "We would always look forward to getting the next entry blank in the mail," he remembered. "Ohio . . . Illinois . . . Wisconsin . . . wherever! I just couldn't wait to get back in that car and get out there on the track again." The top prize for many of these events was about $500. Sometimes every driver who qualified for the main event received a guaranteed sum of $200. Total purses were minimal. Yet, nearly every weekend, drivers with a passion for speed and danger loaded their racecars onto the backs of trailers, hitched them to battered old cars, and traveled hundreds of miles over rough, unpaved roads to compete for honor, thrills, and, most importantly, respect—respect among their peers, and respect among members of a white community that often refused to recognize them.

The greatest African-American driver of the era was Charlie Wiggins, a humble and gifted auto mechanic from Indianapolis. Charlie did not consider himself a great driver, though he won more black auto races than any other competitor during the 1920s and '30s. He also did not consider himself a fighter for social justice, though he forged important friendships with many of the top white drivers at the Indianapolis Motor Speedway and overcame great racial strife to lead a personal crusade against segregation in the field of motor sports.

"The Negro Speed King, that's what they called him," remembered Charlie's wife, Roberta. "All those people would come out to the fairgrounds for those big races. And, my! Charlie always had something to show 'em. Those folks were just crazy about him. Any wife would be scared to watch her husband carry on so. And I was scared for Charlie. But Charlie wasn't scared of nothin'. Charlie was the best."

Charlie's success, both on and off the track, attracted the ire of many segregationists and Klan-backed neighborhood associations in Indianapolis. Chief among them was the White Supremacy League, which routinely left late-night "calling cards" at Charlie's auto shop. Typically these threats came in the form of a brick thrown through the window, a sign torn from its post, or a threatening note left in the mailbox.

The harassment only seemed to strengthen Charlie's resolve, however. Throughout his life he dreamed of one day competing at the Indy 500. His unyielding passion inspired promoters to form the Colored Speedway Association, the group that organized the Gold and Glory Sweepstakes. Throughout the race's twelve-year existence, Charlie established himself as its unequivocal leader, capturing four championship titles and finishing in the top ten for ten consecutive years. His name became synonymous with the greatest aspects of the sport. One driver, Red Oliver, remembered, "Charlie didn't just win the Gold and Glory Sweepstakes. He *was* the Gold and Glory Sweepstakes."

Charlie's story is practically unknown today, even among avid auto racing enthusiasts. The story of the Gold and Glory Sweepstakes is almost forgotten, but it is an extraordinary tale of an ordinary man who elevated his craft, his sport, and his race by simply refusing to give up on his dream. By racing for gold on the track, Charlie Wiggins represented true glory off it.

Auto racing historian Joe Freeman stated, "Charlie and the Gold and Glory Sweepstakes were an exciting part of a cultural renaissance that was sweeping the country at the time. African Americans were beginning to discover and celebrate their own identity in many facets of political and social life. This included the major sporting events of the day. Since Indianapolis was an auto racing town, it only made sense that the African-American population should create a racing event that could bring social significance and pride to that community. The Gold and Glory Sweepstakes became the Indy 500 for the black population."

This story is both engaging and uniquely American. A group of African-American pioneers faced real danger, both on and off the track, in a quest for gold and glory. Their struggles represented the struggles of all African Americans during the era. Their victories were victories in which all African Americans could rejoice. "It had much greater weight to it than just a sporting event," noted historian Richard Pierce. "They tried to show that they deserved increased rights and privileges in their community. And the Gold and Glory Sweepstakes was a major part of that effort."

1.

The Adventurer

She sat alone in a wooden chair as the hours crept painfully by. A large clock on the wall pierced an eerie silence as it struck twelve times. The long day had turned into a longer night. She picked at her blouse, which was covered with tiny clots of brown, hardened blood. She was small, just under five feet tall and only eighty pounds, but her wails of shock and fear were powerful. Hours of ceaseless crying had exhausted her. She slumped into her chair, murmuring, "Why now? Why on earth now?"

At one point she looked down the narrow hall where she was sitting. Usually the "Jim Crow" wing of the Indianapolis City Hospital was bustling with activity. As the state's only public hospital to accept "coloreds," the ill-equipped facility, with only seventy beds to serve the area's seventy thousand black residents, was usually filled to capacity. But on this night, all appeared quiet, "as if everything was standing still," she later remembered. She was forty-two, but the events of the past eight hours seemed to have aged her by twenty years.

Eight hours ago . . . the festivities, the pageantry, the throngs of spectators from across the country . . . all had added to the electric environment. Then, in one horrible instant, it all came to an end. "Why was he always taking those risks?" she wept aloud. Shortly after midnight, an intern emerged from the surgery room, his face covered with perspiration. It was near the end of September 1936, but muggy conditions made the ward feel as though it were the middle of summer. The woman looked up, trembling as she spoke. "How's my Charlie?" He shrugged his shoulders and shook his head. Inside, young doctors using outdated equipment were doing all they could, but there was no word yet on Charlie's condition.

She slid back into her chair and dropped her head back. "What happened?" she wondered. The day had started with such promise. Black journalists had heralded this racing spectacle, the largest of its kind in the country, as "the single greatest sports event staged annually by colored people."[1] Instead it had been the scene of one of the worst accidents in black auto racing history. Visions of the accident flashed rapidly in her head: twisted metal chassis, thick black smoke, and ghastly looks from drivers as they fled the fiery scene. At one point she remembered hearing a voice—that dreadful, screaming voice—the one that yelled, "He's dead. Charlie's dead."

Her husband was not dead, but barely clinging to life. Within minutes of the accident, she had rushed onto the track in time to see drivers and mechanics pull Charlie's limp body from the wreckage. He was unconscious from loss of blood. As paramedics rushed him to the emergency room, she rode beside him, too shocked to speak. She held his head in her lap. Gently she caressed his face.

For hours she sat outside the operating room and waited. The clock down the hall continued to sound . . . one o'clock . . . two o'clock. Charlie Wiggins's wife Roberta slumped in the chair once again and tried to come to terms with the tragedy. "The Negro Speed King . . . Charlie . . . my Charlie!" she thought to herself. "Oh, Lord! What's to become of my Charlie?"

The turn of the century brought sweeping changes in the economic and social life of residents of Evansville, Indiana. The city's population doubled between 1870 and 1890, and doubled again over the next thirty years. Near the riverfront, black clouds billowed from large brick smokestacks, signaling progress for new manufacturing firms. Downtown streetcars and crowded open-air markets were common sights for residents in this, the largest metropolitan area in southern Indiana. Evansville was the southernmost city in the Hoosier state, separated from its Kentucky neighbors only by the murky brown currents of the Ohio River. The "Pocket City," as it was known, exuded both a spirit of Hoosier pride and a flavor and attitude similar to those of states south of the Mason-Dixon Line.

Consistent with these southern notions was the institutionalized segregation of the city's African-American population. Emma Lou Thornbrough, in her book *Indiana Blacks in the Twentieth Century*, noted that Evansville was often considered "the most segregated city in Indiana."[2] All city libraries displayed signs that read "Whites Only." African Americans were allowed to ride only in the back of the city's familiar streetcars. Black children were not allowed on many public playgrounds, and respectable black adults were barred from most city parks. The Majestic Theatre, one of the city's most popular attractions, not only required African Americans to sit in the balcony, it also had a separate "coloreds only" entrance, accessible through a darkened back alley. As well, most restaurants and hotels refused to serve black customers.

All elementary schools were strictly segregated. Two all-black high schools, Clark and Douglass (later renamed Lincoln), were established near the turn of the century. White city officials had debated whether to spend the money to build them. After new state laws in 1878 required that all Indiana counties educate their black residents, Vanderburgh County officials grudgingly accepted the mandate and invested the necessary funds.

In many low-level labor jobs elsewhere in the state—jobs in road construction, coal mines, and limestone quarries—blacks and whites often worked side by side. Not so in Evansville. Lines of segregation in the Pocket City were unquestionably rigid. Most blacks were familiar with the "sunset laws" that prevailed throughout most southern Indiana river towns. These were unwritten laws designed to "keep Negroes in their place" by discouraging them from being out after dark, lest they be subject to threats and acts of violence. One of these river towns, Leavenworth, posted signs notifying all black citizens that if they were on the street after sundown, "they would be annihilated."[3] This attitude often prevailed in Evansville and the surrounding Vanderburgh County area.

Evansville had a history of lynchings and other acts of violence against African Americans. In the decades that followed the Civil War, an all-black community thirty miles north of the city, Lyles Station, had invited many African Americans to escape the oppression of southern states and settle in this "Negro Colony," where they would be allowed to live and prosper. Hundreds of African-American families, all fleeing the racial turmoil of southern Reconstruction, traveled by river to Lyles Station. All had to pass through Evansville.

Segregationists in the Pocket City wanted to ensure that this black influx did not tarry long in Evansville on its journey north. Dr. Carl Lyles, great-grandson of Lyles Station founder Joshua Lyles, remembered, "They would hold public lynchings along the riverfront. Boats passing by could see the bodies of Negroes, beaten and lynched, swinging in the breeze. That was the white man's way of saying, 'Welcome to Indiana.' If blacks thought life was going to be easier north of the Ohio River, they were mistaken."[4]

Segregation in Evansville was most evident in the city's residential zoning regulations. By 1910, nearly 70 percent of the town's 6,300 black residents lived in a designated ten-block area in the heart of the city known as Baptisttown, named for a popular neighborhood Baptist church. Living conditions in Baptisttown were deplorable: no city sewage lines, no indoor plumbing, and no electric lines. Most of the men in Baptisttown worked at the docks. They were known as roustabouts, unskilled laborers, who often toiled under the heavy hand of overbearing, even violent, crewmen.

"The life of a roustabout is the life of a dog," a former slave, George W. Arnold, remembered in an interview with WPA officials during the 1930s.[5] The deck of each boat that pulled into the Evansville port was crowded with passengers and freight. The roustabouts efficiently loaded and unloaded both. African Americans were not the only laborers who worked the docks. Many Irish, Italians, and other immigrants joined

At the beginning of the twentieth century, most blacks in Evansville, Indiana, lived in a segregated ghetto known as "Baptisttown." This is where Charlie Wiggins was born. Courtesy University of Southern Indiana Archives

their black brethren. Together they heaved giant bales of wheat, cotton, and tobacco from passing sternwheelers and packets to the docks below. The days were long. The pay was far below a livable wage. Often the mates who supervised them were cruel. Some roustabouts were beaten until they were crippled. Others died at the hands of their oppressive supervisors. Fights were common. The level of alcohol consumption was high among these weary men, as they struggled to forget their worries.

City council members passed several initiatives during the early part of the century to improve the quality of life in Evansville, including stricter housing laws and better service by the city's public utilities. These new regulations were never enforced in the black community, however.

Ramshackle houses lined the dusty, unpaved streets of Baptisttown. City officials often ignored petitions and other organized efforts by African Americans to improve conditions in the neighborhood. In the midst of a thriving river city, Baptisttown was a stagnant ghetto.

Amid these rough conditions a young couple, Sport and Jennie Wiggins, eked out a modest living. The couple married in September 1896 and worked diligently to support themselves in a one-room apartment on the south side of the black neighborhood. Sport, like most black men in Baptisttown, worked at the docks, unloading heavy crates from the barges that passed through town. Listed in the city directory as a laborer, the twenty-five-year-old Sport toiled for half the wages of his white co-workers. To help earn extra money, Jennie took in laundry from wealthy white families in Evansville. Both Sport and Jennie worked seven days a week just to make enough money to survive.

Two months after their wedding, Jennie and Sport learned that they would soon be expecting their first child. Though excited, Sport knew that his meager pay at the docks would not support the couple and a new baby. He had seen an advertisement on a handbill that touted "fine pay for strong coloreds" in the coal mines north of town. The job required that black workers journey into the depths of the mines. There they would dig and blast new passageways to allow other workers to mine the coal. It was hard and extremely dangerous work, but the pay was more than twice the wage of his job at the docks. So in the spring of 1897, Sport accepted a new position as a coal miner. The job represented far more than new responsibilities and increased pay. All miners and their families lived in neighborhoods specially built for them on the city's northwest side. Though still strictly segregated, these neighborhoods offered far better living conditions, including public utilities and city water and sewage services. That March, Sport and Jennie moved into their first house, a modest two-bedroom home at 306 Magnolia Avenue.

On the evening of July 15, 1897, Sport and Jennie welcomed the newest resident to their home on Magnolia. He was Charles Edwin Wiggins, the first-born son of the Evansville couple. Sport and Jennie would later have three more sons, Lawrence (1898), Walter (1902), and Hershell (1904). From the time he was a little boy, Charlie seemed to possess a natural gift for leadership. According to family accounts, he organized neighborhood races, games, and wrestling matches. Though he was small and thin for his age, he had a reputation as a tough kid with an unwavering resolve, a quality that would characterize him throughout his life.

Historian Boniface Hardin, a friend of the Wiggins family, recalled, "Charlie was an adventurer. He wasn't afraid of doing something that he wasn't supposed to do. If someone told him that something couldn't be done, he'd figure out a way to do it. That was his style . . . an adventurer. Even in his old age, he would tell great stories about his life and all the things he did. You just got caught up with everything he said, and you never wanted him to stop. He had a special kind of courage that was a part of his nature throughout his entire life. Charlie had a spirit people simply embraced." Charlie acted much older than his age. His wife Roberta remembered, "The brothers rarely saw their father, because he worked so much. So Charlie really helped his mama and took care of his brothers. As an eight-year-old, he was feeding a bottle to his brother Hershell and rocking him to sleep. He was very mature, even then."

Though Sport continued to work long hours, the family's circumstances improved. The Wiggins family moved into a new, slightly bigger home on Nevada Street in 1906. Nine-year-old Charlie and his brothers were excited about their new surroundings. But within a few months the family's excitement turned to sorrow. On August 5, Charlie's mother, Jennie, went to bed with a terrible fever. Within three days she was dead, at the age of thirty. If the cause of her death was ever known, it has not survived. The loss seemed to send a paralyzing shock through Sport's body. He became completely despondent. "He wouldn't talk, eat, anything," Roberta recalled. "It was up to Charlie to comfort and care for his brothers. That would be a pretty tough situation for any nine-year-old, and it was particularly hard for Charlie."

Sport returned to his job in the mines the following week, though he never completely recovered from the loss of his wife. More and more Charlie spent his free time caring for his three younger brothers. His days of innocent play in the neighborhood were essentially over. Each day he woke up early to help get his two younger brothers dressed. He then escorted four-year-old Walter and two-year-old Hershell to the homes of a number of neighbors, including Mrs. Mattie Sullinger, a kind but extremely stern neighbor lady originally from Owensboro, Kentucky, just across the Ohio River from Evansville. Some family members

A faded photo, circa 1920, of Charlie Wiggins from his early days in
Evansville, Indiana. Courtesy Mrs. Mildred Overton

recalled that Mattie often carried the Bible with her and offered liberal
doses of discipline and the Scriptures to those youngsters in her charge.

Charlie and his other brother, eight-year-old Lawrence, attended a
blacks-only elementary school located within blocks of their home. As
well as doing his schoolwork, Charlie also helped earn money by shining
shoes each afternoon. After school, he ran to the mines where his father
worked and offered five-cent shines to the supervisors.

His shoeshine business proved to be profitable. By the time he was
eleven Charlie routinely skipped classes to journey into downtown
Evansville and offer shines to many workers at the manufacturing plants.
Often he would walk through the open-air markets on Fourth Street to
watch the energized bantering that flowed between market owners and
shoppers as they bargained over goods and services. He dodged between

the trotting horse-drawn carriages that were the primary means of transportation through the city. In the distance, he heard the trolley cars and their familiar clanging bells. In the midst of this bustling scene, he set up his shoeshine stand on the corner of Main and Eleventh Streets, where crowds of busy white businessmen hurried from one building to another. Mildred Overton, Charlie's niece, noted, "Even as a boy, he was a hustler. He out-hustled all the other shoeshine boys on Main Street. At a nickel a shine, he could bring in about a dollar a day. That was good money for the family back then."

Directly behind Charlie's shoeshine stand was the Benninghof-Nolan Company, housed in a three-story brick structure in the heart of the city. The business was one of the first automobile distributors and mechanical repair shops in southern Indiana. Benninghof-Nolan featured cars from the Overland Auto Company, a car manufacturing firm based originally in Terre Haute, then in Indianapolis. The "horseless carriage" was still a relatively new sight in the Hoosier state, and the cars that rolled out of the Benninghof-Nolan showroom nearly always caught the attention of curious passers-by.

Benninghof-Nolan started as a parts manufacturer and distributor in 1910, and had branched out into wholesale auto sales by 1913. The business was founded and run by two ambitious twenty-year-olds, Henry J. Benninghof and Eugene E. Nolan, who were described in the 1923 *Account of Vanderburgh County* as "prominent among the young and energetic businessmen who are contributing materially to the business advancement of Evansville."[6] Both came from well-to-do families. Henry was the only child of Henry P. Benninghof, a local bank executive and southern Indiana's largest wholesale foreign and domestic wine and liquor distributor. Eugene was the younger of two children and the only son of prominent Evansville businessman John J. Nolan. The elder Nolan was the mayor of Evansville in 1910, and was at various times also head postmaster, vice president of the city's largest bank, and president of the Vanderburgh County Chamber of Commerce.

When Henry and Eugene started Benninghof-Nolan, their wealthy and influential fathers played a major role in the organization of the company. Henry's father was listed in the corporate records as the first company president, while Eugene's father served as its first secretary-treasurer. Both encouraged their young sons to think and act in progressive, entrepreneurial ways. The boys successfully marketed the first operational water truck to city administrators—a truck designed to water unpaved city streets in order to keep down the dust. When the new truck arrived, the two paraded it slowly up Main Street in a grand demonstration. This was one of many unusual and eye-catching promotional strategies that soon established Benninghof-Nolan among the city's most successful businesses.

Each morning Henry and Eugene both stopped to get their shoes shined by Charlie Wiggins. The two wholesale car dealers seemed to take an instant liking to Charlie's hard-working spirit. When Charlie expressed an interest in automotive technology, they invited him to watch their trained mechanics work. Boniface Hardin noted, "Charlie was like a sponge. He watched everything in the garage, asked questions, and soaked up the information into his mind for future use."[7] The mechanics even hired him to wash the cars from time to time, allowing him to earn some extra money.

Every day as he shined shoes, Charlie listened intently to the conversations that emanated from the garage area. He also listened for the sounds of the engines as the mechanics put them through test after test. Though he could not get a close-up look at the adjustments the technicians were making to the engines, he learned to assess malfunctions strictly by the sound the car made. The pitch, rumble, and roar of the engine told Charlie which mechanical adjustments were needed.

One day in 1914, Charlie was talking with Henry Benninghof when the two heard a car sputter, pop, and chug its way down Main Street with great difficulty. Charlie, who was facing away from the car as it pulled up next to the couple, casually mentioned that the car needed a specific technical readjustment, using terminology common only to Benninghof and Nolan's trained mechanics. "He could just tell by the sound," remarked Mildred Overton. "I think it stopped that owner cold. I mean, here's this little black shoeshine boy explaining complex technical specifications in a car engine. And he was doing it strictly by ear. I don't think that the owner knew what to think."

The car pulled into the Benninghof-Nolan garage in need of service. Henry invited Charlie into the service area. He told his head mechanic to look at the engine and give an assessment. Charlie's diagnosis proved to be completely accurate. Henry then took Charlie over to another

Henry J. Benninghof (*left*) and Eugene E. Nolan ran the Benninghof-Nolan Company, an automobile sales and service business on Main Street in Evansville. The two hired Charlie Wiggins as one of the first black mechanics in the city. Courtesy *Evansville Courier* archives

vehicle sitting in the back of the shop and asked the mechanic to start the engine. He told Charlie to listen to the motor and give his evaluation. Charlie listened carefully, and then gave a precise technical explanation. Henry looked at the job order on the car. Right again.

Henry Benninghof walked Charlie into the main office and called for Eugene Nolan. Mildred Overton recalled, "Those two boys, those owners, both of them barely in their twenties, decided to break all the social rules of the day. They decided to give Charlie a chance as an apprentice in the repair shop. At the time it was very rare for a black man to work as a mechanic. But those two boys didn't care. They recognized Uncle Charlie's talents right away and put him to work. That one day changed Uncle Charlie's life forever."

Working as a mechanic for Benninghof-Nolan "changed Uncle Charlie's life forever," his niece Mildred Overton remembered. Courtesy Mrs. Mildred Overton

Back on Nevada Street, Charlie continued to visit the home of Mrs. Sullinger, the neighbor lady who took care of his two youngest brothers. By 1912, Walter was ten years old and Hershell was eight. Both were old

enough now to attend the all-black elementary school in their neighborhood. Neither needed Mrs. Sullinger's care any longer. But Charlie had another reason for visiting. The family's eldest daughter, Roberta, had caught Charlie's eye.

Roberta was a bright, attractive twenty-year-old who exuded grace and charm. Small and shapely, she earned a living as a model for designer dress shops and boutiques around the area. "She was quite glamorous," remembered Mildred Overton. "Uncle Charlie tried to win her affections, but probably felt that she was too good for him. She was a socialite, involved in club meetings and the like. And that was not Uncle Charlie's cup of tea at all."

Roberta's success as a model once earned her a trip to Paris for a fashion show that featured many top American designers. She was ele-

Roberta Wiggins worked as a model and enjoyed a successful career in Evansville and Indianapolis. Courtesy Mrs. Mildred Overton

gant and cosmopolitan, epitomizing many stylish young women in this new Flapper era. She smoked. She drank bootleg liquor. She wore short, European-style dresses with sequins and tassels, and she stayed out late and enjoyed the hot rhythms of the area's top dance clubs. She was creating a promising career and an exciting life for herself that was all her own.

Her lifestyle was in stark contrast to her midwestern upbringing. Her mother Mattie was prudish, austere, and zealous in her self-righteous battles against what she perceived to be a growing plague of sin in America. Roberta's independence directly defied her mother's strict way of life, and Mattie often cried and prayed that her daughter would eventually see the light and put an end to her immoral ways.

Charlie looked upon Roberta's lifestyle in bewilderment. He scarcely understood her need for the glamour, the dazzling nightlife, the fancy clothes, and the freedom to express herself as she pleased. Greasy car parts and smooth-running engines fueled his passions. Roberta's world was completely foreign to him, a magical universe that seemed both strange and exotic. Charlie was smitten.

Though Charlie was young and small—he was only five feet seven inches tall and weighed a hundred pounds—he was wiry and strong. He learned to box at a local boys' club and earned several medals in the junior division. "He hardly had a dime to his name," Overton laughed. "But he was sincere, strong, and ambitious. I think Aunt Roberta must have sensed that, right from the very beginning."

Roberta remembered with a laugh, "When Charlie was younger, he was so handsome. He was really something 'on the market.' So I knew when he started taking an interest in me, I was going to snatch him right up. Oh, my! He was just so good looking. So we got married right away. I was just crazy about him."

Boniface Hardin remembered, "Charlie and Roberta could not have been more different. But they had a way of understanding each other. They supported and believed in each other. When one of them would accomplish something, it was as if they both had accomplished it. That was the magic they shared."

Charlie and Roberta were married on August 27, 1914, and moved into an apartment at 1020 Oak Street. Charlie was only seventeen years old. Roberta was twenty-two. Their marriage came just four months before the birth of their first child, Flay. Roberta's modeling career had been put on hold throughout the pregnancy, and Charlie's two-dollar-a-week income as a mechanic's apprentice at Benninghof-Nolan could not adequately support the couple and their newborn son. So Charlie moonlighted, taking a night job as a railroad porter to feed his family, while working in the garage all day to feed his passion for automobiles.

Five mechanics worked a frantic pace at the Benninghof-Nolan garage. Charlie moved quickly and quietly from bay to bay as the mechanics hollered their orders, like surgeons standing over a room of seriously injured patients. A wrench here . . . a hose there. . . . For nearly

While in Evansville, Charlie met and courted Roberta Sullinger. The two were married on August 27, 1914. Courtesy Mrs. Mildred Overton

two years, Charlie moved his weary, sleep-deprived body from one corner of the shop to the other, grabbing parts and supplies. When there were no supplies to grab, the foreman sent him out on foot to a junkyard seven blocks away. There he rummaged through heaps of rusted old cars to uncover, dismantle, and retrieve needed parts.

"He worked hard, but he was always a happy person," recalled Mildred Overton. "His smile was contagious. He cracked jokes. He really got along well with everyone."

Almost everyone. Though the mechanics accepted the fact that they were working alongside a Negro, attitudes toward him were harsh at times. On one of his first days in the shop, the foreman called Charlie a nigger. Charlie held his tongue and his rage in check. When Henry Benninghof heard of the incident, he issued a mandate to all his mechanics that the word "nigger" would never be used again in his garage.

Still, conflicts arose. One day all of the mechanics approached Charlie in unison and bet him a day's wages that he could not defeat the company's stock boy in a boxing match. Charlie was unaware that the stock boy was a former state champion wrestler who had never lost a match in his career. Charlie refused, attempting to avoid the conflict, but the mechanics' taunts and threats forced him into the impromptu bout.

Charlie and the stock boy faced off in the back lot after work. The mechanics had parked cars in a large circle to form an informal boxing ring. Charlie, small and thin, paced the gravel lot as the 6'2", 220-pound stock boy entered the area. Amid jeers from the mechanics, the stock boy tackled Charlie and flailed wildly at his face. Charlie wriggled free from the strong hold of his opponent and began to move his feet with lightning-quick speed, a technique he had learned in his training at the Evansville Boys' Club. What the mechanics and the unfortunate stock boy did not realize was that Charlie's training in the ring had earned him two regional Golden Gloves boxing titles in the featherweight division. The stock boy's size did not make him a match for his lighter, faster, and more experienced opponent. Charlie struck with hard, fast blows to the face. Within minutes blood trickled from the boy's eyes and ears. Dizzy and disoriented, he fell to the ground.[8] The mechanics, subdued and humbled, helped Charlie carry the boy back into the shop. Time passed. No one spoke of the incident again. "No one at the garage ever called him a name or gave him a hard time after that," Roberta remembered.

It had been nearly ten years since his mother had passed away. By 1915 Charlie Wiggins had grown from a scrawny nine-year-old into a mature, strong-willed husband and father with a job in the field he loved. Jennie Wiggins's death, though devastating to him at the time, seemed somehow to strengthen him and give him the wisdom he needed to help raise a family. "It was as if her spirit had been injected into his soul," recalled Mildred Overton.

Charlie's father, Sport, on the other hand, saw his own spirit sink into a dark abyss. He was still grieving over the loss of his wife and facing the wretched working conditions in the coal mines. A cloud of depression engulfed him. On January 15 Charlie and his brother Lawrence stopped by their father's home to discover him lying on his bed in a feverish delirium.

A winter storm had whipped across the landscape just two days earlier. The two brothers borrowed a neighbor's car and coaxed it through the snow to the nearest hospital. A nurse at the front door sternly refused to admit a colored patient and turned the boys and their sick father back out into the cold. They returned home and called a local black doctor, who arrived later that afternoon. But little could be done. Charlie watched helplessly as his father slipped further and further away. Within two days, Sport Wiggins died. He was forty-eight. Charlie was still a teenager, and already he had watched both of his parents die. His father's death was the first in a series of heartbreaking tragedies that would beset his family over the next five years. The next came the following year.

Good fortune had apparently come Charlie's way in September 1916. That month, Roberta found out that she was pregnant with the couple's second child. Four weeks later Henry Benninghof and Eugene Nolan promoted Charlie to full-time mechanic. His pay was increased to seven dollars a week. He was able to quit his job as a porter and devote himself completely to his career as a mechanic. With a new child on the way and more money in his bank account, Charlie thought it was time to buy a bigger house. But before he and Roberta had an opportunity to shop for a new home, their son Flay fell seriously ill.

For one month the toddler battled intense bouts of fever and searing stomach pains. By November 1, 1916, uncontrollable spasms in his abdomen were causing incessant vomiting. The family doctor diagnosed Flay with tuberculous peritonitis, a severe form of tuberculosis. The child had developed an infection in his abdominal cavity. In the absence of antibiotics, the infection spread quickly, causing pain and swelling.

Flay cried night and day as Roberta attempted to comfort her child. But there was little she and Charlie could do. In less than two weeks, on November 13, 1916, Flay died. A grief-stricken Roberta, now entering her second trimester with her second child, refused to eat—a development that frightened Charlie. "He grabbed me by the shoulders and looked me straight in the eye," Roberta remembered. "He told me that we were going to have to pull through this. Losing that little boy was so hard, but we had to survive somehow." She paused and sighed. "It was just so sad, so sad."

On May 23, 1917, the Wigginses' second son, Lowell, was born. The baby appeared healthy, but during the delivery Roberta experienced complications that caused Charlie's tiny wife to lose a large amount of blood. The family doctor, working in the Wigginses' bedroom, tried hard to contain the bleeding. However, the blood loss caused Roberta to slip in and out of consciousness for two days. Charlie kept a constant vigil over his wife. Fortunately, within a week his prayers were answered. Slowly, Roberta began to regain consciousness and strength. She would survive.

Charlie stayed home with his wife as long as he could. But after two weeks, he received an urgent message from Henry Benninghof: Come back to the shop right away. On April 2, President Woodrow Wilson had declared war on Germany, making official the United States' involvement in the Great War. The call for young, able-bodied men went out throughout the land and was met by a rising wave of patriotism. Recruitment officers mustered in soldiers by the thousands, and Vanderburgh County contributed its share. One by one, young Evansville men, including each of the five mechanics at the Benninghof-Nolan Company, boarded trains bound for Fort Benjamin Harrison in Indianapolis and other training sites and were shipped overseas.

Charlie, too, answered his country's call and gathered his papers together to report to the recruiting station in Evansville. "I've come to enlist and fight for my country," he announced. The officer in charge picked up Charlie's papers and threw them on the floor. "Go home, nigger," he shouted. "This is a white man's war, not a war for niggers. When we need niggers, we'll call you."[9]

Charlie was stunned by the response. Angered and frustrated, he returned to the garage. Over the next year and a half he watched all of his white colleagues at Benninghof-Nolan leave for military training. With each departure, Charlie grew more and more busy at the garage. His extended responsibilities at the shop forced him to spend many long nights leaning over and crawling under the chassis of hundreds of automobiles. Boniface Hardin explained, "Charlie was virtually left alone to make repairs and work on cars. He learned every nut and bolt, every angle, and every part of those cars. Soon there was no doubt that he stood head and shoulders above the so-called experts." After the Armistice in November 1918, a couple of the mechanics returned. But by then it was clear that Charlie Wiggins was in charge of the Benninghof-Nolan garage. Benninghof named him head mechanic, the only African American listed in that capacity in the Evansville area.

At work, things were getting better for Charlie. But at home, they only grew worse. Charlie and Roberta's son Lowell died suddenly on July 11, 1918. Another son, Charles, Jr., born September 5, 1919, died in infancy on February 10, 1920. No cause of death was listed for either Lowell or Charles, Jr., though one family member recalled that the Wiggins family faced many struggles with tuberculosis and other "terrible diseases" in their early years in Evansville.

Dr. Darrel Bigham, in his book *We Ask Only a Fair Trial*, noted that many of the black neighborhoods were "a breeding ground for contagious disease." On several occasions legislators attempted to improve the substandard sewage systems and housing in the black areas, and city administrators passed new housing laws in 1913. But white building owners often ignored the laws.[10] Even members of the Chamber of Commerce, some of whom proposed that the black neighborhoods be leveled and turned into parks for white citizens, were slow to react to the call for relief measures. Members of the Wiggins family were victims of social injustice allowed by the indifference of white policymakers in Vanderburgh County.

Social injustice seeped into the fibers of Evansville's cultural life, as well. In 1906 a stage version of Thomas Dixon, Jr.'s *The Clansman*

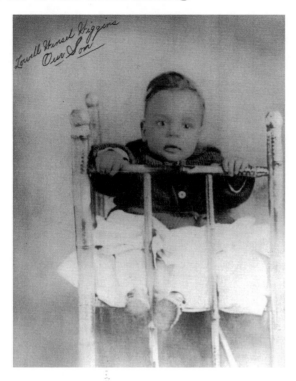

Charlie and Roberta Wiggins had three sons. Lowell, the second child, was born on May 23, 1917. All three of the Wigginses' children died in infancy. Courtesy Mrs. Mildred Overton

debuted at the Grand Theatre, a play the *Evansville Journal-News*, in its "Colored Folks" column, called "an attempt to stir up race prejudice."[11] Nine years later, two films, *The Nigger* and D. W. Griffith's historic *Birth of a Nation*, premiered in Evansville. Two recent lynchings just south of the river, in the Kentucky towns of Henderson and Paducah, were still making headlines. Black civic leaders were concerned that the movies would fuel racial hatred in the city.

Mayor Benjamin Bosse and his staff attended a private showing of *The Nigger*. The film included one scene of a black man burning at the stake and another disturbing sequence near the end in which, as Mayor Bosse pronounced, "a whole flock of Negroes" were burned in one violent rampage. The mayor agreed to ban the showing of the film in Evansville. The theater owner protested, however, claiming that he would lose revenue, since he was unable to find a substitute film quickly. Several white segregationist groups lobbied on his behalf. Eventually the administration caved in. The film opened on August 14, 1915. The local press celebrated its release, claiming that the picture offered "nothing . . . to cause race prejudice on the part of white people against Negroes."[12]

When *Birth of a Nation* debuted four months later, black leaders tried again to get city leaders to intervene, hoping to reverse the precedent set in the summer. The mayor agreed to form a "board of censorship" to scrutinize all films for violent content. But this was only a cursory effort to please black citizens. Support for the picture was overwhelming among whites. Despite an eloquent plea for censorship by members of the local chapter of the NAACP, Griffith's work played to packed houses and received rave reviews in Evansville.

The mounting racial pressures in the city, coupled with personal loss, were almost too much for Charlie Wiggins to take. Evansville had become a very mean city. But it was not until 1922 that Charlie decided to look for new opportunities outside Evansville for his business and his family.

African Americans in Evansville were about to endure some of the worst racial turmoil in the city's history. The Ku Klux Klan had been reestablished in Atlanta in 1915, and in the summer of 1920 Joe Huffington, a Houston, Texas, native and a Klan national organizer, began a push to gain northern support for the Klan. Huffington moved to Evansville and set up an office a few blocks east of the courthouse in a two-story building that had once been a bakery. By the spring of 1922 he had the support of several hundred Hoosiers in organizing a spectacular event at the Evansville Coliseum.

On June 10, 1922, the *Evansville Courier* reported the tremendous success of a rally to promote the Ku Klux Klan. A crowd of more than six thousand lined the streets near the Coliseum. Dr. Caleb Ridley, a Baptist minister from Atlanta, erupted on stage with a deeply impassioned speech on the fundamental principles of a "white, gentile American and Protestant organization." Five hundred hooded, robed men encircled the stage, waving crosses and American flags.

"The first principle of the Klan is that it is a white man's organization," Ridley told the cheering crowd. "Some people think we ought to apologize for it, but we are not going to do it. Some think we are against all who are not white. This is not so. If they attend to their own business, we'll attend to ours. We are not out gunning for anyone, regardless of his color or creed."

Ridley concluded, "Then it is a gentile organization. You know I'm not responsible for being a gentile. God Almighty takes care of that. Our organization is for white, gentile Americans.... Not only is the Ku Klux Klan white, gentile and American, but it is first, last, and all the time a Protestant organization. That doesn't mean that we are bothering anybody about their religion. What we care is that we are not going to mix up with them in this organization." Cheers drowned out Ridley's final remarks. The Hutchinson Brothers quartet broke through the applause with a rendition of "If You Don't Like Your Uncle Sammie, Then Go Back to Your Home across the Sea." The *Courier* concluded that the rally was a success, claiming that the general enthusiasm "brought down the house."[13]

In the weeks and months that followed, local KKK chapters, called "klaverns," were organized in big cities and small villages throughout the Hoosier state. Evansville itself became the home of the KKK in the North. The Klan desired to project a new image of itself. Dr. Ridley promoted it not as an organization of southern renegades from the Reconstruction era, but rather as a congregation of sophisticated community leaders who longed to preserve "the American Way of Life."

According to James Madison in his book *The Indiana Way*, the new Ku Klux Klan "was like the League of Women Voters or the Indiana Farm Bureau. It offered a community of membership, a program of action, and a potential to engage in politics outside the structure of the two major parties."[14] Promoting a social and political agenda thinly veiled in Christian values and American patriotism, the Klan began to infiltrate the highest levels of Indiana politics and civic associations. It targeted "racial, ethnic and spiritual transgressors,"[15] primarily African Americans, Catholics, and Jews. During a period when Prohibition ruled the land, the Klan's moral values struck a chord with many white Protestant Hoosiers. Fears of moral depravity were especially strong in

Evansville, where segregation was already seen as a means of preserving the moral sanctity of the community.

The Klan was moving in to stay. And Charlie Wiggins wanted out.

In July 1922, one month after the Klan rally, Roberta Wiggins's brother, Elvia Sullinger, arrived from his home in Brooklyn for a visit. During the war, he had commanded a Negro army unit in France. Upon his return to the United States, he served with the National War Veterans Association. As part of a program sponsored by the NWVA and the *New York Age* newspaper, Sullinger traveled throughout the Midwest to explore a recent trend among African Americans who were moving from the South to northern cities, such as Chicago, Detroit, Cleveland, and Indianapolis. Sullinger termed the trend "the Negro Exodus"; it would later come to be known as the Great Migration.

When Elvia arrived in Evansville, he was shocked to see the horrific conditions in which many blacks lived. The death of his three nephews, two of whom he had never seen, as well as of Charlie's parents, angered him. He implored his sister and her husband to move out of Vanderburgh County immediately.

Elvia had just visited Indianapolis, where jobs in the manufacturing industry were at an all-time high. At the heart of this manufacturing boom was the automobile industry. More than 250 different makes and models of cars rolled off the Indy assembly lines during the decade, a fact that, no doubt, piqued Charlie's interest. Housing, while segregated, offered amenities superior to the squalid conditions most blacks in Evansville faced. A thriving colored business district allowed African Americans to enjoy their own shops, to dine at their own eateries, and even to watch their own baseball teams.

Elvia's argument must have been convincing. Two months later, Charlie and Roberta borrowed a car, loaded their belongings on a trailer, and braved the dusty, unpaved roads that led from Evansville to Indianapolis. Roberta remembered, "It was like running away from a cloud of sadness." Leon "Al" Warren, a family friend, recalled Charlie's final memory of the Pocket City. "Evansville represented some sad times for Charlie and Roberta. One time, many years after the fact, he laughed and told me that his favorite view of Evansville was the view over his shoulder as he looked back, heading out of town."

2.

The Dawn of a New Opportunity

Hoosier playwright and Pulitzer Prize–winning author Booth Tarkington made a sweeping prediction about automobiles in his 1919 novel *The Magnificent Ambersons:* "They are here, and almost all outward things are going to be different because of what they bring." In perhaps no other city in America was Tarkington's assessment as true as in the city of Indianapolis during this era. In the early twentieth century, most of the country's finest luxury cars—Coles, Stutzes, Marmons, Cords, Duesenbergs—were produced in Indianapolis. The city's explosive success in the manufacturing industry inspired a national business journal to remark, "Naptown's wealth and trade increase materially day by day, making the Hoosier state the Queen of Central Western States."[1]

Charlie and Roberta Wiggins arrived in Indianapolis in the fall of 1922. The couple settled into a home on West Street, two blocks south of Indiana Avenue in the heart of the city's African-American district. Life on "the Avenue," as the neighborhood was known, was far removed from the bleakness Charlie and Roberta had endured in Evansville.

Nearly one-third of the city's black residents lived within eight blocks of Indiana Avenue. The business district featured more than thirty restaurants, twenty-six groceries, tailors, undertakers, barbers, Ward's Sanitarium (a medical facility for African Americans), and the Plaza Hotel. As well, the Avenue was home to the *Indianapolis Recorder*, a nationally distributed black newspaper; national clothing and jacket manufacturers; and the international hair-care empire of Madam C. J. Walker, one of the country's first black female millionaires.

Elvia Sullinger had visited Indianapolis on two occasions in the months following the First World War. In a *New York Age* article he noted that "progressive Negroes" were at the heart of the city's black community.[2] Indeed, African-American life in Indianapolis was far advanced over Evansville. The Indianapolis ABCs, an all-black baseball team sponsored by the American Brewing Company, won the "Colored World Championship" in 1916 and became a founding member of the Negro National League in 1920. African-American churches, part of the bedrock of most black communities, were strong and active. The Senate Avenue YMCA, founded by noted black business leaders including Madam C. J. Walker, was the largest colored YMCA in the country. And black social orders, such as the Elks and the Knights of Pythias, gave African-American residents a sense of pride and heritage.

At the core of this electric social renaissance was the Avenue's music scene. Russell Smith, an early ragtime pianist, first performed in Indianapolis during the 1910s. He directed a city dance orchestra that featured the likes of Eubie Blake and Noble Sissle. (Blake and Sissle composed a stage revue, *Shuffle Along*, in 1921, which popularized dances such as the Charleston and the Black Bottom.) Frank Clay, known in Indianapolis as "the Black Sousa," melded ragtime with his own military-band sound to create memorable works that crossed racial divides. Both Smith and Clay played for black audiences in clubs such as the Washington Theatre and for white audiences in places such as Riverside Park Pavilion. At times they performed in both white and black arenas in a single night.

The 1920s saw a multitude of black jazz clubs lining the Avenue. Prohibition was still in effect, but the laws banning alcohol did little to stem the tide of enthusiasm. Many new dance clubs were established in the heart of the African-American community, including the Indiana

Theatre, the Broadway Theatre, Tomlinson Hall, and the Walker Theatre. Each played host to many favorite local musicians and budding national acts. Indianapolis was a good stopping point for many bands migrating from the South to the clubs on the south side of Chicago. Gennett Records, in nearby Richmond, was one of the first recording studios in the nation to permit African Americans to record jazz (often called "race music"). Noted black musicians Ferdinand "Jelly Roll" Morton, Joe "King" Oliver, and Louis Armstrong each signed their first recording contract at Gennett. Many of these artists and their bands stopped in Indianapolis to perform before heading to the Windy City.

These performances often attracted a mixed audience of whites and blacks, as well as the attention of the mainstream press. Perhaps the *Indianapolis Times* best captured the essence of the buzzing social scene along Indiana Avenue during the 1920s. A *Times* reporter, sent to cover the grand opening of the Hollywood Café, noted, "The inside of the place, after midnight, became bedlam. The music continued to get hotter. As the orchestra members perspired, so did the dancers. Signs of intoxication were evident. No open drinking was seen . . . but several persons found it hard to mount the narrow stairway to the scene of activity. Two Negro women put on some warm stuff billed as 'all that is late.' They sang and crooned some of the 'hottest jazz what am,' intermingled with snappy dancing."

The review concluded, "As soon as the crowd began to grow the small dance floor in the center of the cabaret became overcrowded, and dancers found it much more convenient to dance between the tables and other spots on the floor. After midnight it was practically impossible to obtain a table, and persons lined the front and sides of the soda fountain. [People] danced . . . until light penetrated the windows [the next] morning."[3]

Roberta Wiggins "ate up the social scene," remembered Mildred Overton. "This was her chance to build up her modeling career again. She could also join the nicest clubs and socialize with the important '[well]-to-do' women in the community. I'm sure it was a breath of fresh air for her. Uncle Charlie, on the other hand, could care less about the social scene. To him, moving to Indianapolis meant a chance to work in a place where automobiles were very important to many other folks, just as they were to him."

Upon their arrival in Indianapolis, Charlie answered an advertisement for a head mechanic's position at the garage of Louis W. Sagalowsky on Merrill Street, in a Jewish neighborhood just south of the Circle Monument downtown. Sagalowsky owned a building that stretched across nearly the entire block. The building included shops that specialized in auto parts production, interior work, and general maintenance and repairs. Charlie rode from his West Street home twelve blocks south on his bicycle, because he did not own a car. With a copy of the advertisement in one hand and a box of tools in the other, he knocked on the door of the shop and asked to see Mr. Sagalowsky.

The garage owner had his own unusual "measuring stick" for finding a qualified mechanic. In the back of the shop was a Chrysler Champion. The car seemed to defy fixing. Several candidates for the position had tinkered with it in an attempt to reengineer the engine block and get the car running again. To date, none had had any success. Now it was Charlie's turn.

Charlie attempted to turn the engine over and listened to the low grinding sound that emanated from under the hood. His trained ear sensed immediately that the magneto, a small rotating electric generator, had to be reset. He went to work and realigned a tiny revolving arm on the maladjusted part. But even with that problem fixed, he could tell that something else was not functioning properly. He crawled under the chassis for a closer look.

As his examination went on, it grew dark. Charlie asked to return to the garage the following morning to fix the car. Historian Boniface Hardin remembered Charlie's story: "There were a few snickers at this, as others in the garage knew [the Champion] was impossible to fix. Charlie placed a bet with the manager, who agreed to give him a job if he could fix it."[4]

When Charlie arrived the next morning, he was surprised to see the garage crowded with people, each wanting to see firsthand whether the colored mechanic could repair the troubled Champion. Crawling back under the car, Charlie went to work on the drive chain. The car's engine design had concealed the problem; it could not be seen by simply looking under the hood. Only by crawling under the car could Charlie feel that the chain had slipped from the front end and was ready to break.

Within minutes, he peered out from under the car and asked the manager to send for a new chain. Two hours later Charlie slipped the new chain into place. He started the engine. The exhaust pipe coughed up puffs of black smoke. The engine turned over, popping, whirring, and smoothing itself into a perfect churning rhythm. The sound brought a smile to the face of the mechanic from Evansville with the trained mechanical ear. Louis Sagalowsky also grinned. He had found his new mechanic.

"Superb mechanical ability was really a great American art form," noted automotive historian Joe Freeman. "And this was as much, certainly, a part of the black community as it was of American society as a whole. . . . Automobiles were still a 'New Frontier' at that time. There were no rules, so to speak. Guys who worked in garages were always trying to invent 'the better mousetrap,' trying to come up with a slicker and better solution to make their cars run better. . . . And Charlie Wiggins, particularly, proved that his practical skills were enormous."

All about the city, new cars rolled off the assembly lines. The booming industry in Indianapolis gave rise to a spectacular auto racing event, held on a two-and-a-half-mile brick-paved oval just west of the city. Four Indianapolis automotive pioneers, Carl Fisher, James Allison, Arthur Newby, and Frank Wheeler, had bought a large plot of land five miles west of downtown. There they developed a permanent testing ground and racing circuit that came to be known as the Indianapolis Motor Speedway. The track opened in 1909 and hosted the first Indianapolis 500-Mile Race two years later. The race attracted thousands of spectators, as well as some of auto racing's finest drivers and mechanics. The "Indy 500" continues to this day to be the largest single sporting event in the world, attracting nearly half a million spectators each year.

The *Indianapolis Star* once called Indy 500 drivers motor sports' most intrepid speed demons. Donning a simple leather helmet and goggles, racing's elite manned, and manhandled, customized, high-powered engines that revved at more than 3,800 rpm. Cars often reached speeds of a hundred miles per hour, and drivers battled for position around tight turns. The cars had no power steering. Drivers had to pump their own oil continuously throughout the race, while at the same time applying the brakes, shifting gears, and steering at top speed through a maze of other drivers.

Joe Freeman recalled the rugged conditions in which early racecar

In 1922 Charlie moved to Indianapolis and worked as head mechanic for a south-side garage owner, Louis Sagalowsky. Charlie is pictured here in the center, flanked by two unidentified friends, behind Sagalowsky's garage on Merrill Street. Courtesy Mrs. Mildred Overton

drivers often competed: "Not very many people had a lot of money. So these guys would go out and basically take whatever they could find, and, for a dollar a part, put together a car known simply as a 'Special,' like a 'Joe's Special' or a 'Tony's Garage Special.' Many of these cars were downright aesthetic embarrassments. But those were the conditions many of these drivers and mechanics had to face. As a result, these cars were wildly unpredictable, and in a heated racing competition, they could be dangerous, even deadly."

Donald Davidson, historian and curator of the Indianapolis Motor Speedway Museum in Indianapolis, elaborated on the dangers these fearless sportsmen faced. "You had very few state-of-the-art racetracks back in those days. Most of these locations were simple dirt ovals cut out of the countryside. The tracks were very rough, with lots of holes, lots of bumping and gouging. . . . It would get so dusty out on the track that drivers could not see directly in front of them. They had to look up at light poles or a tree line and judge when the bank of trees began to bend. Only then did they know to start their turn."

Davidson continued, "Drivers didn't have seat belts either. Some drivers would tie themselves in with a rope. Others opted not to be secured to the vehicle, choosing instead to be thrown clear of the car during an accident. Cars were so sturdy that if you got into a flip, it was better to be thrown out on the first turn-over and land on the ground, rather than to ride it out in the car."

Auto racing began in Europe near the turn of the century. But this new breed of American racers captured the attention and enthusiasm of sports fans all over the world. One English journalist noted, "The professional American motor racing 'circus,' with entrants, mechanics, championship cars, and trailers in tow—a colourful, dedicated, unselfconscious bunch of professionals—has no parallel in Europe. It has been playing to audiences large and small, sophisticated and sensation-seeking, since the automobile became an established feature of American life."[5]

Historian Richard Pierce noted, "Racecar drivers were kind of like the outlaws of the Old West—living on the edge of their seat, unpredictable, tough. They were a combination of brains and brawn, which was a new, evolving definition of manhood during the early twentieth century. They were trying to manipulate the physical environment, especially the mechanical physical environment. But they were also conquering the mental, courageous aspect of [the environment], as well. In a special way, they were the maestros of both worlds."

White America widely embraced these dashing and daring young drivers as the sport's popularity skyrocketed. Likewise, many African Americans were enchanted by racecar drivers, their raw courage and their thirst for speed. Unlike white Americans, however, blacks who yearned to hop behind the wheel of a powerful racing engine had no opportunity to do so. Joe Freeman reflected, "There's really an interesting confluence of social change that begins to take effect in American society right after the First World War. Black Americans are staking a new claim on their heritage and on their rights in society. This also included the major sporting events of the day. And in Indianapolis, a town with a strong automotive heritage and a strong racing heritage, it made perfect sense that African Americans would want to pursue those passions in great earnest and create opportunities for themselves."

In 1929, the *Indianapolis Recorder* retold some sketchy details of what was believed to have been the first auto racing event held by African-American drivers. In 1911, four black mechanics in Fort Worth, Texas, borrowed some high-wheeled roadsters and staged a race on a half-mile track. The *Recorder* noted, "It was what might be called a sweepstakes, with no particular limit as to distance. The boys had little knowledge of the racing game, no idea of centrifugal force, but plenty of guts. And when they got the gun, the show began. Crowding began at the first turn, and some close shaves were made on the first lap and by the time the old boats got under headway, things began to happen. And from that time it is a short story. In one, two, three, four order every man jack blew the track at the curves like mud flying from the wheel of a car 'doing forty.' There was no finish, but it was the beginning of auto racing by colored boys."[6]

Charlie Wiggins was one of those young African Americans who envisioned himself competing at the nation's top auto racing events. In 1923 he received permission from Louis Sagalowsky to use a corner of the garage to build his own racing machine. He began with a simple chassis design. He then created each part by hand, using discarded materials from a junkyard located just a block from the shop. Because of his small stature, he had to extend the reach of his pedals, levers, and controls and build a raised seating area to allow a clear line of sight from behind the massive engine block. He even devised a unique oil system using two pumps with a dry oil base—a system several racing mechanics, both black and white, used in later years. He painted a large "23" on the side of the car, short for "23 Skidoo," a popular catchphrase of the day that meant to move out or leave in a hurry. He called it the "Wiggins Special."

Charlie dreamed of one day competing at the Indy 500. But the Indianapolis Motor Speedway, like many social, business, and civic organizations in Indianapolis at the time, was segregated. Presenting an even greater obstacle was the American Automobile Association, the official sanctioning body of auto racing nationwide. The AAA enforced unwritten, but clearly understood, rules regarding minority participation in all sanctioned racing events. According to many personal accounts and reports in the black press, the AAA steadfastly refused to allow an African American to compete for racing's top prizes.

In 1910 Berna Eli "Barney" Oldfield, America's top white AAA driver, competed in a one-on-one match race against Jack Johnson, the black heavyweight boxing champion. The two staged the event merely as a promotional stunt to attract greater interest in the sport and to reap a hefty profit on the sensational hype created by promoters of the event. In their respective fields, both men had larger-than-life reputations and egos to match. Johnson, the boisterous fighter, once boasted, "I'd be happy to beat Mr. Oldfield at his game as easy as I beat Mr. Jeffries [the former heavyweight champion] in the ring. In fact, I've got $5,000 that says I'm a faster driver on any track." To add to the hype, the *New York Times* printed a statement that noted that Johnson "won several victories the previous winter in a southern California Racing Carnival," and that he knew how to handle himself in four-wheeled competition. Oldfield, the burly, cigar-chomping speed champion, could not resist the challenge. He issued a public reply: "I note in today's paper a challenge made by Jack Johnson to race me for $5,000. . . . Automobile racing is my business, and if Johnson or any other man in the world has $5,000 to bet he can beat me, I am ready to meet him."[7]

In defiance of orders from the AAA, the race was held on October 25, 1910, on a dirt track in Sheepshead Bay, New York. In an exaggeratedly macho move, the two men strutted to the starting line prior to the event and shook hands with powerful grips, intending not only to greet but also to intimidate each other. Both winced in pain. But on the track, Johnson was the only one to wince. Oldfield, the seasoned racing great, easily beat his rival. Promoters desired a close finish to give the crowd a more thrilling show. Once during the race, as Oldfield pulled into the pits, an official shouted, "This has gotta look like a race. . . . Let him pass you a coupla times. Then you can take him in the stretch." Oldfield only growled back at him, "I'll give him a beating he'll remember!" As he coasted across the finish line, reporters flocked to his car. He told them, "I can tell you this. When they took old Jack outta that car, he sure wasn't smilin'."[8]

When the AAA got word that the two sportsmen had held the event, it branded Oldfield, America's top driver, an outlaw and immediately banned him from all sanctioned competitions. The organization's leaders were outraged by the apparent mockery the match race made of the sport. Adding to their outrage was the fact that Oldfield was willing to compete against a colored athlete. They issued a statement to the press, saying, "That Johnson affair was simply a crude circus act, and we won't stand still for this kind of farcical behavior in competition. Our decision is final, and we feel fully justified."[9]

Oldfield was hardly fazed by the incident. The renegade driver had great disdain for racing's governing body and was infamous among members of the group for his long history of disagreements and run-ins with it. The following season the AAA reinstated Oldfield, as more and more spectators demanded to see him. In the short term, the stunt did little to detract from the meteoric careers of Johnson and Oldfield. In the long term, however, the racial dispute made the AAA far more wary of possible future events in which blacks and whites might compete against one other. Joe Freeman underscored the point, saying, "If there had not been a hard and fast color line established in the early years of the AAA, one was certainly developed in officials' minds after the Johnson-Oldfield incident."

From that moment on, opportunities for Charlie Wiggins and nearly all other African Americans in auto racing were virtually nonexistent. One exception was "Rajo" Jack DeSoto, a talented black driver from California. He took his nickname from the Rajo head, an engine part often installed on a standard V-8 engine to allow the car to race at speeds far in excess of original technical specifications. DeSoto was a tall, slender youth during his days as a mechanic's assistant for a white racing team on the West Coast. However, by 1923, when he was competing full time, he had ballooned to a robust 245 pounds. Though tightly squeezed into the chassis of his 275-horsepower racecar, he proved that he was a remarkable competitor, building a dirt track racing career that spanned forty years.

Because of AAA mandates, "Rajo" Jack was not allowed to compete against white drivers in sanctioned events. So Jack and many white drivers who admired his skills as a driver and mechanic formed their own "outlaw circuit," which grew popular in southern California. Eventually the group promoted a national barnstorming tour with stops in cities such as Atlanta, Dallas, and Davenport, Iowa. After a Louisville, Kentucky, driver by the name of Joie Ray shattered auto racing's color barrier in 1946, "Rajo" Jack was asked to participate in a series of AAA-sanctioned races sponsored by the Honolulu Chamber of Commerce in

"Rajo Jack" DeSoto was one of America's earliest African-American auto racers. He began his career in California in 1923 and traveled the country on a barnstorming tour throughout the decade. Courtesy Bruce Craig Photos

1954. Though he had lost an eye in a racing accident in 1938, the sixty-year-old driver still captured two victories, demonstrating his unheralded talent.

DeSoto's career as a businessman was varied and profitable. He owned a steam cleaning business, managed several automotive garages at various times in his life, and even managed a trucking company on the West Coast. His racing career, albeit successful, was one of only a handful of documented achievements in black auto racing during the early part of the twentieth century. There would have been even fewer if not for a dedicated group of African Americans who, soon after DeSoto's start in 1923, began a concerted effort to organize colored drivers and mechanics and promote a national circuit dedicated to promoting blacks in auto racing. As historian Joe Freeman described the situation, "You have Indianapolis, a city that's building a reputation as a premier auto producer. As well, you have a black social culture that is in the process of a civic and cultural renaissance. When you brought those two things together, something special was bound to happen."

That "something special" began on August 2, 1924.

William Rucker had a way with people. At least, that is how most remembered the Indianapolis railway worker. A distinguished gentleman who often wore derby hats and smoked nickel cigars, Rucker was seldom sad or discouraged, despite hard circumstances throughout his life. Rucker was born in Murfreesboro, Tennessee, in 1868. As a boy, he witnessed firsthand the brutality of the newly founded Ku Klux Klan. Public lynchings were commonplace in the area. Opportunities were few for the black son of a sharecropper in a city plagued by racial violence.

Rucker took a job with a railway company, working outdoors on the line. Eventually he worked his way up to crew supervisor, the highest position allowed to an African American at the time. By 1910, he had finally saved enough money to move his wife and three daughters to Indianapolis in search of greater peace and prosperity. His experience on the railroad helped him earn a position with the Cincinnati, Indianapolis and Western Railway. There he developed friendships with railroad managers and crew chiefs. His cheerful attitude helped him develop a reputation for hobnobbing. He cultivated many important relationships with both blacks and whites. Eventually he earned a position as the only colored shop manager for the line.

Rucker was also an avid auto racing fan. For several seasons he attended the annual Indianapolis Motor Speedway classic. Family members recalled that he joined other African-American patrons in a small "coloreds only" section of the grandstand, located between turns one and two of the giant two-and-a-half-mile oval. His grandson Paul Bateman recalled, "He always dreamed of seeing a black man compete at the Indy 500. But the social limits being what they were at the time, it just wasn't meant to be."

Boniface Hardin added, "The best thing that a colored man could expect do at the Speedway at that time would be to work as a janitor or to work as the man who sold the soft drinks and hot dogs. There was never any notion that coloreds could do anything more at the Indy 500. Everyone seemed to accept that." He paused. "Everyone, that is, except William Rucker."

Rucker had been familiar with two successful black baseball managers, Charles Isham "C. I." Taylor of the Indianapolis ABCs and Andrew "Rube" Foster of the Chicago American Giants, who, in 1920, banded together to create a professional baseball league exclusively for African Americans. The Negro National League had gained widespread popularity in a short period of time. Paul Bateman recalled, "I think my grandfather wondered why the same thing couldn't be done for auto racing, especially in Indianapolis, where cars and car racing were so popular."

Hardin commented, "In the context of a segregated community, Rucker was saying, 'If we can't be a part of the mainstream culture, let's create our own cultural event. Let's do it ourselves.' And it was that epiphany that precipitated the strength, courage, and motivation Rucker needed to convince others to overcome the social conventions of the day and to strike out on their own."

By 1924 William Rucker was a noted civic leader in the black community. Paul Bateman remembered, "He always walked proudly down the Avenue puffing on a cigar and tipping his hat to all the pretty ladies. He was a real mover and shaker. All of the top political candidates wanted him to speak on their behalf. Of course, his interests were with the black community. Depending on the candidates' views, he might be a Republican one year and a Democrat the next. He always worked the system to his advantage."

That spring Rucker decided to use his hard-earned community influence to create a unique new sporting venture. One afternoon he called a meeting in the back office of a popular billiard parlor located at 455 Indiana Avenue. The proprietor of the establishment, Harry N. Dunnington, was a sound business manager and a good friend of his. Also attending the meeting was Alvin D. Smith, a specialist in promotion and event planning who ran his own advertising agency on Michigan Avenue one block east of Indiana Avenue. As well, Rucker sought help from Robert L. Brokenburr, one of the city's most celebrated black attorneys, who once served as part-time legal counsel to Madam C. J. Walker.

The smoke from Rucker's cigars filled the room. On the top of a filing cabinet in the back corner, a Starr phonograph player (manufactured in Richmond, Indiana) played tinny "race records" of jazz music. Each man listened eagerly as Rucker began to unveil his plan. He wanted to form an organization that would stage and promote national auto racing events exclusively for African-American drivers and mechanics. He asked all the men in attendance to become the founding members of a group he dubbed the Colored Speedway Association.

"Automobile racing was as American as apple pie at the time and very exciting," Joe Freeman commented. "Black folks looked to become part of mainstream society during the 1920s, and they knew—especially in Indianapolis—that racing was an important part of the American experience. They were determined to carve out a place for themselves in that arena. The dam was about to break, and the Colored Speedway Association made sure it did."

Dunnington would serve as general manager, running many of the day-to-day business activities of the CSA through his Indiana Avenue offices. Brokenburr would help with legal matters, and his status as a civic leader would gain them needed support from white civic and government officials. Smith would be the Association's director of publicity. Two additional black business leaders, Earnest Jay Butler and George LeMon, were brought in later to assist Smith as advertising agents for the group. Rucker himself served as the Association's president, earning the nickname "Pres." "Rucker had the knowledge and the power to pull together the talents needed to start such an organization," remarked Boniface Hardin. "Where he needed help was in the financial area. 'Pres' needed some support from the white community. And that's where his own personality and political savvy came in handy."

During his first few years with the CI&W Railway, William Rucker had built a solid working relationship with the line's chief mechanical engineer, Oscar Edward Schilling. Now, in the spring of 1924, Rucker strolled up the tree-lined walks of tiny Flackville Township (now Eagledale) to pay his co-worker a visit. Schilling's home on Pershing Street was less than a mile from the Indianapolis Motor Speedway. Each May

Original members of the Colored Speedway Association, founded in 1924. From left to right: (seated) Harry Dunnington, William "Pres" Rucker, George LeMon; (standing) Oscar E. Schilling, Earnest Jay Butler, Alvin D. Smith, Harry A. Earl. Courtesy Mrs. Mildred Overton

Oscar would sit on his front porch and listen to the constant roar of engines, as drivers and mechanics prepared for the annual Memorial Day staging of the Indy 500. Schilling, an avid sports enthusiast with a deep passion for fishing, hiking, and hunting, as well as automobile racing, promoted a number of races each summer at Walnut Gardens Speedway, a one-mile dirt oval carved into a cornfield in Mooresville, a few miles southwest of Indianapolis.

Schilling appreciated the hard work and dedication needed to become a success in any business venture. He had worked his way up through the ranks of the CI&W line while studying drafting and engineering through the International Correspondence School. Jack

Schilling, his son, remembered, "He got promoted quickly through the ranks, because he was such a hard worker. But there were others who worked hard, too . . . black fellas . . . who couldn't get promoted because of their race. Dad never much liked that."

The Schilling family was Catholic. Oscar, in particular, showed great disdain for the political antics of the Ku Klux Klan and other segregationist groups. "I think Dad felt a closer bond to the blacks and the Jews because of the social pressures of the day," Jack Schilling commented. Like William Rucker, Oscar Schilling enjoyed a fine cigar. And on a mild spring day in the spring of 1924, the two sat on Schilling's porch smoking cigars and discussing Rucker's proposal for a colored racing circuit. The idea appealed to the railroad manager. "Dad always felt that a good idea was a good idea. He didn't care whether a black guy or a white guy thought of it," Jack noted.

Schilling asked Rucker to return the following week to meet his friend and fellow CI&W executive Harry A. Earl, a steam-engine specialist with the line. Earl was a motor sports enthusiast who was the manager and promoter of the Walnut Gardens Speedway. "If ever there was a guy interested in auto racing, it was Harry Earl," Jack Schilling remembered with a laugh. "Harry was quite a speedster himself. Even in his passenger car, he just could not seem to stay within the posted speed limit. And that got him into a bit of trouble from time to time. He used to tell police these tall tales that the soles of his shoes were too thick, and he could not feel the accelerator very well with his foot to tell how fast he was revving the engine. One officer actually made him shave down the sole of his shoes, so that he could get a better feel for how fast he was going.

"Dad and Harry were always the best of friends, but I think Dad thought Harry was always a damned fool," Jack reminisced. "One time Harry took his own passenger car down the dirt roads of Mooresville at nearly seventy miles per hour. He hit a rut in the road and just completely destroyed that fine car he owned. The wreck broke Harry's leg and damned near killed him. He was laid up for nearly six weeks after that little escapade. I guess you could say that Harry was addicted to speed. That's probably why he was so involved in the Walnut Gardens Speedway."

As a teenager Jack Schilling worked as a ticket taker when his father and Harry Earl promoted races at Walnut Gardens. He recalled, "The area was developed into a large park, with picnic grounds, walkways, and the like. The track was located on the northwest corner of the park. We sold tickets to get into the park, and then charged additional money to go see the races. The races were held each afternoon around 1:00 or 2:00. I'd run around yelling, 'Tickets for sale. Get your tickets for the big race.' The crowds would start coming in about nine in the morning and stay all day.

"There were bleachers around the track that held 250–300 people, and we'd sell out all the time. Lots of folks would just stand around the fencing and watch, because we sold out all the tickets. Entertainment was kinda scarce back then. So these races were the biggest things going down in that neck of the woods. My dad was not as big an auto racing fan as Harry, but I think both of them saw the popularity of racing and the strong investment potential in the sport."

Rucker spent nearly an hour explaining his plans for a colored racing circuit to Harry Earl. The white railway executive listened intently to Rucker's pitch. What Rucker did not realize, however, was that Earl did not need to rely on Rucker alone to tell him that African Americans had the ability to build and drive powerful racecars. He had seen their skill firsthand. When the Walnut Gardens Speedway was not in use, Earl allowed local drivers to test new models and engine designs on his track. One of the mechanics who frequented the Mooresville speedway was Charlie Wiggins. Harry Earl often watched as Charlie, in a car he had designed himself, roared around the dusty surface at speeds nearing seventy miles per hour. The top white drivers on the AAA circuit, using the best equipment available at the time, raced at speeds only slightly higher than Charlie's average. Impressed by his fortitude and ingenuity, Earl showed great enthusiasm for the untapped potential of black auto racing talent in Indianapolis. He was an eager participant in William Rucker's new plan.

Jack Schilling remembered, "Harry and Dad were always looking for new investment opportunities in racing. They would round up investors and maybe even use a little of their own money to get a race circuit organized and promoted. They could then take a percentage of the gate receipts to earn some money back on the events."

Rucker returned to Dunnington's office with good news: Schilling and Earl pledged to contribute $50,000, mostly through outside investments, in the Colored Speedway Association. "The meaning behind this association was highly significant," remarked historian Richard Pierce. "This group was not just a province of the drivers. It was not just a province of the promoters. This organization was a province of the community. It's not about auto racing. It's about what a black community said to a white community: that we, too, can master this Machine Age, and that we can master this craft. It said, in effect, 'We are brave, too. We are courageous, too.' And more importantly, it said to a white community that we had the wherewithal in *our* community to support *our* drivers. We will come and see them. We will support them. We will promote them and celebrate them. And that took the meaning of the Colored Speedway Association far beyond the traditional notion of sports in society."

The first act of the Association was to create a sporting event the likes of which had never before been seen in black culture—a hundred-mile test of speed and endurance to be held on a one-mile dirt track at the Indiana State Fairgrounds in Indianapolis. It was scheduled for Saturday, August 2, 1924, as part of the city's weekend celebration of Emancipation Day. That July, quarter-page newspaper advertisements began appearing in black newspapers throughout the Midwest: "Get Reservations Now to See the World's Fastest Colored Drivers Dash for $2,500 in Prizes in the First Annual 100-Mile Auto Race—Daredevil Stunts, $1,500 in Fireworks and other Events Planned—General Admission $1.00, Reserved Seats $2.00, Grandstand $1.00 and $1.25."

Rucker had a keen sense of the promotional ballyhoo of the era. Malcolm Hannon, a twenty-three-year-old chauffeur for Indiana Avenue billiard-parlor owner George Graham, was the first driver to sign up for the race. To add to the legitimacy and grandeur of the event, Rucker and Harry Earl wanted to ensure that Hannon was able to get behind the wheel of the best car available, what drivers called "getting a good ride." By calling in some favors with mechanics at the Indianapolis Motor Speedway, Rucker and Earl secured for Hannon a Barber-Warnock Ford Special, a car that had finished fifth in the 1923 Indy 500. Rucker then parked the car outside Harry Dunnington's billiard parlor, along Indiana Avenue, for all passers-by to see. Most black residents of Indianapolis had never seen a genuine Indy 500 racecar up close. Crowds gathered every day to catch a glimpse of the powerful racing machine. Posted on the car was a sign that trumpeted the big event: "Don't miss the excitement of the first annual 100-Miler, the only event staged exclusively for Men of our Race."

The stunt with the Barber-Warnock car certainly attracted local interest and attention to the event. But Rucker needed an added promotional boost nationwide. So he contacted the biggest name in black sportswriting, Frank A. "Fay" Young, sports editor for the *Chicago Defender*. Young was the country's first full-time black sportswriter. He began his career with the *Defender* in 1907 and gained national acclaim during a short stint with the *Kansas City Call*, when he covered the Kansas City Monarchs, the Negro National League's baseball powerhouse, and their celebrated pitcher, Satchel Paige.

Young was sharp-witted and gruff, yet wrote with eloquence and color. He wove his columns into a grander cultural fabric, so that each victory by a colored athlete was considered a victory for all blacks in American society. His syndicated columns were some of the most widely read articles in all of black journalism. Rucker knew that he needed Young's help to make the Colored Speedway Association's inaugural event a national success. Young had earned an ornery reputation for going against the mainstream establishment. When he learned that the lily-white American Automobile Association refused to recognize the Colored Speedway Association as a legitimate organizing body for auto racing, he immediately took interest in Rucker's initiative and pledged his support for the group.

As race day neared, Young began a series of essays in the *Defender*'s weekly "Fay Says" column. On July 5, 1924, he wrote, "This auto race will be recognized throughout the length and breadth of the land as the single greatest sports event to be staged annually by colored people. Soon, chocolate jockeys will mount their gas-snorting, rubber-shod speedway monsters as they race at death-defying speeds. The largest purses will be posted here, and the greatest array of driving talent will be in attendance in hopes of winning gold for themselves and glory for their Race."[10] Initially William Rucker had christened the event the Fame and Glory Sweepstakes. But Young's ability to be both graceful and grandiose, coupled with his passion for alliteration, inspired Rucker to rename it the Gold and Glory Sweepstakes.

On race day, August 2, Young added to his own hype. "Just now everybody is buzzing about the big automobile derby in Indianapolis— the biggest sports event of the season so far. . . . Now word comes from Indianapolis that twenty-six or more drivers will enter the elimination trials and on Saturday afternoon, fifteen will face the starter in the first big annual derby. It is certainly to be some race, and we are hoping that it is a whale of a success, because it opens a new field of sport for our fans and it opens a new field for our drivers."[11]

Young's reports, along with the Colored Speedway Association's local efforts, had worked. In the last two weeks, the number of drivers entered in the race increased from ten to twenty-six to forty. Entry forms poured in from all areas of the state, as well as from Chicago, St. Louis, Cleveland, Dayton, and New Orleans. All entrants would compete in time trials for fifteen coveted spots in the main event. Ticket sales also began to soar. Alvin Smith's Michigan Avenue office soon overflowed with more orders than his three-man promotion team could handle. He sought help from more than a dozen establishments to promote ticket sales and distribute travel information. Businesses along the Avenue, such as Strowder's Grocery, McKenzie's Pharmacy, and Fennell's Cigar Stand, lent their support. Out-of-town fans, especially from Chicago, requested that the Colored Speedway Association charter special trains and book additional hotel space for the weekend celebration.

The Indiana Business Association issued an appeal to all local businesses to close for half the day to encourage patrons to attend the race. In an interview with the *Indianapolis Freeman,* Rucker proclaimed, "This is only the beginning. It is entirely possible that there will be races similar to the 100-Mile race in different sections of the country. It is time that members of my Race are becoming famous as racing drivers."[12] Joe Freeman noted, "The promoters did everything they could to make the population understand that this was the biggest event that might ever come to the region, so you'd better make sure that you're a part of it all. This hype created an excitement level that was simply extraordinary. They wanted to make this thing into a county fair, an automobile race, a revival meeting, and an annual convention all rolled into one. And they succeeded."

On race day, the scene reflected a brilliant kaleidoscope of color, sound, and grandeur. Prior to the big event the Association staged a parade up Indiana Avenue, with drivers and race officials proudly waving to a crowd of thousands that lined the streets. Lucius Haeden, owner of the Haeden Motor Car Company of Chicago (touted in the black press as the country's only "Race owner" in the automobile industry), was the parade's grand marshal. Bands marched and played rousing renditions of popular military numbers, such as the *George Washington March*. Colorful floats added to the festive nature of the parade. At the end of the parade route, streetcars lined the Avenue, preparing to transport spectators to the Indiana State Fairgrounds.

When Rucker and the other Colored Speedway Association officials reached the track, an incredible sight met their eyes: more than twelve thousand spectators jammed the Fairgrounds grandstand. Most were dressed in their finery, with men sporting suits and ties and women wearing extravagant dresses and hats. "I think everyone realized that they were on a stage," noted Richard Pierce. "Not only the drivers, but also the spectators knew that they had to show the white community that we can do anything you can do, and we can do it with class, with style. They were saying, in effect, 'All of us, drivers, promoters, and spectators, are part of the event. We're part of this social celebration.'" Many curious fans poured into the infield of the track for a closer look at the pit area. Others grabbed a bird's-eye view, perching high among the steel rafters that supported the roof of the grandstand. Passenger cars sported license plates from places as far east as Pennsylvania and as far north as Minnesota.

Journalists from every major black newspaper crowded into a small tower that overlooked the starting line. Pathé News, a mainstream newsreel organization from Hollywood, sent a cameraman to record the historic event. Charles L. Patton, a local photographer, gathered all of the drivers, mechanics, and race officials at the starting line for a panoramic photograph of the pageantry and pride that characterized the day's events. The social significance of the day was not lost on Frank Young. His syndicated report on August 2 stated, "This Gold and Glory event is the dawn of a new opportunity, another step forward, the brushing away of another barrier, another obstacle met and surmounted by our group in the realm of sports."[13]

Leon "Al" Warren, a grocer and delivery-truck driver from Indianapolis, participated in the early years of the Gold and Glory Sweepstakes. He remembered, "To drive out there with all those folks cheering … it was a feeling I just can't describe. We never could ride with the white boys. Now we were finally getting a chance to compete in a sport we loved. We were representing ourselves as drivers, and representing all of us as a people. The feeling of accomplishment was really something … just kinda overwhelming, really."

The fifteen cars that took the starting line that day were a wild array of makes, models, and designs. "You had some drivers with top-notch cars that raced at the Indy 500," remarked Joe Freeman. "Then you had some drivers in these strange creations: the body of a Ford, the engine from a Duesenberg, and other parts from who knows where. The same could be said of the drivers. You had a handful of guys who really had a lot of experience behind the wheel. Perhaps these guys were chauffeurs or guys who would help racing mechanics drive cars during test laps. Then you had others who were simply guys down at the local garage who had a lack of experience, but also a lack of fear. They were the dangerous ones. It was a pretty crazy, and sometimes a pretty scary, mix of people and cars."

Indianapolis Motor Speedway historian Donald Davidson echoed, "Nobody had any money. A driver just sort of scraped together whatever he could. You didn't have magazines where you could order parts or go to specialty shops and buy the equipment. You just built your own stuff, and you went to the junk heap or took stuff off your passenger car, bolted it into your racing engine, and off you went. There was really very little testing done in these situations either. Most of the drivers simply drove the car up and down the street a few times, then took the thing out to the track and ran it. It was a very rugged time in auto racing history."

Among the drivers who competed in the 1924 event was Jack "Long Shot" Sargent, a St. Louis driver who tied a rope to the front bumper of his "Shield Special" and towed it behind a Model T more than 250 miles from Missouri to Indianapolis. Also included was William Walthall, chief mechanic for the American Giants Garage in Chicago. Andrew "Rube" Foster, the great Negro National League baseball manager and owner of the garage, co-sponsored Walthall with the *Chicago Defender*. Together they agreed to pay the race's $50 entry fee and arranged the loan of a AAA-sanctioned racecar to Walthall—a Marmon similar to the vehicle that had won the very first Indy 500. Another driver, A. J.

Several drivers in the inaugural Gold and Glory Sweepstakes pose on
the Indiana State Fairgrounds track on August 2, 1924. Courtesy Mrs.
Mildred Overton

"Demon King" Russell, was a pit-crew mechanic for a white driver in
New Orleans. He was in Chicago for a series of Midwest races in which
his Louisiana team competed. The head mechanic of Russell's team
brought two cars to the Chicago events and offered one to Russell for the
Gold and Glory Sweepstakes.

The most colorful driver on the starting line that day was William
"Wild Bill" Jeffries, a beefy Chicago bondsman and real-estate broker.
Jeffries weighed more than 225 pounds and had designed a special
chassis in his racecar to accommodate his wide frame. He drove a
$12,000 Ford Frontenac, considered a high-priced, high-end car in any
racing circuit. Most drivers built their own cars or simply borrowed cars
from willing white car owners. Jeffries was one of the only black drivers
who could afford to purchase his own top-of-the-line Indy racecar.

The burly bondsman was known for his deep pockets and his flamboyant nature. Away from the track, he dressed immaculately in tailor-made suits and gold jewelry. He had his own chauffeur to pilot a series of elegant Stutz automobiles, expensive passenger cars built for speed. Roberta Wiggins remembered that "Wild Bill" was "always walking around like he owned the place." Black journalists in Chicago heralded the talented driver as "the Black DePalma," comparing his skills to the celebrated white Indy 500 driver Ralph DePalma, who was the fastest qualifier at the Indy 500 in 1920 and 1921.[14]

Many drivers and promoters were suspicious of how the ostentatious Jeffries was able to have so much money at his disposal. Even the most successful bondsmen and real-estate brokers of the time could not afford the luxuries Jeffries enjoyed. Drivers and spectators at the Gold and Glory Sweepstakes recalled some of the more "creative" ways "Wild Bill" earned extra money to feed his all-consuming passions. "No black man ever walked around looking the way 'Wild Bill' did," remembered Al Warren. "Back then there was only one way for a colored businessman in Chicago to make that kind of money, and that was through the Mob."

Jeffries's office, near Thirty-fifth and State Streets in Chicago, was located in a neighborhood often referred to as the Black Metropolis or the Black Belt. During the 1920s, when the Chicago Mafia ran city politics, several agencies operated illegal gambling establishments. The success of these "policy stations," as they were known, stemmed largely from booking agents, or "bookies," who often ran an illegal numbers racket from the back room of an established facility, such as a restaurant, a billiard parlor, or a cigar shop. Author Dempsey Travis, in *An Autobiography of Black Chicago*, noted of Jeffries's neighborhood, "Underworld characters, jazz, prostitution, alcohol and dope moved through the residential sections of the black community the way the Illinois Central Railroad ran through the little towns and cities between Chicago and New Orleans. Vice first surrounded and then infiltrated the 'Black Belt.' It was all but impossible for black families to escape the stench of corruption and immorality, because it was operated under a protective political umbrella."[15]

To many, Bill Jeffries had earned a respectable reputation in the Black Metropolis as a reputable real-estate broker. In other circles he was considered a "kingpin" along the Black Belt, an organizer of a variety of numbers rackets for the Mafia within the African-American community. Police and city government officials were completely aware of Jeffries's underground policy station, as they were of so many of the popular gambling rings of the day. But with a few friendly financial kickbacks and "donations," most officials were willing to look the other way.

Like Rucker in Indianapolis, Jeffries desired to create an organization dedicated to promoting African Americans in auto racing. Following Rucker's model, Jeffries co-founded the Chicago Colored Speedway Association, headquartered in the Johnson Building at 3520 State Street in the center of the Black Metropolis. The Chicago CSA was on the second floor, just above the Dreamland Ballroom and Café, one of the swankiest clubs in black Chicago. Musicians such as Louis Armstrong, Joe "King" Oliver, Ethel Waters, and Bessie Smith performed there nightly. Dempsey Travis noted that the location was "the heart of the 'Black Belt' and the center of sporting life in Chicago."[16] Mob presence was strong in the area. The Dreamland itself was owned by gangsters. Two other clubs two blocks away, the Sunset Café and the Plantation, were owned by members of Al Capone's Mafia syndicate.

William Bottoms, the business manager of the Dreamland, was a savvy black businessman and a talented cook who had a passion for fast cars and good food. (He left Chicago in 1934 to become the head chef for heavyweight boxing champion Joe Louis.) Bottoms was a good friend of Bill Jeffries. When Jeffries talked of creating a Chicago racing association for African Americans, he asked Bottoms to join him as acting president of the group. Jeffries served as vice president.

The *Chicago Defender* once noted that Bottoms and Jeffries were "the best of friends and the greatest of rivals."[17] The two promoted and drove in Colored Speedway Association events for nearly a decade. Backed by a seemingly endless stream of funds from the Dreamland, Bottoms and Jeffries drove the finest racecars money could buy. While Bottoms typically stayed near Chicago to keep his eye on the day-to-day business of the club, Jeffries toured the Midwest in his $12,000 "Dreamland Ford Special."

"Auto racing in the 1920s was a very, very expensive sport, just as it is today," said Joe Freeman. "Drivers were scraping along on very little and took any financial contribution they could get in order to get a stronger, faster car. . . . And it really makes sense that gamblers and

Mafia men might contribute to this cause. Since so few drivers had good cars, they were the ones who stood a better chance of winning. By financing a car, a sponsor could expect a payback of something like half of all winnings. Plus, if they were smart, they also had a number of bets running on the side to make more money. In big races like the Gold and Glory Sweepstakes, the windfall for a sponsor could be quite significant."

Averitte Corley, a spectator and the nephew of Bobby Lee Wallace, an early participant in the Gold and Glory Sweepstakes, remembered the nature of the gambling racket associated with the races. "There were several racketeers with what you might call a very successful operation running along Indiana Avenue during the mid-1920s. There was one fella named 'Goosie' Lee and another by the name of Archie Greathouse. Those guys ran the numbers circuit in Indy. Then there was Aratha Edlan, the owner and proprietor of the Panama Tavern on the Avenue. All those guys had a numbers game going. Each was like a cross between a state lottery and a bookie. They'd even sponsor cars and drivers at the event itself. It was a way to support more drivers and generate more business. A number of social pressures were keeping these guys from making a solid, honest career. Aratha Edlan was a pharmacist with a degree from Butler University. But he had a hard time making it as a pharmacist outside of the black neighborhood, due to segregation. So a lot of these guys turned to the illegal gambling racket to make good money. And, boy! Did they ever make good money."

Corley concluded, "These numbers men got in thick with a number of Chicago Mafia types who were big-time sportsmen. They all sponsored racing teams and drivers. A lot of the black drivers were chauffeurs and mechanics for these guys. And several of them received support from the Mob or the racketeers, both in Indianapolis and Chicago. That's how a lot of the drivers could afford to compete at the Gold and Glory Sweepstakes."

Conspicuously missing from the starting lineup at the inaugural Gold and Glory event was Charlie Wiggins. Those closest to the Indianapolis mechanic and driver offered three different explanations for his absence. Both Al Warren and Red Oliver noted that it was Charlie's nature to be a perfectionist. Even though his speeds were quite impressive, he was possessed by what Joe Freeman called "the demon tweak," the urge to make ceaseless, subtle refinements to the car and all its parts. "He was like an artist," Al Warren remembered. "Even though most of us would have considered ourselves ready to race, Charlie just didn't consider his car to be in top condition. So he decided to hold off that first year."

Charlie's wife, Roberta, recalled some intense encounters with Bill Jeffries of Chicago. "Wild Bill" had worked closely with Rucker and the Colored Speedway Association in Indiana to ensure that the group had appropriate backing and qualified drivers coming from the Chicago area. Roberta suspected that Jeffries might have placed some pressure on the Association to keep Charlie out of the inaugural race. "Charlie and 'Wild Bill' didn't see eye to eye, you might say. Bill was always talking big and flaunting about. Charlie didn't much care for that. . . . While he always respected Bill as a driver, Charlie never much liked his ways."

Boniface Hardin remembered another story Charlie once told him. "There was a bit of a run-in Charlie had with 'Pres' Rucker in 1924. Rucker was trying to promote the Gold and Glory as an elite race. For some reason, Charlie's size really turned him off. I mean, here's this five-and-a-half-foot guy that everyone in the garage called 'Wee' Charlie. Rucker had some preconceived notion of what a tough, aggressive driver should look like, I guess. Rucker told Charlie that he was too small, therefore he couldn't compete. It didn't seem to matter whether or not Charlie could race at top speeds. It was just, 'You're too small, so go home.' Of course, Rucker later realized what a huge mistake he'd made. But for that first race, Charlie was forced to be a spectator, not a participant."

Without Charlie in the starting lineup, fifteen of the country's fastest African-American drivers revved their engines, and the dust began to rise at the Indiana State Fairgrounds track. Each racer fell in line behind the pace car, driven by Harry Earl. At 1:30, the green flag dropped. The 1924 Gold and Glory Sweepstakes was officially under way. In an earlier time trial, Bill Jeffries had earned the pole position, the number one starting spot on the inside of the first row, where all race drivers hope to place. Jeffries, in his speedy four-cylinder Ford, tore around the first turn at an average speed of seventy-five miles per hour. In the second lap, however, an Indianapolis driver, Ben Carter, driving a "Sneider Special," overtook Jeffries. Carter's move thrilled the local fans,

The start of the first Gold and Glory Sweepstakes at the Indiana State
Fairgrounds on August 2, 1924. Courtesy Indiana State Archives—
Indiana Commission on Public Records

who, in the words of Frank Young, "gave a mighty shout and just went
dippy."[18]

Only ten laps into the race, a number of drivers, including Carter
and fellow Indianapolis driver Malcolm Hannon, pulled into the pit
area for minor adjustments. Another Indianapolis mechanic, William
Buckner, took the lead, with "Wild Bill" Jeffries only three seconds
behind. More cars began to drop out. Frank Young noted that the ill-
fated vehicles were "smoking like a 'Big Bertha' gun after it has been
discharged." For forty-eight laps, Buckner fought through the dust and
the competition to hold a slim lead. But when his car hit a large chuck-
hole in the dirt track, he lost a tire. The car began to spin, eventually
settling in the weedy infield along the back straightaway. Jeffries was
now in the lead. As he passed by the grandstand, he waved to the crowd.

"Isn't that just like 'Big Jeff'?" quipped a journalist from the *Indianapolis Freeman*.

Jeffries's lead was short-lived, however. Four laps later he signaled to his pit crew that his car was malfunctioning. On lap 53 of the hundred-lap affair, he pulled into the pits and never pulled out again. A large rock had shot through his engine block and severed the main water line. The crewmen could not repair his car in time to allow him back into the competition. Frank Young lamented, "Chicago's best hope for a championship just went goodbye."[19]

Ben Carter was out in front of the pack again until engine problems forced him back into the pits on the sixty-fifth lap. Mechanics worked frantically to make the necessary repairs. Falling five laps behind, he gunned his engine at full speed in a desperate attempt to catch up. His

William "Wild Bill" Jeffries was a flamboyant, cigar-chomping racketeer from Chicago who distributed bootleg liquor throughout the black neighborhoods of the Windy City. He used his underworld contacts to purchase his own $12,000 Ford Frontenac racecar and competed in the inaugural Gold and Glory Sweepstakes in 1924. Courtesy Mrs. Mildred Overton.

Malcolm Hannon, a chauffeur from Indianapolis (*seated, right*), captured the first Gold and Glory championship in 1924. Courtesy Mrs. Mildred Overton

move proved to be costly. On lap 80, while navigating through a thick cloud of dust and black exhaust spewing from the cars in front of him, Carter misjudged the first turn and collided with the guardrail that circled the infield. The car took out thirty feet of fence, then flipped completely over, an accident drivers called "turning turtle." He was thrown clear of the wreck and knocked unconscious. According to reporters, he "soon revived, badly shaken up and bruised."[20]

With ten laps to go, all but three of the fifteen cars had dropped out of the race. Still in the competition were Malcolm Hannon, George Graham's chauffeur, who was driving the 1923 Indy 500 car, and John A. Simmons and Hugo H. Barnes, two other Indianapolis drivers. The race for first was hotly contested. Simmons, in second place, pulled within two seconds of Hannon, who was leading at lap 95. The crowd was on its feet. Even the hard-bitten journalist Frank Young found himself "daffy with excitement."[21]

Simmons remained close behind Hannon during the final lap. As Young described the scene: "Ninety-ninth and no change. They round the first turn. [Hannon] gains four car-lengths. Necks crane. People shout with frenzy. Hannon feeds the Barber-Warnock Special plenty of gas and breezes home, the national champion, winner of the first big 100-mile derby for colored drivers, just two seconds ahead of his nearest rival."[22]

Hannon finished the race in one hour, thirty-four and a half minutes, an average speed of 63.5 miles per hour. He captured a $1,200 first prize. Simmons took home $500 for second place. Famed boxer Jack Johnson presented a large silver cup, the championship trophy, to Hannon at the Gold and Glory gala ball, which was held that night. More than six hundred people attended the festivities, at which Kioda Barber's Ten Jazz Kings performed. But the real star of the evening was Hannon, who continued throughout the night to answer questions from journalists and to pose for pictures.

Looking on were William Rucker and the members of the Colored Speedway Association. "They had to have felt an incredible feeling of accomplishment," Richard Pierce remarked. "Auto racing had always been such an important part of Indianapolis's culture. And to that point, it had remained strictly a white enterprise. Now blacks could stake a claim in that heritage. They were now a bigger part of their city's culture. They were now a bigger part of Indianapolis."

3.

100% American

By 1924 Charlie Wiggins's business had grown. He serviced many of the cars owned by families in the black neighborhoods. As well, he had gained a loyal clientele of wealthy white businessmen, politicians, and civic leaders who entrusted their high-priced luxury cars to Charlie's mechanically skilled hands. David Curtis "D. C." Stephenson, an executive in the city's booming coal industry, never visited Charlie's garage. But he was typical of the kind of client Charlie served—a young, charismatic millionaire manager who seemed to epitomize the promise of never-ending prosperity in Indiana's new fast-paced manufacturing economy. Stephenson also had a passion for fine automobiles. The three-car garage of his mansion in Irvington was filled with expensive touring cars.

No doubt Stephenson knew many of the wealthy whites who visited Charlie's shop. But the two never crossed paths, at least not directly. Their businesses were only seven blocks from each other. But their ideologies were worlds apart. Charlie was a man committed to creating new opportunities for African Americans through auto racing. Stephenson was a man committed to squelching such initiatives. Charlie was a black sportsman and entrepreneur. Stephenson was the Grand Dragon of the Ku Klux Klan.

The Klan's venomous attitude toward African Americans was infamous and deeply rooted, dating back to the days immediately following the Civil War. Threats, beatings, and lynchings were commonplace among the KKK's "Old Order." While acts of terrorism continued throughout the 1920s, the attitudes that spawned such acts were now tempered by others that were subtler and potentially more far-reaching. Stephenson represented a "new breed" of Klansmen, a more "sophisticated" group that sought power through the manipulation of civic and political organizations, rather than control through threats and physical violence. But this hardly meant that he was willing to consort with African Americans on any level. For a white car owner to give his business to a black mechanic such as Charlie was not acceptable in Stephenson's eyes. The new segregationist attitudes may have been more "sophisticated," but they were still segregationist attitudes, nonetheless.

On the surface there were no direct ties at all between Charlie Wiggins and D. C. Stephenson. And yet the careers of the two entrepreneurs were remarkably similar. Both men started from very humble beginnings. Charlie struggled to raise his three brothers while working as a shoeshine boy. Stephenson, a self-proclaimed "nobody from nowhere," was a struggling salesman of typesetting equipment. Both began their careers in Evansville. Charlie worked for Benninghof-Nolan, while Stephenson joined Joe Huffington, the national Klan representative in Evansville, to organize a political platform for the KKK in Indiana and throughout the Midwest.

The same month Charlie and Roberta moved to Indianapolis, Stephenson got a call from the Klan's national office in Atlanta asking him to take over the Indiana headquarters from Huffington and move operations to the state capital. Charlie Wiggins and D. C. Stephenson set up shop in the downtown area within weeks of each other. Charlie was quiet, and Stephenson was bombastic. Yet both had charisma, which made them popular in their respective fields. At the beginning of their careers, neither man could have had a clear idea of his own destiny, but skill and circumstance were about to catapult each of them into the national spotlight. Though there were no direct confrontations between them, the waves that followed in the wake of their success collided on many occasions, creating a maelstrom of racial strife.

D. C. Stephenson arrived in Evansville in 1920, hoping to make a fresh start after a number of failed business ventures in Oklahoma. He opened a shop to sell typesetting equipment, but soon heard of a lucrative opportunity as a stock salesman for Citizens Coal Company, a local coal brokerage firm. Stephenson had served with a training unit in Massachusetts during the First World War. To make his résumé seem more appealing, he altered some facts of his military record. His embellished army career was colorful and exciting, with many toe-to-toe confrontations with Germans on the front lines of France. According to his enhanced records, Stephenson was a genuine war hero, just the type of bold leader the Citizens Coal Company of Evansville needed.

According to historian William Lutholtz, Stephenson was "a supersalesman, an aggressive, likable man who always appeared in public well-dressed and physically impressive. He could talk business and politics with well-read citizens, usually holding a strong opinion of his own to share with them. But he could also talk with average people on their own terms without seeming to patronize them."[1] Stephenson's charm, coupled with an incredible boom in coal production and demand during the early part of the decade, made the stock salesman an overnight success. He was promoted quickly through the ranks and soon became a partner in the firm.

He was also interested in the social and political activities of the community. Many Indiana men of the time joined fraternal orders. Stephenson, driven by power and an inflated ego, decided to create his own social organization and serve as its president. By June he had organized a group of Evansville war veterans into an enthusiastic fraternity that promoted American patriotism and actively campaigned against "foreign influences" that, in Stephenson's mind, were a growing threat to the American way of life.

In the autumn of 1921, D. C. Stephenson met Joe Huffington, organizer of the Ku Klux Klan in the North. In an interview with the

New York World, Stephenson remembered his first encounter with Klan organizers: "I was in Evansville in the fall of 1921, where my friends were a crowd of fine young men. Nearly all of them had joined the Ku Klux Klan. I was against it. . . . They kept after me, tho, and explained to me that the Klan was not an organization which took Negroes out, cut off their noses, and threw them into the fire. Nor did they tar and feather people or oppress them in any way. I was told that the Klan was a strictly patriotic organization. . . . They finally convinced me the Klan was a good thing, and I joined."[2]

In the Klan, Stephenson saw an opportunity to build his own power base. It was a large and rapidly growing organization that included influential politicians and civic leaders on its membership roster. The KKK had a religious and political agenda similar to his own, celebrating patriotism while attempting to eliminate foreign enemies. Among the "enemies" identified by the Klan were Catholics, who followed the mandates of a foreign leader (the Pope), and Jews, who did not follow the "correct" teachings of the Protestant faith. Another target of the Klan's (and Stephenson's) ire was African Americans, a group that, according to Stephenson, needed to be "put in their place"—a separate, segregated place—in American society.

While Charlie Wiggins was busy building cars and earning a reputation as a talented mechanic at the Benninghof-Nolan Company in Evansville, just six blocks away Stephenson was busy building the Klan into an influential social organization and earning a reputation as a savvy power broker in city politics. As Klan membership grew into the thousands, Evansville mayor Benjamin Bosse and other city officials called on Stephenson for advice and support. Stephenson's hard work and political influence impressed leaders at the Klan's national headquarters in Atlanta. When it came time for the Klan to make a push north to the state capital, they chose Stephenson over Huffington to lead the Indiana Klan and organize a statewide social and political agenda for the KKK in the North.

In 1922, Stephenson settled into his new Indianapolis apartment house on Seventeenth Street and began to explore the social and political landscape of his new hometown. He found in Indianapolis the perfect climate in which to promote the Klan's agenda. The population was made up predominantly of white Protestant families. Jewish and African-American neighborhoods were already segregated. William Lutholtz noted, "Behind the Christian zeal of the white majority was a sense of ethnic and racial superiority. Among the most enlightened, there was a sense of duty, of responsibility to lead the 'weaker' races to a better way of life. Farther down the social ladder, there was a simple fear that blacks, Catholics and Jews should not be allowed to get away with too much."[3]

Historian and author James Madison analyzed the social climate of Indiana during the early 1920s: "Nearly 95 percent of all Hoosiers were born in Indiana, and statewide, nearly 97 percent were white. There was a prevailing attitude among this vast majority of white, native-born Hoosiers that in order to maintain the integrity, safety, and prosperity of

David Curtis "D. C." Stephenson came to Indianapolis in 1922 and organized the Midwest regional headquarters of the Ku Klux Klan in a downtown office building. By 1924 he was widely considered one of the most powerful political figures in Indiana. Courtesy *Indianapolis Star* archives

life in Indiana, there must be an effort to keep the state 100 percent American. And in the minds of this ethnic, religious majority, there was a group of 'others' who threatened this way of life—people who were less than 100 percent Americans, out to undermine all the moral principles that the majority held near and dear."

Fanning the fire of those fears was the fact that Indianapolis had the largest percentage of African-American population of all states north of the Mason-Dixon Line. Nearly 10 percent of the city's population was African-American, an even higher percentage than in Chicago or New York City. Historian Richard Pierce pointed out, "This black population was growing. And they were very active within their own community. This was perceived as a tremendous threat to the white Protestant majority. As a result, Indianapolis became a segregated city in the 1920s in a way it had never been in the past and to a much larger degree than it had been in the past. The color line became harder, stricter, less fluid. Stricter segregation was one of the ways the majority contended with these 'outsiders.'"

Most of the majority feared that these "outsiders" were beginning to have an impact on the community. Black nightclubs played to mixed audiences. Some black businessmen, like Charlie Wiggins, routinely served white patrons. Black neighborhoods were growing and extending into white neighborhoods. The Jewish community was also growing. Membership in the Catholic Church grew within the city's thriving Italian and Irish districts. Catholic business leaders were growing increasingly influential in community affairs. Some of the white Protestant majority looked upon all of this with horror. Intense, irrational fears began to rise. The time was right for D. C. Stephenson and the Ku Klux Klan.

As racial tensions simmered in Indianapolis, Chicago driver and race promoter William "Wild Bill" Jeffries began planning for the Dreamland Derby, Chicago's version of the Gold and Glory Sweepstakes. John Owens, president of the National Motor Speedway Association and an official of the Hawthorne Speedway on the southwest side

By 1924, more than one-third of all white Protestant males in Indiana were members of the Ku Klux Klan. Large Klan rallies, like this march in Anderson in 1922, were a common sight in many Hoosier cities. Courtesy Swift Collection—Ball State University archives

of Chicago, signed a contract with Jeffries to allow the newly formed Chicago Colored Speedway Association to hold a daylong series of racing events on September 14, 1924.

Always the audacious showman, Bill Jeffries talked his partner Bill Bottoms into allowing him to park his $12,000 Ford Frontenac racecar in the lobby of the Dreamland Ballroom and Café, downstairs from the headquarters of the Chicago CSA, in an effort to promote the Dreamland Derby, just as William Rucker had parked Malcolm Hannon's car on the Avenue. Serving a high-profile clientele of both black and white patrons, the Dreamland had earned a reputation as one of the finest "black and tan" clubs in the area. Jeffries's car stood in stark contrast to the elegant art deco design and colorful murals that lined the walls. Certainly the sight of a racecar in the lobby must have caused quite a commotion. But Jeffries knew that residents of Chicago's Black Belt were always hungry for a good story. Also, Jeffries himself was always hungry for self-promotion. The racecar stunt sufficiently fed the voracious appetites of all.

Word hit the pages of the *Chicago Defender* on August 9: "Chicago is to have its first 100-mile automobile derby race under the auspices of the Chicago Colored Speedway Association. . . . The news is spreading like wildfire, and race enthusiasts, especially those who witnessed the first big national auto derby in Indianapolis, are awaiting the printing of tickets."[4]

The event would feature a number of racing attractions, including a ten-lap qualifying event, a twenty-lap feature, and a match race between the top African-American qualifier and George Beck, a white driver the *Defender* called "one of the fastest on the dirt track circuit."[5] The Dreamland Derby, the main feature, was a fifty-lap event that would spotlight many of the top drivers from the Gold and Glory Sweepstakes and include additional entrants from Chicago, Michigan, and northern Indiana. As race day neared, more and more articles appeared in the *Defender*. "There are thousands of people who have never seen an automobile race like this before. All are glad of the opportunity to witness the running of this grand colored racing spectacle. . . . Chicago is looking forward to this event, which marks a new era in the local sports world, a triumph for men of Color."[6]

Gold and Glory champion Malcolm Hannon and second-place finisher John Simmons, both Indianapolis drivers, wired their entries to the Chicago Colored Speedway Association's headquarters at the Dreamland Café. Another young driver, Chicago cabbie Norbert Wiley, captured the attention of *Defender* journalist Frank Young. In one report, Young reasoned that Wiley would gain a distinct advantage over the competition because "it is his natural instinct to drive through heavy traffic, after having driven in taxicabs through Chicago's busy streets."[7] William Carson, an employee of the Beck Auto Truck Manufacturing Company of Hammond, Indiana (owned by the white dirt track champion George Beck), also entered, driving one of Beck's homemade racecars. Bill Bottoms himself entered in a $10,000 Duesenberg, while his partner Jeffries touted to journalists that his own powerful $12,000 Ford Frontenac would "surely cop the Dreamland title and avenge the loss in Indianapolis."[8] In all, twenty-five African-American drivers entered the main fifty-mile event.

Conflicts arose in the days leading up to the Chicago race. Harry Dunnington, general manager of the Indianapolis Colored Speedway Association, had written Jeffries to congratulate him and Bottoms for their initiative in Chicago. He also planned, apparently at Jeffries's request, to come to the Dreamland and help organize the race and the Association. At first Bottoms and Jeffries welcomed the support of their Indianapolis counterpart. But relations between the two organizations eroded when Dunnington suggested that both Bottoms and Jeffries, as the promoters of the race, should voluntarily eliminate themselves as participants. His advice, transmitted through a series of letters, did not settle well with the two Chicago men. Egos and tempers flared. Ties between the two organizations were soon cut. As a result, a small contingent of drivers from Indianapolis refused to participate in the Dreamland Derby. The *Indianapolis Freeman* reported Dunnington's side of the story, stating that the Chicago race smacked of impropriety, due to the fact that the promoters were also participants in the event (though the articles failed to explain exactly how Dunnington thought the promoters might rig the race).

The *Chicago Defender* backed Jeffries, publishing a scathing article about Dunnington and the Indianapolis Colored Speedway Association. "Harry Dunnington of Indianapolis is doing everything to dissuade Hoosier drivers from entering, because he was not called in to 'show' the Chicago promoters how to run the race."[9] The disagreement between Dunnington and Jeffries made for spicy reading in the black press. The rift ignited a fiery feud between the two racing organizations and sparked an intense rivalry between the top drivers in Chicago and Indianapolis, each side trying to prove that it was the faster and more talented.

Even without Dunnington's help, plans for the Dreamland Derby were made. On race day, an estimated fifteen thousand spectators crowded into the grandstand at the Hawthorne Speedway to enjoy the spectacle. Indianapolis Colored Speedway Association president William Rucker was in attendance, an indication that perhaps the two auto racing organizations found a way to overlook their disagreements for the sake of the sport. Organizers of the Chicago association honored Rucker before the start of the day's events. The *Chicago Defender* reported that Jeffries and Bottoms presented Rucker with a gold medallion and other "special gifts" in appreciation for his "giving birth to the idea of having auto races for Colored people."[10] A carnival atmosphere surrounded the speedway. Boxer Jack Johnson was on hand to present the championship trophy, just as he had done in Indianapolis. A gala dance was planned at the Dreamland Ballroom following the day's festivities. Despite their conflicts with the Indianapolis association, Jeffries, Bottoms, and the Chicago Colored Speedway Association had created a racing event just as impressive as the Gold and Glory Sweepstakes.

Then disaster struck. In a twenty-lap preliminary race, Norbert Wiley, the Chicago cab driver, captured the checkered flag. As Wiley completed his victory lap around the track, a few excited fans, including Fred Shaw of Chicago, ran onto the track to congratulate him. The stunned driver swerved to avoid Shaw, but at seventy-two miles per hour, neither Wiley nor Shaw had time to avert an accident. Wiley's car hit Shaw, then skidded out of control, flipping over on its side. Shaw was killed instantly. Wiley was listed in critical condition at Provident Hospital, where he died later that night. William Carson, in his "Beck Special," went on to capture the Dreamland Derby championship in the fifty-mile feature. But Wiley's wreck earlier in the day deflated the sense of celebration that had once energized the crowd.

"Death, the Grim Reaper, mowed down two men at the Hawthorne race track Sunday," Frank Young reported. "The victim [Shaw] was carried on the radiator 40 feet and dropped under the front left wheel of the car, causing it to leave the ground. Wiley was thrown into the air 25 feet, and after a full two seconds, he fell clear of the wreckage." Young went on to describe how Wiley's split-second reactions had avoided even greater disaster, as he swerved to avoid another spectator, Fred Shaw's brother Robert, who had also run onto the track. Young called Wiley's efforts "heroic."[11]

Two days after the race, Wiley's cab, draped in black, led the funeral procession through his hometown of Chicago Heights. Hundreds of citizens turned out for the funeral. The *Defender* eulogized, "Wiley was born and raised in this small town, and people of both races all knew him as one of the most ambitious boys in the town. . . . His wife, Mrs. Jennie Silverman Wiley, who witnessed the accident from the grandstand at the track, collapsed and was brought by friends to Provident Hospital, where she remained with her husband until death claimed him at 2:15 A.M. Monday." The article concluded, "Wiley died as he had lived, a true hero."[12]

Fueled by Ku Klux Klan propaganda, segregationist attitudes began to spread quickly throughout the Hoosier state. Klan rallies in cities like Muncie, Franklin, Valparaiso, Martinsville, and many others attracted hundreds of loyal followers to daylong events that typically included patriotic parades, large picnics, fireworks, and long orations on the virtues of "100% Americanism."

The largest Klan rally in U.S. history was held in Kokomo, Indiana, a town of thirty thousand residents sixty miles north of Indianapolis. On July 4, 1923, reporters from some of the state's leading newspapers claimed that as many as two hundred thousand people had attended the day's events. A more conservative estimate, offered even by some Klan publications, put the figure closer to fifty thousand.

D. C. Stephenson, the man appointed by the KKK's national head-quarters to lead the northern movement, flew to the rally aboard an open-cockpit biplane. The plane dipped suddenly downward and swept low over the crowd. Stephenson waved to the thousands of men, women, and children who waited eagerly for his arrival. As he climbed down from the cockpit, the crowd cheered wildly. Later that day, in a formal ceremony, he was appointed supervisor of all Klan activities in a twenty-one-state region. Standing on a large stage with representatives from the national Klan office in Atlanta, Stephenson accepted numerous tokens, gifts, and the sacred gold-orange robe and hood bestowed only on the privileged few who earned the title "Grand Dragon." He then grabbed the microphone, as well as the collective attention of all in attendance, and launched into a long-winded speech, "Back to the Constitution," in which he preached the importance of protecting America from "the forces of evil at work in our communities today."[13]

"The Klan brought to the surface a number of common stereotypes that have been a part of the mainstream culture from the very beginning of [U.S.] history," stated James Madison. "By the 1920s these racial and ethnic stereotypes were intensified. At that time most white Protestant Americans were not embarrassed at all about expressing these stereotypes, racist jokes, ethnic pictures and cartoons, even in the mainstream press. In fact, it was simply an act that was unthinking, as natural as the air they breathed. The Klan used these stereotypes to play off the fears that were a part of the life and mind and heart of many white Protestant Americans."

D. C. Stephenson was gaining a stronger voice in Indiana. He once bragged that he was a master of mass psychology. Aiding his efforts to reach the masses was a widely distributed Klan newspaper, *The Fiery Cross*, published in Indianapolis. In addition, the Klan produced and distributed a number of records at the Gennett Studios in Richmond. (Oddly enough, Gennett Studios also produced some of the earliest "race records" featuring African-American artists, such as Louis Armstrong and "Jelly Roll" Morton.) Klan recordings featured new lyrics written to well-known hymns, such as "The Old Fiery Cross" instead of "The Old Rugged Cross," but also included several original works, such as "That's Why I'm a Klansman" and "Daddy Stole the Last Clean Sheet and Joined the KKK." Klan members distributed most of these records themselves at rallies and other official functions. Many recordings became very popular within this highly specialized market. For D. C. Stephenson, each record and newspaper sold was another extension of his voice, exhorting and enticing recruits to his growing army of supporters. The master of mass psychology was getting his word out. And the white majority in Indiana were listening.

As the Ku Klux Klan gained momentum throughout the state, Klan rallies often grew intensely rowdy and cruel. On June 2, 1923, a Klan march through Muncie, Indiana, sixty miles northeast of Indianapolis, was the scene of a near riot. George R. Dale, editor of the *Muncie Post-Democrat*, was one of the few newspapermen who dared to oppose the Klan openly in print. As a result, the Klan targeted Dale as an "Enemy of America." In a dramatic first-person account of the June march, Dale reported, "The Klan marched, two thousand strong—armed, arrogant, and overbearing. Citizens in all walks of life were insulted and assaulted.

Under the hypocritical guise of requiring honor to the American flag, citizens were required to remove their hats and humble themselves before the Invisible Empire, Knights of the Ku Klux Klan. . . .

"John O'Neill, a gallant captain of the A.E.F. who saw hard service overseas, was brutally assaulted by a gang of Klansmen. He went down fighting but was taken to the hospital, where eleven stitches were taken in his lacerated cheeks. The blow that rendered him unconscious was struck from behind by a Klansman. He was dragged from his automobile, where he was seated with his young wife, when he refused to raise his hat to a masked horsewoman, who was desecrating the flag by sitting on it, the flag being draped over the rear end of the horse. . . . Former prosecuting attorney Frank Mann was standing in the courthouse yard when the parade went by. He wore his hat and refused to obey the 'hats off' order. 'Go get him!' was the command from the ranks of Hundred Percent Americanism. Six men left the Klan mob and made a rush for Mr. Mann, who stood his ground. As they approached, Mr. Mann reached for his pocket for his knife, and the cowardly Klansmen, thinking he was about to shoot, turned tail and ran."

Dale went on to describe assaults on several other community members who were unfortunate enough to cross the Klan's path that evening. Other anti-Klan newspapers, such as the Catholic publication *Tolerance,* picked up Dale's story and ran it in full. Banner headlines appeared over the article: "Klux Has the Whiphand Here! Muncie, Indiana, Shows What You May Expect!" Dale's article concluded, "The real purpose was to make everyone take off their hats to the Klan, not to the flag. Patriotism and courtesy demand the removal of hats when the color bearer of some military or naval organization passes, but no other organization on earth is empowered even to request such a proceeding, much less a law-breaking, murderous outfit like the Ku Klux Klan."[14]

Klan activity intensified in the state capital, as well. James Madison stated, "There were a large number of Klan members in those neighborhoods of [Indianapolis] near the African-American districts. These white neighborhoods were the most fertile territory for the recruitment of new Klan members. Most whites in these neighborhoods were fearful that blacks were going to move into their neighborhood and threaten their property values and their way of life." He concluded, "Most were hopeful that the Klan was going to be their method, their voice, their means of stopping black movement into their neighborhoods. In their minds the Klan was going to keep their neighborhoods free of African Americans and keep the area '100 percent American.'"

The Ku Klux Klan was not involved in every segregationist attitude or act of racial or ethnic violence in Indiana. But the Klan's increasing strength in the state and region gave momentum to the radical behaviors of extremist groups. One such was the White Supremacy League, an Indianapolis social order founded in January 1923. On January 19 the group published an informal manifesto in the *Fiery Cross* that extolled the virtues of white supremacy: "We have no animosity toward Negroes, but have a marked respect for the Negro who keeps his own kind, who does not display an anomalous desire for 'social equality,' and who respects the white authority of the United States."[15]

The group billed itself as a "neighborhood improvement organization." More specifically, the White Supremacy League's main mission was to discourage black families from moving into white neighborhoods. Its tactics consisted of letters and verbal threats directed at black families who attempted to do so. Occasionally the league went beyond threats. In July 1924 an African-American family, despite warnings, moved into an all-white neighborhood. Members of the White Supremacy League tossed a hand grenade through the window of the family's home. Within days of the incident, the league circulated petitions through the neighborhood that blared, "Do you want a nigger for a neighbor?"[16]

Another white neighborhood organization in Indianapolis was the Capitol Avenue Protective Association. Many members of the group lived close to the black neighborhoods near Indiana Avenue. As the black neighborhoods began to expand, white citizens grew increasingly uncomfortable and looked to the Capitol Avenue Protective Association as a shield to protect their streets from unwelcome "outsiders." Around their yards, they erected "spite fences," large, menacing spiked fences to separate themselves from the black neighborhoods.

Other civic organizations, such as the White Citizens Protective League, put pressure on the Indianapolis city council to impose a new residential zoning ordinance. The group argued that, "in the interest of public peace, good order and the general welfare, it is advisable to foster the separation of white and Negro residential communities." The proposed ordinance declared it unlawful for white persons to establish residence in a "portion of the municipality inhabited principally by Negroes," or for Negroes to establish residence in a "white community," unless that person received written consent from a majority of the persons of the opposite race inhabiting that neighborhood. Most in the city council were aware that a similar statute enacted in Louisville had been struck down as unconstitutional. And yet, amid a crowd of eight hundred cheering, hand-clapping, foot-stomping spectators who poured onto the floor of the council chambers, council members and the mayor signed the ordinance. The White Citizens Protective League proclaimed, "Passage of this ordinance will stabilize real estate values . . . and give the honest citizens and voters renewed faith in city officials." Lawmakers declared that critics would study the new ordinance with "open minds and hail with delight this step toward the solution of a problem that has long caused deep thought and serious study by members of both races."[17]

The Indianapolis chapter of the National Association for the Advancement of Colored People immediately challenged the constitutionality of the law. The case went before the Marion County Superior Court in November 1926. As expected, the judge cited the U.S. Supreme Court decision on the Louisville case and declared the Indianapolis law unconstitutional. But while it failed to accomplish its main objective, the White Citizens Protective League, as well as other white civic organizations in Indianapolis, had proved that it was an active force in city and state politics.

With each threat or act of violence by these white civic organizations, a cry of moral outrage went up from the vast majority of Catholics, Jews, and African Americans in the city and state. Yet few were willing to act against such frightening social and political powers for fear of severe repercussions. The *Indianapolis Freeman* wrote of the frustrations that plagued the black community. While its editors encouraged colored citizens to fight for the right to live where they chose, they did yield certain points. "We have learned to forego some rights that are common, and because we know the price. We would gain but little in a way if certain places were thrown open to us. We have not insisted that hotels should entertain our race, or the theaters, rights that are clearly ours."[18]

There were some who did fight back. An Irish Catholic immigrant, Joseph Patrick O'Mahoney, published a weekly newspaper, the *Indiana*

Catholic, which became one of the state's leading voices against the practices of the Klan and Klan-backed neighborhood associations. *Tolerance,* the nation's most widely distributed newspaper, dared to obtain (often by illegal means) Klan membership rosters and publish the names of prominent civic leaders it found in them. Both the *Indianapolis Freeman* and the *Indianapolis Recorder* warned of the Klan's efforts to take over Indiana politics. A handful of individuals, such as Dr. Lucian B. Merriwether, a successful black dentist, and Dr. Guy L. Grant, a distinguished physician, decided to take on the white citizens' groups in hopes of exposing the illegal nature of their acts. Noted black attorney Robert Lee Brokenburr argued repeatedly in court that many of their mandates were unconstitutional.

Others took a quieter, less confrontational stand. Charlie Wiggins had turned Louis Sagalowsky's auto repair shop into a thriving business. He attracted a large clientele, including many wealthy whites who owned large luxury automobiles. "This was unusual for the times," stated Richard Pierce. "For Charlie to attract a large white client base meant that he had to be able to provide exceptional service that many whites felt they could not get from their own community. For them to 'cross over,' so to speak, was a testament to Charlie's skills. In that regard, he was more than an economic success. He was a social success, as well."

Charlie's reputation attracted not only the regard of white car owners, but the attention of the White Supremacy League, as well. A black mechanic's presence in a Jewish shop owner's garage caused a stir among members of the organization. They often left late-night "calling cards" to show their displeasure toward a Negro who refused to "keep to his own kind." Charlie's wife Roberta remembered, "We got some notes. Some were like 'Stop, Nigger.' Others were 'Beware, Nigger,' stuff like that. One time they tore down the sign in front of the garage. Another time they threw rocks through the window. A time or two they hid in the bushes, two or three of them. They'd jump out and attack Charlie when he went out." She paused, and then continued, "He'd fight them off every time. He'd just get mad. But I'd cry." Another pause. "Ever try to get the blood out of your husband's shirt? That was the worst thing of all."

Charlie weathered the threats and acts of violence with quiet strength and fortitude. "He seldom spoke of any problems he encountered," remarked his niece Mildred Overton. "I think he finally found his true calling [as a mechanic], and he wasn't about to let anybody take that away from him." In fact, the encounters with League members only seemed to strengthen Charlie's resolve. When Louis Sagalowsky announced in 1924 that he was stepping down from the day-to-day duties of the company, Charlie asked to buy the auto repair shop and run it himself. Sagalowsky agreed. Charlie Wiggins, an experienced twenty-seven-year-old mechanic, now owned his own garage. "This was his dream," Roberta said. "He was floating high, and nothing was going to bring him down."

Throughout Indiana, political candidates were gearing up for the state elections of 1924. D. C. Stephenson and the Ku Klux Klan were gearing up, as well. In one six-month period Stephenson's team recruited more than twenty-five thousand new Klan members statewide. Klan officers once reported more than 2,200 new members in a single week. In the summer of 1924, as black Indianapolis celebrated the inaugural Gold and Glory Sweepstakes, the Klan celebrated its most recent membership total. More than one-third of all white Protestant males in Indiana now belonged to the Klan. That proportion reached nearly 40 percent in Indianapolis. Stephenson had the support of a half-million registered voters, enough to swing the outcome of an election in his favor.

In an effort to garner greater voter support, many candidates for public office aligned themselves with the Klan. The most notable of these was Ed Jackson, Indiana's secretary of state and a Republican candidate for governor in 1924. Jackson was a good friend of D. C. Stephenson. Their homes in Irvington Township were only blocks from each other. Stephenson often invited Jackson with him on "business trips" aboard his large yacht on Lake Erie. When Jackson announced his candidacy, Stephenson lent the candidate his top-down Lexington touring car to canvass the state and to greet potential voters.

Many Republicans that spring tried to build a strong alliance with the Ku Klux Klan. One strong anti-Klan Republican, Indianapolis mayor Samuel Lewis Shank, attempted to break ranks with many in his own party by running against Ed Jackson in the May primaries. Shank frequently sparred with Klan officials in the state capital. He passed city ordinances prohibiting masked parades and enforced a Board of Public Safety ban on cross burnings. He even barred the women's auxiliary of the Ku Klux Klan from using the spacious Tomlinson Hall for a highly touted statewide rally. The Klan retaliated with vehement articles in the *Fiery Cross*, in which they accused Shank of aiding bootleggers and criminals.

On the day of the primaries, Jackson and the Klan jumped to an early lead in Indianapolis. Jackson received 38,668 votes in Marion County, easily defeating Shank, who garnered 20,306 votes. The rest of the state soon followed suit. Shank proved that an anti-Klan stance was lethal to an Indiana political candidate in 1924. As candidates worked toward the general elections in November, all sensed the Ku Klux Klan's icy grip on the state's political future.

The night of Jackson's primary victory, D. C. Stephenson wanted to send a powerful message to the entire state. More than seven thousand fully clad Klansmen and Klanswomen gathered for a victory celebration at the Indiana State Fairgrounds. They then marched from the city's north side thirty blocks south, waving flags and singing patriotic hymns, right down Indiana Avenue in the heart of the city's black district. Hundreds of African-American families watched in dismay as the Klan flexed its political muscle right through the heart of their own neighborhood.

"It was an awesome statement," noted James Madison. "The Klan was saying, in essence, 'We are Indianapolis. We are 100 percent Americans. We can go wherever we wish. We have the power to do so.' They were trying to show just who they were as Klansmen and where they stood in Indiana society. As well, they wanted to show that African Americans were simply powerless. This was truly symbolic and significant, something that ran directly in the face of all African Americans in that community."

Among the onlookers that night were Charlie and Roberta Wiggins, who had come to a club on the Avenue to enjoy a concert. "It was a nightmare," Roberta remembered, and refused to talk any more of the incident. The *Indianapolis Freeman* wrote of the Klan march, "Many reputable citizens who have been deceiving themselves by holding that

Indiana governor
Ed Jackson was a
member of the Ku
Klux Klan and a good
friend of Klan leader
D. C. Stephenson.
Jackson and a Klan-
backed Republican
ticket swept into
political power in
Indiana in 1924.
Courtesy Indiana
Historical Society

the Klan is merely an innocent, misguided, un-ambitious, temporary organization are now wondering about how long they have been asleep. Indeed, they are becoming aroused to the fact that while they slept, a real enemy has taken possession."[19]

With a lock on the Republican ticket, the support of the Klan, and Stephenson on board as a political advisor, Jackson steamrolled his way across the state. Reporters noted that he seemed to proceed "with su-preme confidence" in the eventual outcome of the November election. As the campaign heated up, Jackson's opponent, Dr. Carleton McCul-loch, publicly announced the Democratic Party's tough new anti-Klan stance. "The Republican Party has been captured by the Ku Klux Klan, and has as a political party for the present, ceased to exist."[20] When reporters pressed for a response to McCulloch's accusations, Jackson simply declined to comment. He continued to grin and wave, knowing that his friend Stephenson was pulling all the necessary political strings back at Republican headquarters.

Both the *Indianapolis Freeman* and the *Indianapolis Recorder,* two longstanding Republican newspapers, had, since their inception, proudly thrown their support behind "the party of Lincoln." Early in 1924, however, *Freeman* founder George Knox and *Recorder* editor Marcus Stuart found themselves denouncing the Republican Party for the first time. Knox, along with Freeman B. Ransom, general manager of the Walker Manufacturing Company, decried the acts of the Klan's political machine: "The Ku Klux Klan has captured, boot and breeches, the Republican Party in Indiana and has turned what has been historically an organization of constitutional freedom into an agency for the promotion of religious and racial hate. Nobody now denies the Ku Klux Klan is the dominating power in Indiana Republican politics. In fact, the Republican Party exists in Indiana today only in name. Its place has been usurped by the Klan with Klan purposes and leadership and issues. The fight in the future will be purely a contest between the Klan and anti-Klan forces."[21]

Their words had a powerful impact on the black community. On election day many African Americans in Indianapolis found themselves voting the Democratic ticket for the first time in their lives. The increased tally for Democratic candidates had little influence on the outcome of the election, however. Jackson easily won the governor's race, by nearly a hundred thousand votes. An entire slate of Klan-backed political candidates swept into office, including nearly all of Indiana's thirteen congressional representatives, half of the Indiana legislature, and many county offices.

Dr. Madison commented, "On one hand we have an image of the 1920s as an era of speakeasies, jazz, and bathtub gin. And on the other hand, in the midst of this decade of great openness, we have brewing a time of great intolerance, especially among the white Protestant majority in Indiana. They are now organized in powerful ways to eliminate this group of people deemed 'less-than-100-percent Americans.' Those organizational efforts produced positive results for this group in the state elections of 1924. . . . The lines of color and religion in Indiana, lines that have always been fluid and changing over time and circumstance, were about to grow harder and more volatile."

The *Indianapolis Freeman* wrote of the governor-elect, "Mr. Jackson poses as a Christian man of sincerity. One wonders how he feels in the role of Dr. Jekyll and Mr. Hyde. Whatever his qualms of conscience, there is no escape from his Klan identification." Ed Jackson smiled and declared, "The good people of Indiana have spoken." As the mainstream press trumpeted Jackson's victory, D. C. Stephenson began working on an agenda for the new administration. The Klan's political machine was at its zenith. Stephenson bragged, "I am the law in Indiana."[22]

For African Americans in the midwestern United States, the social climate went from bad to worse. Reports of threats and violence blanketed the pages of the black press. African-American property owners near Cleveland, Ohio, had come under siege already that winter, when armed, masked Klansmen stormed into the homes of several wealthy black property owners. The *Cleveland Call-Post* reported one such case: "An alleged attempt was called to the attention of the city commission by R. R. Dobey, an aged colored citizen, possessing real estate holdings of considerable value. Dobey said he was warned Sunday to leave the city within 48 hours, and a burning cross was left at his front gate. . . . The authorities have ordered the police to make a special effort to round up the bands of nightriders responsible for the disturbance. It is said the nightriders are operating in the interest of certain real estate dealers who are eager to force Negro property owners to sell their holdings or flee from the section."[23]

Similar accounts of intimidation and violence came from other northern cities. Under a *Chicago Defender* banner headline "Klansmen Burn Girl" a report read, "Race citizens residing in the notorious Maxwell Street district on the West side were terror-stricken late Wednesday night when white gangsters, parading as Ku Klux Klan members, hurled bricks and gasoline bottles into the home of Mrs. Artice Baldwin . . . and set fire to two automobiles on the premises with gasoline torches. The bricks were soaked in gasoline and lighted. Miss Annie Mae Larue, a member of the Baldwin home, was burned on the arm from the explosion of one of the gasoline bottles hurled through a front window. The explosion awakened the tenants in the building. Panic-stricken, they rushed to the windows and saw a Paige touring car parked in front of the house in flames."[24]

Historian Boniface Hardin recalled the vigilance most African Americans practiced during the era. "A colored person had to know the terrain. You were taught from childhood what you could do and what you couldn't do. You were taught what you were to say if you were in the company of black people only and what to say if you were in the presence of white people. There was a line you knew you couldn't cross. And that line was very thin and always moving. So you always had to be on guard."

African Americans in the spotlight of social and civic life in Indiana exercised extreme caution. Leon "Al" Warren, a competitor in the Gold and Glory Sweepstakes, recalled, "We stayed to ourselves for the most part, and that didn't seem to disturb the white boys at first. But we were trying to create a racing event just as big and important as the Indy 500. When we began to have some success, I think we were looked at pretty closely by some white folk. . . . It was like they were saying to us that we could be successful, but not *too* successful. That was the line we had to walk." When asked if he had experienced any threats or confrontations personally, Warren replied, "Not directly, per se. But a lot of times I'd be hauling my car to a racing event in Wisconsin or Illinois, someplace like that. And often I'd get stopped by police, who made me show all my paperwork on the car, my entry form for the race, and other things like that. I was even told once by a county cop not to come back through his particular county on the way home, especially at night. I'm not sure if that was a threat or a warning. But I made sure I took another route home that day."

"It's one of those side-by-side things," remarked Dr. Pierce. "On one hand you have the organizers, promoters, and drivers of the Gold and Glory Sweepstakes working to create a sustained endeavor and a symbol of pride in the black community. And on the other hand you had the simultaneous rise of segregationist attitudes, fueled by groups like the

Ku Klux Klan. Both of these social phenomena were coexisting, and many times colliding, with one another."

"It was a tense time for all African Americans," Hardin echoed. "And we sought outlets for those tense times. We embraced our own heroes, people who could achieve great things during these tough times. We could all live vicariously through their examples. Jack Johnson, Marian Anderson, Jesse Owens, these people exemplified the possibilities we could all hope to achieve. And in their own special way, the drivers of the Gold and Glory Sweepstakes represented that same thing to us."

It was a time for heroes—men and women who were not afraid to step to the forefront and make a social statement through their words and actions. By the spring of 1925, fans of the Gold and Glory Sweepstakes were celebrating a hero who would quickly garner the attention of many auto racing enthusiasts, promoters, and public officials. Some would thrust him into the national spotlight. Others would attempt to bring him down. A soft-spoken mechanic on the south side of Indianapolis was about to make history.

It was Charlie Wiggins's time to shine.

4.

The Negro
Speed King

The 1925 Gold and Glory Sweepstakes dawned bright, cloudless, and warm. By 10:00 A.M. the temperature had soared to ninety degrees, topping out near a hundred by midafternoon. Journalists from the *Indianapolis Recorder* predicted that the temperature on the track would be far higher than even the sweltering heat experienced by the spectators in the stands. *Chicago Defender* journalist Frank Young described an ice cream cone that had melted and dripped down his arm only moments after he had purchased it. Despite the hot weather, however, Young went on to write that August 8, 1925, was "a perfect day for the racing game."[1]

As the drivers gathered near the pit area prior to the race, the press, as well as many young drivers and mechanics, clamored around Chicago's Bill Jeffries and Indianapolis's own Malcolm Hannon, the two drivers favored to win. Charlie Wiggins, a rookie entering his Wiggins Special racecar at the event, focused his attention on another driver in the field, Bobby Lee Wallace. A twenty-two-year-old Hamilton County, Indiana, native, Wallace had been racing cars since he was sixteen. He had gained valuable driving experience, first as a chauffeur, then as an ambulance driver heading a first-aid training unit for the Indianapolis Fire Department. Wallace had valuable experience on the track, as well. He had spent a number of hours training with a talented new breed of Indy car driver—a fraternity that included eventual Indy 500 champs Howdy Wilcox and Bill Cummings.

Wallace's light complexion fooled many white race officials, and according to family members, he was able to move about freely in the garage area at the Indianapolis 500-Mile Race and other AAA-sanctioned racing events. Participants in the Gold and Glory Sweepstakes remembered that "black blood" flowed through Wallace's past. His mother's family hailed from Roberts, a "Negro colony" in Hamilton County, just thirty miles north of Indianapolis. The Wallace family had roots in the "freedman's settlement" near the town of Arcadia dating back to the 1820s. Nearly every member of his mother's family had a light complexion. Wallace's father, a Lancaster, Pennsylvania, native, was also fair-skinned. When Bobby Wallace and his brother Raymond were born, neither had outwardly showed their African-American heritage. "Bobby looked as white as any of them AAA guys. None of them ever even considered that he was black," recalled former Gold and Glory driver Al Warren. "It wasn't like he was trying to hide it or anything. He was always proud of his heritage. I think it was one of those things where no one asked, and he didn't tell. That's how he was able to work with the white drivers so much."

Averitte Corley, Wallace's nephew, grew up in the same house with the talented mechanic and driver, who was known simply as "Uncle Lee." Corley recalled, "During his chauffeur days he got to know the ins and outs of auto mechanics. He was good—top-notch. As they went on in their careers he and Wiggins were greatly respected by the white drivers and mechanics at the Indianapolis Motor Speedway on 'Gasoline Alley.' They were mechanical geniuses without the degrees. They were so good that most of the white drivers and car owners openly welcomed them in the pit area. Those guys were like brothers in the pits. But on race day, they were not allowed to be a part of the action."

When Wallace was not speeding around a midwestern dirt track, he was often speeding away from the law. Corley laughed as he recalled, "Uncle Lee had spent much of his early life working with bootleggers.

"BOB WALLACE"
1934.

Charlie's good friend and chief rival on the Gold and Glory circuit was Bob Wallace. An extremely talented African-American driver and mechanic, Wallace had a very light complexion that allowed him to compete unrecognized in several "whites only" races during the 1920s and '30s. Courtesy Indianapolis Motor Speedway archives

Back when Prohibition was in full force, he used to run whiskey for members of Al Capone's gang. There were two guys named Walter and Ollie Kelly from Capone's group. They would hire him to take a car from Lake County, up near Chicago, and run the booze to Evansville, Richmond, and other places around Indiana. He always used to drive a car with two gas tanks. One of them was a fake, of course. It was filled with whiskey. He'd run for some pretty rough characters back then. They liked to hire Uncle Lee because he could always outrun the state police. A lot of the Gold and Glory drivers did that kind of thing back then. Their mechanical aptitude and their ability to drive quickly got them plenty of good jobs and good money with the Mob." Corley remembered that his uncle seemed to have lived a fast, full life, even before the age of thirty. "He was no angel. Few of them were, really," Corley smiled.

By 1925 Wallace was one of the wealthiest black mechanics in the Midwest, thanks largely to his powerful connections with members of the Chicago underworld. Corley once recalled a confrontation Wallace had with his father, an ordained A.M.E. minister. Wallace returned home after a successful liquor run across the state. He arrived at his parents' humble home driving a new Stutz Bearcat and wearing a full-length fur coat. "Grandpa was completely outraged by his actions," Corley stated. "Uncle Lee tried to give my grandmother a large wad of bills and told her to put it away for safekeeping. She and my Grandpa would have nothing to do with it. For years, he and my grandparents were at odds with one another."

Even if the police were fast enough to apprehend Wallace, the crafty mechanic always had a way of getting out of trouble. Corley recalled one time when a county sheriff caught Wallace red-handed with a carload of illegal alcohol. "They took him in and called my grandparents. They were beside themselves with grief that their son had been arrested. But the next morning, he just walked right in the front door. When my grandfather asked him what happened, he flashed a smile and a badge. He had been made a deputy sheriff! The booze was mysteriously gone." When asked what special arrangements had been made for Wallace's release, Corley only answered, "I guess you could say that it was just the politics of the day."

On the track Wallace had built strong friendships with many of the top drivers and mechanics at the Motor Speedway. Arthur and Louis Chevrolet, two young brothers and car owners, frequently visited him and shared automotive advice. It was Wallace's contacts with these and other drivers, mechanics, and car owners that some years later allowed him to spend time at the garages of the top drivers at the Indianapolis 500-Mile Race. According to Corley, during the 1934 race, Wallace was working with a crew on a car sponsored by Stokely Foods and driven by Deacon Litz. The car, a four-cylinder Miller, was a two-man vehicle, with a driver who manned the wheel and controlled the brakes and a mechanic who rode alongside and pumped oil and gas through the engine line. According to Averitte Corley, Litz's riding mechanic fell ill either before or during the race. In any case, Wallace was reportedly in the pit area when the mechanic announced that he would be unable to compete. Litz then turned to Wallace, the most seasoned mechanic in the immediate vicinity, and told him to "suit up." Bobby donned the white mechanic's outfit and leather helmet. Litz told him to pull the goggles over his face and remain quiet while the team introductions were made. Apparently not a single AAA official noticed that a light-skinned African American was manning the gears for the racing team. Bill Cummings went on to capture the checkered flag that year. Litz finished fourth with an average speed of 100.749 miles per hour.

Whether Wallace actually competed at the Indianapolis 500-Mile Race or not is debatable. Apparently another (white) mechanic by the name of Robert Wallace attempted to pass himself off as a riding mechanic for a racing team during the decade. No official records exist to confirm or deny the black Bobby Wallace's participation in the 1934 Indianapolis 500-Mile Race. His light complexion and his expert mechanical skills certainly would have made him a likely candidate to compete as a riding mechanic for Deacon Litz or any other driver at the Speedway. Regardless of whether or not Wallace took official laps at the Indianapolis Motor Speedway, the fact that an African-American driver would even have the opportunity to be considered a legitimate competitor at the Indy 500 says a lot about his mechanical ability and driving skills, as well as the respect he commanded among many white drivers at the Brickyard.

At the 1925 Gold and Glory Sweepstakes, Charlie Wiggins knew he would likely face stiff competition from drivers such as Jeffries and Hannon. But Wallace would be a tougher challenge. In Charlie's opinion, Wallace's extensive driving experience made him a true competitor for the championship trophy. Moreover, Wallace's car, a Ford Frontenac similar to "Wild Bill" Jeffries's speedster, was a top-of-the-line Indy racecar that had finished in the top ten in the 1924 Indy 500. In the final hours leading to the big event, Charlie spent a large part of his preparation time talking with Wallace.

Roberta Wiggins recalled, "Charlie could just look at Bobby's car and tell that he got it right. The engine, the transmission, everything was built for speed and endurance. Bobby and Charlie talked a lot in those early years . . . just two professionals talking shop, you know. I think Charlie learned a lot from Bobby, and, in turn, Bobby probably learned a thing or two from Charlie. In the end, the two were always fierce competitors, but they both had a great respect for one another. That's what made their relationship special."

When the green flag dropped, signaling the start of the 1925 race, Charlie gunned his engine and rushed to the front of the pack. He ran neck-and-neck with Bill Jeffries, as "Wild Bill" held a slender lead. Malcolm Hannon was close behind. Bobby Wallace fell deep into the pack. Thirty laps into the event Charlie battled to within four car-lengths of Jeffries. During the forty-third lap, two drivers, Hugo Barnes of Indianapolis and "Doc" White from Keokuk, Iowa, collided on the northwest end of the track. The collision caused a cloud of smoke and dust, marring the drivers' view as they rounded the third turn. "Wild Bill" and Charlie weaved and navigated their way through the tangled mess of bent chassis and flaming engines. Meanwhile, Wallace kept a slow, steady pace, skillfully steering clear of the wrecks as the smoke dissipated.

Several drivers battled for the top position. Jeffries and Charlie remained in the top five throughout the race. Suddenly dark smoke began to billow from under Jeffries's hood. A hard head and a heavy foot were too much for his high-revving engine block. He blew a piston rod and came to a sudden halt along the backstretch. Charlie passed him, looking back to see the Chicago driver cursing and waving his fists wildly as his car coasted off the track and out of the competition. Then he noticed something else. Bobby Wallace was gaining on the pack. By lap 85, Charlie and Wallace were neck and neck, battling for fourth place. Charlie pushed his foot to the floor, giving his Wiggins Special every-thing he had. But after eighty-five long, hard miles of driving, Charlie's engine finally gave out. He pulled into the pits as smoke rolled out from under the hood. A couple of desperate attempts to restart his motor failed, and he was forced to call it quits. As he sat on the edge of the inside fence row, he watched as Bobby Wallace overtook the entire field and finished nearly one minute ahead of the competition.

The *Indianapolis Recorder* reported, "Every one of the pilots shared in the glory of the event. But it was Bobby Wallace of Indianapolis, at the wheel of his 'Trey of Hearts' Ford Special, who carried off the lion's share of the gold in the Gold and Glory Sweepstakes."[2] Wallace crossed the finish line in 1 hour, 32 minutes, 26 seconds, for an average speed of 64.9

The 1925 Gold and Glory Sweepstakes was Charlie Wiggins's first professional auto race. He finished fifth, the lowest finish of his entire career. He later won four Gold and Glory championships in a ten-year period. Courtesy Mrs. Mildred Overton

miles per hour. As he stood at the winner's circle, he waved to the crowd and gleefully accepted the $1,250 first-prize check.

The top four finishers collected a cash prize for their efforts. Charlie just missed out on the prize money. The rookie's eighty-five-mile mark earned him a fifth-place finish. But he earned a greater prize that day, a valuable lesson learned from the winning strategy of Bobby Wallace. Al Warren explained, "Races aren't won by the guys who run the fastest. They are won by the guys who run the *smartest*. Some guys would go out there and just run their cars into the ground, while others knew just what their car could do and not do . . . when to speed up, when to lie back, when to push to the front of the pack. Smart drivers are the ones who are going to win the most races. Charlie's the one who taught me that. And he said he learned it from Bob Wallace back in '25."

Bobby Wallace went on to win three of the next ten Colored Speedway Association events that year. Charlie returned to his garage to make some necessary readjustments, both to his car and to his racing strategy. He vowed not to make the same mistakes the following year. "He told me he was going to make 1926 a special year," Roberta remembered. With his mistakes behind him, Charlie Wiggins quietly asked himself if he had the skills needed to earn a place among black auto racing's elite.

His answer would come on the afternoon of August 7, 1926.

The faint rumble of thunder could still be heard in the distance. The summer storm that had pounded Indianapolis for ten long hours throughout the night and early morning of August 7, 1926, was now subsiding. By 6:00 A.M. the last of the dark, rolling clouds had disappeared over the horizon, giving way to brilliant, pink-orange sunlight.

In the middle of a sweltering summer, the rain brought cool relief to the fifteen thousand African-American auto racing fans who had gathered at the Indiana State Fairgrounds. For nearly a week, they had been coming from across an eight-state region to witness the third annual running of the Gold and Glory Sweepstakes. While a lucky few found lodging in the city, most camped out near the track and weathered the storms and the oppressive heat.

Roberta Wiggins remembered the day well. "It was so steamy that day . . . hot and rainy. We didn't even think that we were going to have the race, because the rain was so bad [the night before]. It was funny to watch Charlie. He was nervous and excited all at once. He was out of bed really early that morning, looking out the window, watching the clouds. I told him that pacing about wasn't gonna make the clouds go away. But he wasn't listening. His mind was on his car and the race." Roberta finally sent him to the shop to work off his nervous energy and mentally prepare for the race. The south-side garage owner felt he had something to prove that day. For three years Charlie had tweaked and tuned his racecar, the

Wiggins Special, to near perfection. Lap after lap, he had made test runs at Walnut Gardens Speedway. Every part of the car had been carefully crafted to fit tightly and run smoothly. He had rebuilt the engine and had retooled the chassis. His oil tank held his own special mixture of motor oil and castor oil. His fuel tank was loaded with a low-grade airplane fuel. The body, carefully hand-hammered to a smooth finish, was sleek and aerodynamic. A long exhaust pipe stretched the length of the car, giving the machine a rocket-like appearance. Charlie's niece, Mildred Overton, remembered, "Uncle Charlie's cars looked like they were built to fly."

As the morning sunlight streamed through the windows of the shop, Charlie gazed intently over every part and joint one final time. Lost in concentration, he almost did not hear a car horn honking outside the building. Sitting outside was his brother Lawrence, who had traveled from Evansville to watch him compete. Hopping out of an old Model T that Charlie had rebuilt for him, Lawrence helped his older brother push the Wiggins Special out of the garage. Together they carefully tied a rope to the front bumper of the racecar. Then they towed it behind the Model T forty blocks north to the Indiana State Fairgrounds track.

The two entered the main gates of the Indiana State Fairgrounds complex and made their way to the track with the Wiggins Special in tow. Charlie was surprised to see the large number of drivers and mechanics who had gathered in the pit area. There were fifty-nine drivers, a new Gold and Glory Sweepstakes record. All crowded into the small outdoor garage area. A nervous energy saturated the atmosphere as mechanics worked frantically on last-minute adjustments to their cars. All knew that only twenty would survive the qualifying rounds and advance to the main event. Charlie backed his brother's Model T into the pit area and wedged his racecar into a small space provided for him by race officials. Then he lifted the hood of his Wiggins Special and began to run through his final technical checks.

As the temperature began to rise, steam hovered thick above hundreds of puddles, turning the speedway into a muggy sauna. The growing crowds, decked out in their finery, stepped carefully around the muddy spots near the ticket booth. Black veterans of the Great War wore their dress uniforms and stood at attention in the stands as a military band played patriotic numbers in a pre-race tribute. Leaders of the National Association for the Advancement of Colored People, who had

Charlie Wiggins built his first Wiggins Special in Louis Sagalowsky's garage in 1923. He later entered that car in the 1925 Gold and Glory Sweepstakes, his first professional auto race, and finished in fifth place. Courtesy Mrs. Mildred Overton

arrived the night before from New York City, were seated alongside race officials and wore colorful ribbons bestowed on all special guests of the 1926 Gold and Glory Sweepstakes.

Frank Young served as the grand marshal of a special parade held prior to the big race. In the grandstand, he was seated next to members of the Chicago American Giants and the Indianapolis ABCs, two well-known Negro National League baseball teams. Team owners had agreed to postpone a doubleheader originally scheduled for that day. Barnstorming stunt pilots performed aerial acrobatics, followed by music from the Atlanta Gospel Chorus.

"Pres" Rucker and the Indianapolis Colored Speedway Association had once again created a spectacular event that celebrated the ingenuity and courage of the African-American spirit. As in the past, the pre-race hype in the black press was sensational. "The fastest cars in the land will make the first lap of the big grind, and the race will be on. Many will remember the exciting finish during the first race two years ago, when Hannon, the fierce champion, pushed his steed to a finish so thrilling that several women fainted and had to be carried from the stands. The Speedway Association is doing all in its power to make this race a huge success and stamp it as the one big sports event of its kind in the world."[3]

Gamblers in the crowd were taking bets on the drivers. Bobby Wallace was a two-to-one favorite to repeat as Gold and Glory champion, having already captured one award at the Roby Speedway in northern Indiana earlier in the year. Bill Jeffries and Malcolm Hannon, the two fastest qualifiers in the preliminary heats, were also frequently picked by gamblers to capture the checkered flag.

Virtually no one noticed Charlie Wiggins. The south-side mechanic and second-year competitor finished eighth in the early qualifying rounds. His Wiggins Special, the gold car built completely by his own hands and painted with a proud 23, seemed a homely creation in comparison to the powerful Indy 500–tested machines driven by competitors such as Jeffries, Bill Bottoms, and Malcolm Hannon. On a lark, Charlie painted on the side of his car a caricature of Felix the Cat, one of his favorite comic strip characters. The sight of the cartoon cat on the side of his racer caused other drivers to dub his car "the Black Cat." Charlie liked the name, and it stuck. Names for Charlie were as colorful as they were for his cars. The newspapers called him "Wee Charlie," noting that his tiny stature had required him to construct a special chassis that extended the pedals and lifted the seat, so that he could guide his machine with greater ease. Bill Jeffries reportedly scoffed at Charlie's car as the two pulled their racers to the starting line for the beginning of the showdown.

The green flag dropped. The engines roared. The adrenaline flowed. And the race was on. "Wild Bill" Jeffries, in a pure white Fronty Ford with a bold number 1 painted on the side, stormed to an early lead. The crowd sent up an enthusiastic roar. Drivers reacted to the cheers and gunned their engines at full power. Twenty high-revving, piston-pounding engines roared past the grandstand. "I remember the start of those races very well," recalled Mildred Overton. "The roar was so loud and deep, you could feel it in your stomach. Boy, was it thrilling!"

Action from the 1926 Gold and Glory Sweepstakes at the Indiana State Fairgrounds in Indianapolis. Courtesy *Indianapolis Recorder* Collection—Indiana Historical Society

Charlie Wiggins kept a steady pace. Two, then five, then eight drivers passed him as he established a position on the inside of the track, just a few seconds behind the pack. "Charlie always knew how to position himself well in a race," Al Warren remembered. "He used to say that no one remembers the guy who leads the race at the beginning; only the one who leads the race at the end."

By the fortieth lap, Charlie had fallen to tenth place. And yet he continued to drive patiently . . . so patiently. For twelve long months Charlie had been hiding an engineering secret that he felt would ultimately give him the advantage over his fellow competitors. His secret was about to be revealed to the crowd and to the rest of the field.

Sixty laps—sixty miles—into the hundred-lap race, Bill Jeffries still maintained the lead. But a sudden cheer from the Indianapolis crowd caused "Wild Bill" to look back. Charlie Wiggins, who at one time had been nearly a lap behind, was now gaining on Chicago's premier black driving talent. For ten laps the two drivers battled for the top spot. By lap 70, Jeffries held only a slim, one-car-length lead. In the fourth turn, Charlie finally revved his engine to full power. He overtook "Wild Bill" right in front of the grandstand. Thousands of spectators screamed.

The Chicago driver soon began to fall behind Charlie. Looking down at his gas gauge, Jeffries realized how Charlie was able to gain so much ground on the competition. Charlie had built his engine to run on a more efficient mixture of oil and airplane fuel. While other drivers needed pit stops to refuel, Charlie's engine could go the entire distance—one hundred long, hot, grueling miles—without ever stopping for fuel or oil. In lap 75, Jeffries's hard driving finally forced him into the pits for refueling. He was five laps behind Charlie by the time he reentered the track. Charlie had outmaneuvered his opponents by out-engineering them. Roberta Wiggins noted, "Charlie always knew that competitions were not only won on the track. They were also won in the garage in the weeks and months prior to the race."

By the ninetieth lap, Charlie had coasted to an easy lead. A valiant effort by Bill Jeffries helped him gain three laps on the field, causing the crowd to stir near the finish. But in the end, Charlie Wiggins cruised across the finish line two laps ahead of Jeffries and the rest of the field to capture the 1926 Gold and Glory Sweepstakes championship. Despite efforts to restrain the crowd, police officers were unable to stop dozens of overly enthusiastic spectators from storming onto the track to congratulate their hometown hero. The *Chicago Defender* reported, "A wild burst of applause greeted Wiggins from his home towners, some of whom lost their heads and broke like a bunch of wild steers, women and men, running across the track, despite the yells from the cooler heads, warning them of the impending danger of getting killed, as Carter, Jeffries, Smith and Dawson were still in the race for second, third and fourth place honors."[4]

Race officials remembered the deaths of two men at the Hawthorne Speedway in Chicago in 1924 in similar circumstances. Thinking quickly, Colored Speedway Association official Harry Earl grabbed the checkered flag and ran toward the fourth turn, waving the banner frantically. He successfully stopped all the remaining cars before they reached the crowd, and awarded each driver a finishing place exactly as they stood at

Charlie and Roberta Wiggins posed aboard the Wiggins Special after Charlie captured the 1926 Gold and Glory championship. The win earned him the title "the Negro Speed King." Courtesy Mrs. Mildred Overton

the time he stopped the race. Second-place honors went to Ben Carter, who had led Bill Jeffries by only two seconds.

The winner's circle was a melee of excited activity. Charlie and Roberta smiled as photographers snapped pictures of the couple posed in Charlie's car with the championship trophy perched on the hood. The *Indianapolis Recorder* noted, "Charles Wiggins, driving his own make of racing automobile, a Wiggins Special, never going to the pits for gas, water, nor oil, never stopping for tire changes and driving a steady race, won the third annual Gold and Glory Sweepstakes, which carries besides the beautiful silver cup and the large cash prize, the national dirt track championship for 100 miles. Needless to say, Indianapolis went wild, because one of her own drivers won, and also because the one that won had built his own iron steed."[5]

Frank Young commented on the new champion in the following week's edition of the *Chicago Defender:* "'Wee Charlie' Wiggins, that plucky young mechanic from Indiana, had to build a special seat in his chassis to boost his tiny frame. But at the end of this grand Gold and Glory event, it was not the mechanics that mattered, but the mechanic himself. . . . Wiggins crossed the finish line well ahead of the pack, sending a great roar through the crowd, welcoming their hometown champion."[6]

Auto racing historian Joe Freeman reflected, "One hundred miles on a rough, rocky, dusty dirt track is a long way. And it will tire out even the strongest of guys. And when you have somebody like Charlie who only weighs a hundred pounds, a small, wiry fella, that one hundred miles had to be a real experience. The fact that he even survived is an accomplishment. To win the race is truly spectacular."

Mildred Overton remembered the excitement. "What a thrill it was for me to be a part of all that as a young girl! I had always looked up to Uncle Charlie. Now here were all these people cheering him, celebrating his accomplishments. It was like they were sharing in a joy that had been a special secret of mine for all those years. Now everyone could see what I saw . . . that Uncle Charlie was a very special guy."

"There was a dance that night at Trinity Hall. Charlie was the man of the hour," Al Warren recalled. "They put posters up all over Indiana Avenue. Everywhere you'd go, you'd see Charlie's picture with the title 'National Champion.' He was a local boy, the guy everyone in the neighborhood knew. His victory was like a victory for all of us. We could all relate to it and whoop it up, just like we'd done it ourselves."

His victory in the 1926 Gold and Glory Sweepstakes sparked an explosion in Charlie Wiggins's racing career. Dayton . . . Chicago . . . Cleveland . . . Detroit . . . Keokuk, Iowa . . . Langhorne, Pennsylvania . . . South Bend, Indiana . . . Charlie won seven of the nine Colored Speedway Association events in the rest of the 1926 season. Never before in black sports had an athlete risen to national acclaim so quickly. The shy garage owner from Indianapolis often backed away from media interviews. And yet Charlie continued to find his name in bold print in the headlines of sports pages in the *Kansas City Call,* the *Chicago Defender,* the *Pittsburgh Courier,* and other prominent black newspapers.

One reporter commented that Charlie Wiggins's efforts "broke down the walls of oppression," creating "a new breed of sports hero among members of our Race."[7] A reporter from the *Indianapolis Recorder* dubbed him "the Negro Speed King,"[8] a popular moniker that soon found its way into nearly every major black newspaper in America. "Charlie never said much," Roberta Wiggins remembered. "He let his driving do the talking. The reporters were the ones who made a big to-do about Charlie and turned him into a racing celebrity. Truth be told, I think Charlie would have preferred to stay in his garage and work quietly on his cars and race on the weekends. Period." She shook her head and laughed. "'The Negro Speed King.' . . . He never could get used to that. I think that name made him very uncomfortable."

When Charlie *did* speak publicly, his comments typically centered on the social injustices practiced by the AAA, particularly their unwritten but clearly understood rules barring African Americans from sanctioned competitions against the nation's top white drivers. At the request of the Colored Speedway Association, Charlie once made a public statement to the *Chicago Whip.* His comments were supposed to focus on his recent win in Detroit. Instead Charlie told the reporter, "We have the desire and skill to compete with the nation's best. The AAA folks just don't want to see that. That's why we must work to prove our ability within our own ranks, so that we can show the rest of the world that we belong."[9]

All auto racing events not sanctioned by the American Automobile Association were considered "outlaw" races—events that had absolutely no bearing on AAA-sanctioned competitions. All drivers and mechanics on the Colored Speedway Association tour were outlaws, according to the AAA. Any record set in an outlaw event would be ignored in AAA publications and documents.

Historian Richard Pierce noted, "If you picked up a copy of the *Indianapolis Recorder* in 1926, you'd read giant, front-page articles about the Gold and Glory Sweepstakes. As well, you'd see references to Charlie

Wiggins as the 'Jack Johnson of auto racing.' Then, by contrast, you'd go and pick up a copy of some mainstream papers, such as the *Indianapolis Times* or the *Indianapolis Star,* and there would be virtually nothing about the Gold and Glory events." The AAA gave the mainstream press much of the nation's racing information. Its influence as a public relations machine at the time was significant. The AAA did not simply attempt to discredit the Gold and Glory Sweepstakes. They went even further. They wanted all traces of Charlie Wiggins and the Colored Speedway Association to be erased from existence, at least in any official racing context.

Charlie's remarks fanned the fires of rage among members of the White Supremacy League, as well. The property damage to Charlie's garage and the threats of physical violence increased as Charlie's career blossomed. "A lot of us would like to say that we'd stand our ground during the tough times," Al Warren stated. "But when you start getting notes that say, 'We're gonna kill you,' that's pretty tough to take. Would you stand your ground then? Most wouldn't. But Charlie sure did. There weren't no fear in his bones, no backin' down at all. He knew what was right. And to him, right made might."

When the Ku Klux Klan held a regional rally in Indianapolis, the White Supremacy League helped with the organization of the event. Touting the city as "the Racing Capital of the World," members of the League wanted to celebrate its rich racing heritage. The group produced a number of gold pendants to hand out as souvenirs to out-of-town visitors. On one side of the pendant was an image of a racecar with the words "Indianapolis 500" engraved along the edge. On the back were the letters "KKK." There is no evidence that either the Indianapolis Motor Speedway or the American Automobile Association knew about or approved of the creation and distribution of the pendants. Still, the actions of the White Supremacy League underscored the prevailing attitudes among mainstream auto racing enthusiasts regarding minority participation in AAA-sanctioned events.

The achievements of Charlie Wiggins, Bobby Wallace, Malcolm Hannon, and other black drivers began to raise an initial, subtle awareness among mainstream racing fans that a colored man could indeed possess the knowledge and skills to drive a racecar competitively. Charlie underscored the point during one of the final Colored Speedway Association events of 1927, held in Quakertown, Pennsylvania, on October 2. Charlie easily won the championship of the fifty-mile derby, outdistancing the competition by nearly two laps. What made the win so sensational was that Charlie reportedly finished the race at an average speed of 81.6 miles per hour. Just one week earlier, Frank Lockhart, a talented white competitor driving a top-of-the-line Miller racecar, had set a one-mile dirt track speed record at the Cleveland Speedway with a speed of 82.826 miles per hour. Charlie came within 1.2 seconds of eclipsing the world record, a feat that received great attention in the black press. "As the records fall, so too, will the barriers that keep us from the great racing traditions in America," Sol Butler from the *Chicago Bee* proclaimed.[10] No mainstream, white-owned newspaper included any coverage of the race or mentions of Charlie's noteworthy accomplishment.

"Charlie surely didn't want to admit it, but he was becoming a hero to the black folks around here," Al Warren stated. "I knew he wasn't comfortable with the publicity and all. But I think he realized that folks were coming out to see the races and see *him*. He never said much, but I was so very proud of him. We all were."

Indiana governor Ed Jackson took the oath of office in January 1925. For the governor's friend, Ku Klux Klan leader D. C. Stephenson, Jackson's win in the November election was a coup. The KKK Grand Dragon began to map out a social and political agenda that pushed toward greater segregation in state and national government. Stephenson, ever ambitious, was hardly ready to rest on the laurels bestowed upon him after the election. He next set his sights on Indiana's 1925 municipal elections. Indianapolis mayor Samuel Shank, the adamant anti-Klan politician who had run against Jackson in the May 1924 primaries, was up for reelection. Stephenson's organization had been a thorn in Shank's side for the past three years. Shank was out to destroy the powerful Klan once and for all. And Stephenson was out to destroy Shank . . . once and for all.

Stephenson picked a Klan-backed Republican candidate, banker and lawyer John L. Duvall, to run against Shank in the May 1925 primaries. Duvall had organized the city's first suburban bank, the Haughville Bank, and was serving as Marion County treasurer when he aligned himself with the Ku Klux Klan. Strongly supported by Klan dollars, Duvall ran an aggressive campaign. Shank rigidly stuck to the same anti-Klan platform that had spelled his defeat in the race for governor the year before. With the popularity of the Klan at its peak in the city and state, Shank stood no chance. Duvall easily captured the May primaries and went on to defeat Democrat Walter Myers in the November elections.

Stephenson seemed to hold ultimate control of city and state politics. He had served as an advisor to Governor Jackson and now Mayor Duvall. The new mayor could make several key appointments, such as the chiefs of the police and fire departments. Stephenson was at the height of his political power. His influence on local and state policy issues could be seen immediately. The residential zoning ordinance that placed tremendous restrictions on African Americans who wished to move into white neighborhoods was the work of Klan-backed special-interest groups. Mayor Duvall signed the bill into law despite the fact that he and other city-county council members were fully aware of its unconstitutionality. Ultimately struck down in the courts, the bill reflected the segregationist attitudes that prevailed among many white civic leaders.

The Klan's populist politics spread throughout other areas of social life in Indiana, as well. Since the turn of the century, Indianapolis had battled tremendous overcrowding in its schools. Poorly maintained, overcrowded facilities had many administrators and parents debating the future of the city's school system. At the time, Indianapolis High School (later renamed Shortridge High School) was a completely integrated facility. It was also considered the premier college preparatory school in the city. As the black neighborhoods began to expand into the area, many white families grew concerned about the rising minority population. They turned to the Ku Klux Klan and other segregationist groups for support.

In 1921, and again in 1923, Indianapolis voters had passed a bond issue that would allow for the construction of a new elementary and high school designated for African Americans. Fierce fighting by organizations such as the NAACP and local black leaders, including Robert

Brokenburr, had staved off the creation of a segregated high school in the city. But as the Ku Klux Klan gained widespread support, and white citizens' groups grew in number and power, the initiative gained new momentum. "We are not only white, but you just bet your life we are going to stay white," one Klansman told a reporter. "Whenever a man goes to mixing God's colors he gets into trouble, an' he is not only doomed, but he is damned and . . . ought to be."[11]

At the time, the city was battling a fierce tuberculosis scare. The painful and still untreatable disease was taking a terrible toll on many in the city, particularly in Indianapolis's African-American districts. Inadequate sanitation services in the black neighborhoods contributed to the spread of the disease. In 1920, an African-American man was five times more likely to die of tuberculosis than was a white man. The Indianapolis Chamber of Commerce seized upon this fact and, in a petition to the Indianapolis Board of School Commissioners in 1922, made tuberculosis the focal point and the battle cry of all segregationists in the city. "Our children should not be exposed to this terrible menace," one white mother told a reporter.

The clamor soon grew to a fever pitch. And by the end of 1925, with Mayor Duvall, the school board, and many members of the city-county council backing the initiative, an urgent push was on to complete construction of a segregated high school in Indianapolis. Brokenburr, the NAACP, the local black press, and others vehemently fought the project with no success. Crispus Attucks High School opened in 1927 and continued as the city's only all-black high school until 1969. Disgusted by the city's actions, Dean William Pickens, a national officer with the NAACP, said, "Violation of the unalienable rights of colored people to life, liberty and the pursuit of happiness is more flagrant and vicious in Indianapolis and Indiana than in any Northern or Western city and state. . . . The laws and customs in Indianapolis are reprehensible."[12]

"The us-versus-them attitude was at its peak in 1925," remarked historian James Madison. "Indianapolis, like any other city in the United States, had struggled with the issue of race for many, many years. But this was something altogether new and more vicious, more volatile. It seemed that literally day by day, more and more restrictions were being placed on African Americans—restrictions that were designed to keep them out of practically every area of mainstream society during the

1920s. By 1925, particularly after the city elections, the Klan's rise to power was at its peak. And this made things very, very difficult for African Americans who dared to battle this increasingly rigid color line in Indianapolis and Indiana."

The fight for racial equality was a quiet, subtle battle for most African Americans in Indianapolis. A direct confrontation with a segregationist juggernaut that included D. C. Stephenson, the Ku Klux Klan, and many Klan-backed civic and political leaders would have been dangerous and even life-threatening. Therefore, many black leaders tried for smaller victories in hopes of slowly eroding racial injustice. Organizers, drivers, and promoters of the Gold and Glory Sweepstakes adopted just such a strategy. Historian Boniface Hardin commented, "These men had a dream that someday there would be an opportunity for black folks to drive in the Indy 500. There would be an opportunity to show that they belonged. Someday there would be a change. But they knew they had to prove that they could organize and compete within their own ranks first. This was their first goal, their first victory. This would be a signal to the establishment—and to themselves—first and foremost. That's where they began to break down the color line. That's why they needed a leader like Charlie Wiggins, whom the fans loved and the white establishment respected for his mechanical ability. He was a natural hero for the circuit and for the black community."

"The folks sure loved Charlie," remembered Al Warren. "A lot of the black drivers looked to Charlie as kind of a leader. I really don't think he wanted the attention, but people liked him and liked the rivalries with guys like Bill Jeffries and Bobby Wallace. The Speedway Association was always trying to hype up these rivalries and things, because they wanted to get more people out to the track. I think Charlie knew deep down that if the circuit did well, he could do well and finally break down the color barrier in auto racing."

To keep the circuit revving at full speed, Charlie agreed to work with the Colored Speedway Association promoters to stage outrageous stunts in an effort to attract more spectators to the track. "This was a common practice among all auto racing promoters at the time," stated racing historian Joe Freeman. "Promoters . . . were really a wild bunch. The truth was often bent beyond belief. There were all sorts of tricks they used to get fans into the stands. Many drivers were billed as 'the greatest in the world,' or 'the Russian national dirt track champion,' even though Russia never had a dirt track champion at the time. There was an enormous amount of hype similar to the circus coming to town. . . . 'Thrills, Chills, and Spills'. . . 'Death-Defying Acts' . . . 'Drivers Skidding on the Edge of Disaster' . . . all that type of language was used to add to the mythical stature of these drivers."

The Colored Speedway Association staged a large number of promotional stunts, including a series of match races between Charlie "the Negro Speed King" Wiggins and "Wild Bill" Jeffries, and between either Charlie or Jeffries and the top local black driver in the region. In one race Charlie agreed to drive a five-lap solo race against the clock while blindfolded. The scheme was a common one among drivers in the racing profession at the time. Small holes or slits were cut into the blindfold just before the race began, without the audience's knowledge. While the crowd gasped, Charlie easily steered his way around the track. The stunt, though deceptive, was wildly popular among the fans. Al Warren recalled, "At first we were just getting good fan support in Indianapolis, in Chicago. There was always the big city rivalry going there: which city had the better drivers, that kind of thing. But then we started getting eight thousand fans in Dayton, ten thousand in Cleveland, twelve thousand in Detroit. It was a sight to watch."

Charlie and the Colored Speedway Association continued to find new and unusual ways to promote black auto racing to the widest possible audience. In 1928 they developed an elaborate stunt unlike any in auto racing so far. Throughout the history of the sport, no woman had ever competed in any official racing competition. Late one night, after a long CSA meeting at the new Madam Walker Theatre and business complex on Indiana Avenue, Charlie came home, sat Roberta down on the edge of the bed, and told his wife that she was about to make history.

"I couldn't believe my ears when he first told me!" Roberta recalled. "Charlie cooked up this notion that I should compete in a ten-lap match race against one of the top male competitors at a race in Cleveland. I told Charlie right then and there what I thought about that idea . . . 'No way,' I said. I told him to drop the subject, but Charlie had other plans."

"The idea of Aunt Roberta driving a racecar was not as far-fetched as many might think," Mildred Overton noted. "She visited the garage a lot and helped him when he worked on his cars. When he took the car out for testing, she often drove test laps for him. She would tell him stuff about how the engine was doing, whether it was riding rough, things like that. She was very small, but she could handle a powerful motor. She was one tough cookie, that's for sure."

No one understood Roberta's steely determination and fiery temper better than Charlie did. The week before the race in Cleveland, the drivers gathered for a series of meetings. Charlie saw his old rival, "Wild Bill" Jeffries, and began to tease him. He told the Chicago car owner that his $12,000 racer was no match for a Wiggins Special, even with a woman behind the wheel. When the boisterous car owner erupted at Charlie's claim, several drivers took notice, as did a reporter from the *Cleveland Call-Post*. Mildred Overton recalled, "Jeffries said something to the effect that a woman had no business being near an automobile. Well, you know that didn't settle well with Aunt Roberta. She really didn't like Jeffries anyway. And she sure wasn't going to put up with that."

Charlie had orchestrated the perfect scheme to get Roberta to agree to race against Jeffries in the Cleveland match race. The following day reporters gathered around as Charlie announced the special pre-race attraction. Roberta remembered, "I'll never forget that race in Cleveland. There, in front of all those reporters, Charlie told 'em that he'd stake the race's purse that old 'Wild Bill' couldn't beat me in a one-on-one heat ... *me!* I'd driven Charlie's cars during warm-ups and all, but I ain't never raced in a competition like that." She paused, and then chuckled. "The papers called me 'the Mystery Woman Driver.' Ha! ... No woman had ever competed in auto racing before. It was quite a stunt. We had nearly fifteen thousand people come out that day just to see me get in that car. Charlie was just loving it, I could tell. All I could think was, 'What in the world am I doing here?'"

When race day came, the "Mystery Woman Driver" was grand marshal at a parade in her honor prior to the big event. Charlie and Roberta rode in the back of a convertible, waving to the adoring crowds that lined the streets of Cleveland's black neighborhoods. Earlier that morning, Roberta had eaten an unusual breakfast of cantaloupe and ice cream. After two hours in the summer heat, she began to feel ill. Her stomach turned. Her vision narrowed. While waving to the crowd, she paused to look at her husband. And then she fainted. Charlie gathered his wife's limp body into his lap and ordered the driver to rush to the nearest hospital. When the couple arrived at the emergency room, the doctor on call made a surprising discovery. Roberta was pregnant.

"I woke up right away, and I felt pretty good," Roberta remembered. "I told Charlie I wanted to go on with the race. I didn't want all those

As a promotional stunt in Cleveland in 1928, Charlie and the Colored Speedway Association trumpeted a special match race that featured "a fearless mystery woman driver." That "mystery woman driver" was Charlie's wife, Roberta, who learned how to drive a racecar under Charlie's tutelage. Courtesy Mrs. Mildred Overton people to think I was backing out on them. But Charlie refused. He said it was too dangerous for me. I begged him, but he still wouldn't let me race. I looked into his eyes, and I could tell he meant it. We *did* go back to the track, and I drove a lap or two by myself in Charlie's car and waved to the crowd, but that was it. My racing career was over."

It had been eight years since the death of the Wigginses' third son, Charles, Jr. The couple's early life together had been filled with sorrow as they watched each of their three infant sons die of disease. The news of Roberta's pregnancy in 1928 injected a new vigor into Charlie's life. Friends noted that the pleasant but quiet mechanic was now "gabby" and walked through his garage whistling and singing. He vowed to spend more time at home and withdrew from two Colored Speedway Association events the following month in order to spend more time with Roberta.

Roberta was far more circumspect than her husband. Mildred Overton said, "She'd had a terrible history of health problems, and she was afraid that something awful might happen here, as well. Uncle Charlie seemed to be oblivious to it all. It was kinda like he was saying to himself, 'If I ignore the danger, it doesn't exist.' I think that worried Aunt Roberta even more."

The couple's worst fears were realized six weeks later. Charlie returned from his garage late one night to find Roberta doubled over on the floor with severe stomach pains. Blood was on the carpet. Later, at the hospital, Charlie stood despondent over his wife's bed as an emergency room physician told the couple that Roberta had suffered a miscarriage. Worse yet, the doctor explained that Roberta's fragile health would not allow her to bear any children. Each word penetrated Charlie's soul like a sharp punch to the stomach. Exhausted, Roberta fell into a deep sleep. Charlie slumped over and gently caressed his wife's face.

On the track Charlie seemed invincible. But away from the cameras and the celebrations at the winner's circle, his soul was awash in sorrow and seemingly infinite pain. As a child he had faced the death of his mother and the depression that consumed and killed his father. As a young man he had watched helplessly as his three young sons succumbed to dreadful, painful diseases. He had been assaulted. His property had been damaged. His life had been threatened.

And now this.

The "Negro Speed King" was falling hopelessly behind in a race in which he had no control of the outcome, no control of his fate. The thought made him angry, sad, and completely overcome with grief. As Roberta slept, Charlie took her hand, bowed his head, and cried. Years later he told a reporter, "I never feared danger of any kind on the track. But I feared for Roberta like nothing I've ever known."

Officials of the Colored Speedway Association were worried as well. One of their competitors and drawing cards, Charlie Wiggins, had withdrawn his name, missing the final two races of the 1928 season. Rumors began to fly that Charlie might never return to auto racing. Bill Jeffries had captured the 1928 Gold and Glory Sweepstakes in a thrilling race that attracted thousands to the Indiana State Fairgrounds. Yet attendance in other markets had dropped during the latter part of the season. There was even talk that Jeffries and his partner, Chicago night-club owner Bill Bottoms, might buy the Colored Speedway Association and move its headquarters to Chicago. CSA president William "Pres" Rucker made a statement to the *Indianapolis Recorder* reassuring the Indianapolis media that the world's premier black auto racing association would stay in Indianapolis, the world's premier racing city. Business manager Harry Dunnington and 1924 Gold and Glory champion Malcolm Hannon echoed Rucker's remarks. But without more talented drivers like Charlie, Rucker was, no doubt, concerned about the league's future in Indianapolis.

Charlie's brother Lawrence had a far greater concern. He had noticed Charlie slipping into the same dark shadows of despair that had haunted and eventually devoured the soul of the boys' father, Sport Wiggins. Lawrence feared that his older brother might never recover from the tragedies Charlie and Roberta had faced. Shortly after Roberta's miscarriage, Charlie's friend Al Warren saw Lawrence walking down Michigan Avenue, in the heart of the African-American district, and called out to him. "I asked if Charlie was giving up on racing. And he told me, 'I'm worried that he might just give up . . . period.' Well, what do you say to something like that?"

Four days after her loss, Roberta came home from the hospital. Depressed and exhausted, she spent much of her time in bed. Charlie was edgy and noticeably upset. One friend remembered that he went nearly a week with no sleep. And then, according to Roberta, his mood seemed to change. He was quiet, but more determined somehow, as if he had come to some sort of resolution. Late one night he woke his wife and pulled a chair to the side of her bed. "It was two in the morning, but Charlie was ready to talk," Roberta remembered.

According to Roberta, Charlie grabbed her hand and spoke slowly, never taking his eyes off her. For Roberta, the two-hour conversation that followed was sacred. She promised Charlie never to tell a soul what they discussed in those quiet early morning hours. By the time the sun rose, Roberta knew that Charlie had come to terms with what she called "his personal demons."

Later that morning the sun seeped through the gaps in the gnarled wooden walls of Charlie Wiggins's garage on Merrill Street. The large, barn-like doors creaked as they opened slowly. As the sun poured in, a solitary figure stood in silhouette in the doorway with his toolbox in his hand. The shadowy figure made his way to the racecar sitting in the back of the garage.

Social pressures . . . personal tragedy. . . . Somehow Charlie Wiggins would reengineer his life just as he had retooled his racing engine. He hopped into the cockpit and started the motor. The roar shook the rafters of the old building. And for the faintest second, a small grin flickered across a hardened face that had been so solemn for so long.

Charlie Wiggins had taken a long trip through hell. Now he was finding his way home.

5.

Charlie's Gang

The gravel pavement popped and crackled under the rolling tires as Charlie Wiggins pushed his customers' ailing cars from the garage area into the large open lot that encircled his establishment. The summers could be brutal inside Charlie's garage. The sun through the southern windows made the workshop unbearably hot during the long, sultry Indiana afternoons. A small black electric fan whirred at high speed in one corner of the workbench, providing only a faint respite from the steamy conditions. During these warm days, Charlie often moved his business outdoors. He pushed each car into a wide, shaded yard, where faint breezes brought brief relief to the hardworking auto mechanic.

Young men gathered in the gravel yard nearly every day to share a Coke and a laugh with Charlie. Some of these young men were black. Others were white. All were brought together by an unquenchable passion for automobiles and a deep respect for the talented mechanic. They were known as Charlie's Gang. "Charlie made you feel like you was family," Sumner "Red" Oliver remembered with a smile. "He'd always tell these bad jokes, and sometimes he'd razz you a bit. But he'd also take the time to show you what he'd be doin'. And any of us who knew anything about cars knew we'd better listen up, because Charlie would teach ya all kinds of important stuff. Whether he was working on a racecar or an old Model T, that man knew more about engines than anybody I'd ever met."

Leon "Al" Warren was a delivery truck driver and one of Indianapolis's first African Americans to earn a pilot's license. He owned a family grocery store not far from Indiana Avenue. "I guess you could say I was a bit of a jack of all trades," Warren remembered. "But my real passions were flying and auto racing. It's just something about the speed, I think, that gives me such a thrill. That's why I wanted to get into the racing game. I was a young guy—probably nineteen or twenty years old—when I first started going over to Charlie's garage. I had so many different jobs to bring in money that I'd have to get over there really early in the morning. Charlie was always there around six, so I could spend a few hours with him then. Charlie was considered a real hero around these parts at the time, especially among us black kids. To study under him was great . . . and a real privilege."

Warren continued, "Charlie was great. Everybody loved Charlie. Charlie was so good to take the time to explain things to you. For a top-notch driver to do that to an impressionable young man like me really had an impact. My brother and I eventually saved up enough money to buy an old Chandler—just a regular passenger car. We brought that car to Charlie's garage, and he'd let us keep it in his shop. We'd work on that thing just about any free moment we had. And Charlie would always work with us to teach us how to make the car run better. That old car was great. Charlie really helped us get her up and running smoothly."

Warren remembered the first time he entered a car in the Gold and Glory circuit, at a race in Mitchell, Indiana, in 1930. "If you're a rookie and the other drivers know it, the older, more experienced ones will try to play mind games with you a little bit. They'd say things like, 'Don't come on my side, or I'll run you right off the track.' One driver, Bill Buckner—he was a local boy—he was a tough son of a gun. He drove this big ol' Duesenberg racer that looked like a tank. I tried to pass him in that race, and he intentionally swerved his car right into the side of mine to see if I'd flinch. It was kinda like playing a game of chicken on

Some members of "Charlie's Gang" hit the road for an auto race near Chicago in 1933. From left to right: (*kneeling*) Andy Kirk, Leon "Al" Warren, Sumner "Red" Oliver; (*standing*) Andrew Pryor, Charlie Wiggins, and Charles "Dynamite" Stewart. The two men standing on the far right are unidentified. Courtesy Mrs. Mildred Overton

a dusty racetrack going seventy miles an hour. He was testing me. They all were, really. Charlie warned me before the race that guys will always dare you to knock the chip off their shoulder. It was all a game. Still, when you get a guy like Buckner coming at you at full speed like that, it's a real 'gut check.' Well, I didn't back down from him. I sped up and he hit me in the side of the car. We both flew up over the bank and off the track. I landed on my side, sliding across the grass. Buckner buried the nose of that Duesenberg right into a big mud bank . . . completely crushed his engine block." Warren paused to reflect. "Served him right, dammit!" he laughed. "My car was screwed up for weeks, but at least then people knew that I wasn't going to back down from anybody."

Leon "Al" Warren was one of Indiana's first licensed black pilots. Warren was also a talented racecar driver and a devout member of "Charlie's Gang." Courtesy Mrs. Esther Ewing

The war of words and macho mind games were common in all auto racing during the era, particularly on the colored circuit. Al Warren explained, "All the guys were in open cockpits. And we'd be so close to each other, some of the guys would lean over and yell at us. It was usually some nasty, stupid thing, like calling your mother names. Sometimes you'd get a driver in front of you who would intentionally try to skid into the bank more than usual, so that he could throw more dust and dirt up in your face. I've even been driving side by side with someone, and the two of us have been so close that the other driver has reached out and tried to punch me in the side of the head. Can you believe it? I mean, here's a guy who is trying to manhandle a car with no power steering at a very fast speed. He's pumping oil as fast as he can. He's trying to handle the brakes. And then in the middle of all that, he's trying to reach over and punch me. Now that's tough!"

In order to gain the experience and toughness needed to steer through such a heart-pounding experience, most young drivers needed to apprentice themselves to a seasoned driver and mechanic, and most in Charlie's Gang did. Shadowing Charlie Wiggins during races, or "stooging," as the young mechanics called it, was a privilege that many young black drivers treasured. Charlie gave many young apprentices the opportunity to steer in the cockpit as he towed the racecar from one racetrack to another. His pit crew consisted of many eager young men who crowded under the hood as Charlie readied his Wiggins Special for battle. "To this day stooging for Charlie is still one of the fondest memories of my life," smiled Red Oliver, who got his start as an eigh-teen-year-old mechanic for Dayton, Ohio, car owner Johnny Varee in 1929. He met Charlie Wiggins at the 1933 Gold and Glory Sweep-stakes. The two became fast friends.

"I was only twenty-two when I started working for Charlie. I started driving Charlie's cars in practices at Walnut Gardens. But I ain't never raced in any real competitions. We got to a race in Winchester, and Charlie brought two cars to the race. And he says to me, 'Red, you're racing my other car today.' I was so nervous I thought I was going to throw up. There was this large crowd all around cheering and all. I looked around and told him, 'I ain't never drove in a competition like this.' He said, 'Yeah, you're all right. You're ready.' The other guys gave me a hard time because I was a rookie, but Charlie told me, 'Don't let 'em bluff ya. You got what it takes.' He said that, but I was so scared."

Oliver continued, "They dropped the flag for qualifications. It was really dusty. I could hardly see. But I did it. I made the starting field . . . proved I was a driver that morning. Charlie leaned over to the guy with the official scorecard and said, 'That's Red Oliver. Don't forget it.' That's what Charlie did for me, and I'll always be grateful for that as long as I live." Oliver's career in the auto racing industry as a driver and a mechanic lasted another forty years. He became the first African American to work as a mechanic at the Indianapolis Motor Speedway when he joined George Bignotti, Jackie Howerton, and the Patrick Racing Team in the 1970s.

Just down the street from Charlie and Roberta's home lived Charles Stewart, a tall, thin factory worker who, as a child, would sneak into the Indianapolis Motor Speedway to catch a glimpse of the speeding engines from a small hideaway beneath the bleachers near the second turn of the giant 2½-mile oval. Stewart grew up to earn a supervisory position on the second-shift line at Inland Container Corporation in Indianapolis. He spent his days focusing on quality control issues, walking ceaselessly around the facility, all the while dreaming of making laps in a racecar around some midwestern dirt track.

Because he worked the second shift, much of his day was free to spend as he liked. Most of that time was spent at the garage on Merrill Street. "Lord, you couldn't go over to Charlie's garage without seeing Charlie Stewart," Roberta Wiggins remembered. The former Gold and Glory champion showed Stewart how to piece together a powerful racecar using only discarded parts from the local junkyard. The first "Stewart Special" made its debut on the black auto racing circuit sometime in the early spring of 1933. "The thing was a disaster," Roberta laughed. "It was built well enough, but Charlie Stewart had a heavy foot. He kept pushing it too hard, and it finally fell apart. He was always doing that, despite what Charlie kept trying to tell him. He was so hard on his cars, Charlie finally started calling him 'Dynamite,' because he kept blowing up engines."

As Charlie's business continued to grow, he moved some of his clients' cars to a large garage behind his new home on Indianapolis Avenue. "His work kept him so busy that he could have literally worked all day and all night," noted Charlie's niece, Mildred Overton. "Uncle Charlie was a hard worker. He was also extremely nice, and couldn't turn anyone away. That's why he had so much work to do."

Of course, wherever Charlie went, "Dynamite" Stewart, Al Warren, Red Oliver, and the rest of his loyal following were close at hand. But when a group of rowdy, messy mechanics came to call at the Wiggins household, Charlie's wife set some clear ground rules for Charlie's Gang.

"Aunt Roberta was a sophisticated society girl," remarked Overton. "She'd try to hold these social club meetings and tea parties at the same time Uncle Charlie's friends were milling about working on cars. It really upset her to have all these greasy, rough-talking men hanging around her house. So she went right out there and had a talk with them all. She was tough. She wouldn't back down from any of them."

Sumner "Red" Oliver was first exposed to auto mechanics in his hometown of Dayton, Ohio. He later refined his skills under the guidance of Charlie Wiggins. Courtesy *Indianapolis Recorder* Collection— Indiana Historical Society

Charlie gave his close friend Charles Stewart the nickname "Dynamite" because he drove his cars so hard that he blew up his engines. Courtesy Mrs. Mildred Overton

Overton continued, "She was tiny, only 4'11" tall, but she went out back once and laid out some ground rules for those men. No yelling. No profanity. No loud equipment operation during her club meetings. This was serious stuff. I'm not sure what she would have done if someone would have given her any lip, but none of them did. If they came into the house to use the restroom, they had to take their shoes off and wash their hands and faces before entering the house. She commanded respect. They all called her 'Miss Roberta.' No one dared to mess with her."

The "Negro Speed King" and "Miss Roberta" had a tremendously positive influence on the men associated with the Gold and Glory Sweepstakes. The young drivers and mechanics on the circuit grew and matured with the help of the Indianapolis couple. "The drivers were becoming ambassadors of the sport and of their race," noted historian Richard Pierce. "They grew to understand the nuances and subtleties of the deeper meaning of the sport. They had a responsibility to more than themselves, and Charlie and his wife understood that. They were saying to these young men, 'You are on a stage. You must display courage. You must display class. You must show that, in every arena, you belong with the top drivers at the Indy 500.' The life lessons that came from Charlie's garage were not as overt as that, but the subtle meaning behind the message was that we, as a people, *will* perform, and perform well, with the world's best."

In their own way, Charlie and Roberta Wiggins represented the backbone of black auto racing coast to coast, epitomizing the spirit and courage of the African-American population in the midwestern United States. The results of their actions would be seen for decades to come. Joie Ray was a happy thirteen-year-old when Charlie Wiggins captured his first Gold and Glory crown in 1926. The success of Charlie and others on the Colored Speedway Association tour inspired Ray to pursue a career in auto racing. Known later as "the Jackie Robinson of Auto Racing," Ray broke the AAA's color line in 1946 by becoming the first African American to compete in official, sanctioned racing events.

"I grew up in Louisville," Ray noted. "And I remembered all the stories about Charlie Wiggins, Dynamite Stewart, and those guys that created the Colored Speedway circuit in the Midwest. Times were rough back in those days. I remember hearing of times when promoters would bring the black racers into town, charge a dollar to get in, get several thousand people to turn out, then slip out of town with the gate receipts while the race was going on. Sometimes when that happened, some person would announce to the crowd that someone had stolen the money, and then they'd pass the hat for donations in order to give some prize money to the winner of the race."

Ray's first racer was a sprint car he won in 1946 through a gambling operation. As he told *Open Wheel* magazine reporter Terry Reed, "I was in my dad's office, reading the classifieds in a racing paper. There was this four-cylinder Dodge for sale out of Macon, Georgia, for $450. Here came the numbers writer. He said, 'Are you going to play your number today?' I said, 'Give me 450 for a dollar. If this number comes up, I'm going to buy me a racecar.' We talked no more about it. That afternoon he came back with a big laugh on his face, and he threw $500 on my

Joie Ray earned the nickname "the Jackie Robinson of auto racing" for breaking the AAA's color barrier in 1946. He raced alongside many of the members of "Charlie's Gang," including Charles "Dynamite" Stewart and Sumner "Red" Oliver. Courtesy Mr. Joie Ray

desk. Numbers paid 500 to one. I said, 'What was the number?' He said it was 450."[1]

During the 1940s, in the early years of his racing career, Ray traveled with noted Indy 500 drivers Bill Cantrell and Chick Smith and experienced relatively little overt racism ("Cantrell, Smith, and those guys were my friends, and they watched my back," he remembered). He noted, however, that his predecessors often had a more difficult time. "The Gold and Glory boys would travel from town to town for these colored-only races. And hotels would not accept them. Restaurants would not serve them. Those guys ate a lot of baloney sandwiches back then . . . just stuff they could take with them in the car."

Ray remembered reading stories of Charlie Wiggins's exploits and hearing word of "the great colored driver from Indianapolis," who, as Ray put it, "drove with the mean speed of an Indy car driver." He noted, "Building a racecar from scratch is one thing. Having that car perform, like Charlie's did, is another. Back in that era there were a few great homemade cars, like Charlie's 'Wiggins Special.' There were others that were not so good, like a driver I knew who built a car named 'Basement Bessie.' We all called it that because he built the entire car in his basement, then couldn't figure out how to get it out once he had the thing finished."

Ray continued, "The big challenge was to keep the car running well race after race, especially when rough tracks would tear up the car and ruin all the time and hard work you put into it." One of Ray's early cars, a "Joe's Special," was similar to those that competed in the Gold and Glory Sweepstakes. "It was tough running cars in dirt track competitions. Your body was exposed from the chest up. There was no roll bar or anything. And when the dust, dirt, and gravel kicked up, it felt like someone was throwing marbles or shooting a BB gun at you. The Gold and Glory drivers had even less technology and protection than I did, so I know how tough it must have been for Charlie and those guys to succeed in dirt track racing at that time."

Ray concluded, "I didn't have the chance to study directly under Charlie, but I drove with Charlie Stewart, Red Oliver, and others who worked and drove with him. All of us had seen and understood how Charlie had been a pioneer. He showed us, in his own way, that you can do some pretty amazing things if you believe in yourself and create opportunities for yourself. No doubts. No fears. That was Charlie. Thank God he was there to pave the way for me."

The popularity of the Indianapolis 500-Mile Race and other racing events sparked a national fascination with automobiles that reflected the high-revving hubbub of a freewheeling industrialized economy. One direct beneficiary of this overflowing exuberance was the Gold and Glory Sweepstakes, black auto racing's crown jewel, which continued to attract the largest crowds and the largest purses in the sport for African American drivers. The actions of officials at the Colored Speedway Association's headquarters, now located on the second floor of the new Madam Walker business complex at 617 Indiana Avenue, had broad effects on the sporting scene, as well as the social scene, in the midwestern United States during the latter half of the Roaring Twenties.

As more and more Gold and Glory events were staged throughout the Midwest, an unusual and diverse cast of characters soon found themselves drawn into the world of the Colored Speedway Association and its top drivers. Some white car owners agreed to share their powerful machines and their expertise. Also, many top African-American mechanics shared their automotive knowledge with drivers at the Indianapolis Motor Speedway.

"Indy 500 drivers were bringing their cars to Charlie Wiggins's garage all the time," remembered Al Warren. "You have to understand that there is a family among racers, no matter your color, religion, whatever. Charlie was a good driver with a fast car, and that's all any driver, white or black, cared about. . . . When Charlie helped them white boys, I don't think he ever saw it as bridging racial gaps or anything as big and important as that. He was just helping friends and fellow drivers, that's all."

"There's a kind of fraternity in automobile racing that pervades the sport," echoed racing historian Joe Freeman. "It's a common experience that includes a certain element of danger, excitement, and mechanical skills. This combination, which makes the sport so exciting and attractive, also helps its participants transcend the racial tenor of the times. In a city like Indianapolis, which was not particularly known for its racial tolerance during the era, the ability for blacks and whites to come together around the sport of auto racing speaks to the significance of the sport and complexity of the relationships between these men."

Among the white drivers who worked with and drove for Charlie Wiggins was Harry MacQuinn, a talented young mechanic and driver who competed in ten Indy 500 races and finished in seventh place in both the 1938 and 1941 competitions. He later became the chief steward of the Indianapolis Motor Speedway during the 1950s. During his early years at the speedway, MacQuinn drove a four-cylinder Miller with

Indianapolis 500 competitor Harry MacQuinn (*left*) was a good friend of Charlie Wiggins and sometimes drove Charlie's Wiggins Special racecar at dirt track competitions around the Midwest. Courtesy Mrs. Mildred Overton

a design similar to that of Charlie's own Wiggins Special. MacQuinn also competed in many dirt track events around the Midwest, driving a variety of car makes and models.

According to the Wiggins family and backed by historian Boniface Hardin, MacQuinn entered a race in Louisville, Kentucky, in 1928 and asked Charlie if he could borrow the mechanic's famed car in return for a share of the potential winnings. Charlie agreed, with the stipulation that he himself would drive the car during its pre-race qualification laps in order to give the car a proper shakedown for possible mechanical malfunctions. "This was a common practice at the time," stated Richard

Pierce. "But it was certainly not a common practice for a black man to shake down a car at a 'whites only' event. But Charlie was adamant. He reserved that right for himself."

Pierce continued, "Charlie was saying, in essence, 'I can loan you my car. I'll build it. I'll fix it. And I'll let you take it out for the competition. But the bottom line is that the car is mine, and I know it better than anyone else. So I reserve the right to conduct a proper shakedown of the vehicle myself.' Just think about how difficult it must have been to negotiate that kind of relationship with another driver, especially a white driver, at the time. That's a kind of temerity that few blacks in the early twentieth century had: the ability, as Charlie did, or perhaps the courage, which Charlie obviously did, to pull it off."

When fans at the Kentucky Speedway discovered that a black man was driving the car during qualifications, many began to shout protests to race officials. When speedway management declared that Charlie, as the owner of the car, had a legal right to run the qualification laps, an angry mob began to form near the pit area. With little effort they soon broke through a poorly secured area of the track.

Race officials acted quickly and ordered the Kentucky militia to arrest Charlie for his own protection. A team of officers warded off the enraged fans as two policemen spirited Charlie away in a paddy wagon. At police headquarters the captain suggested he stay in a cell until nightfall, at which time he would find it easier to slip out of town unnoticed. In the meantime, official documentation had to be made of the arrest. The captain filed a detailed report. For the record, he listed a reason for Charlie's arrest: speeding.[2]

One of Charlie's favorite stories revolved around another young man who often came to visit. He was a teenager Charlie knew simply as Johnny. They met during Charlie's early years in Indianapolis, when he first began to take his homemade racecars to Walnut Gardens Speedway for testing. He often noticed a slender young white teenager standing by the wooden fence and watching intently as he raced around the dirt track. One day after Charlie completed his test laps, Johnny introduced himself to the mechanic and offered his help keeping time, cleaning the cars after heats, and running errands. Charlie accepted.

The two men shared many interests, including hunting, fishing, and, of course, automobiles. The Walnut Gardens Speedway was located only one mile from Johnny's home in tiny Mooresville, Indiana. Roberta remembered that Johnny seemed "pleasant and personable" and seemed to possess a genuine love for the sport. She also noted that he tended to bombard Charlie with ceaseless questions about the intricacies of building racing engines.

While some members of Charlie's Gang were lifelong friends of the Wiggins family, many others passed in and out of Charlie's life quickly. Johnny was one of those young men who spent many long days at Charlie's garage and at the track, but later grew up and moved on. Over the years, Charlie lost touch with him. Then, one day in July 1933, he opened his morning paper and was shocked to see Johnny's picture on the front page. The headline read "Public Enemy Number One." The young man with the passion for fast cars was the notorious gunman and bank robber John Dillinger.[3]

One devoted member of Charlie's Gang was Bill Cummings. As a gangly teen, Cummings worked in a fish market on Illinois Street just a few blocks north of Charlie's garage. Each afternoon after work, Cummings would run down to the garage to help the talented mechanic and share in the camaraderie of the men at the shop. "Guys would come and guys would go," Roberta Wiggins recalled. "But Charlie could tell that Bill Cummings was something different . . . something special."

Charlie often allowed Cummings to clean the cars, work on the engines, and warm up the cars as Charlie tested new parts and procedures. He even gave Cummings his first chance to sit behind the wheel of a racecar. With great zeal, young Bill leaped into the cockpit of the Wiggins Special and imagined himself crossing the finish line at the Indianapolis 500-Mile Race.

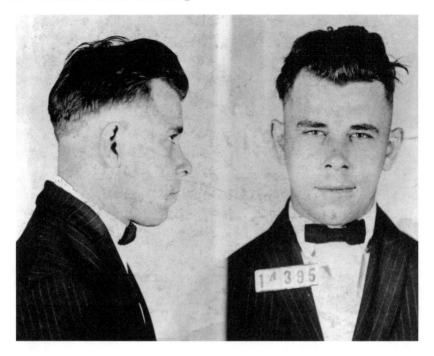

In his youth, John Dillinger was a friend of Charlie Wiggins and shared the mechanic's passion for fast automobiles. Courtesy Indiana State Archives—Indiana Commission on Public Records

By 1930 Bill Cummings no longer had to imagine himself a top Indy car driver. He had become one. Driving an eight-cylinder yellow-and-black Duesenberg, Cummings qualified for his first Indy 500 in May 1930 and surprised many race officials by finishing fourth, one of the top finishes by a rookie at the annual racing event. By 1934 he had earned the nickname "Wild Bill" and was widely considered one of the top competitors in all of auto racing. That season Michael Boyle, the business manager of Chicago's International Brotherhood of Electrical Workers—Local 134, gave him the use of a four-cylinder Miller that was sleeker and faster than any he had driven to date. It was a challenge for Cummings, however, because it was much smaller than the standard V-8 engines he had piloted in the past. The car was, in fact, very similar

1934 Indy 500 champion Bill Cummings first sat in a racecar in Charlie Wiggins's garage. He later helped Charlie and Bobby Wallace promote the Gold and Glory Sweepstakes and other African-American auto races throughout Indiana and the Midwest. Courtesy Indianapolis Motor Speedway archives

in make, model, and handling to a car he had once sat in many years earlier—a Wiggins Special.

Charlie once told historian Boniface Hardin, "Bill came by and asked me if I would want to come by the garage at the [Indianapolis Motor] Speedway and check out the car, which I did on several occasions." Hardin recalled that Cummings finally offered Charlie a job working on his pit crew, an offer applauded by other members of Cummings's racing team. "But the AAA officials wouldn't allow it," Charlie stated. So Cummings and he worked out a secret arrangement whereby Cummings would hire Charlie to work as a janitor. "It was the only 'official' way a colored person could work at the track during those days," Charlie remembered.[4]

Throughout the month of May Charlie worked each day in Cummings's garage, sweeping floors and taking out the garbage. Then at night, when the AAA officials had left the track, Roberta recalled, he assisted the rest of the crew by crafting top-of-the-line engine parts to create a finely tuned racing engine. On race day a record crowd was in attendance. Charlie was there, too. "He sat in the 'coloreds only' section near the first turn and cheered 'Wild Bill' to victory," Red Oliver remembered. All were thrilled as they watched Cummings rev his powerful engine around the track at speeds averaging more than 104.8 miles per hour, the fastest in Indianapolis 500 history. Throughout the race Cummings held a slender lead, using Charlie's technique of pacing the car during the race to conserve fuel and tires. Near the end of the race, twelve drivers still kept pace on the lead lap. Then, in one final burst of speed, Cummings left the competition in his exhaust-filled wake, as he pushed his car at top speed across the finish line.

Hundreds of photographers, race officials, pit-crew members, and excited fans closed in on Cummings's car as he pulled into the winner's circle. Noticeably missing was Charlie Wiggins, who quietly slipped out a large gated exit and returned to work at his garage. In a series of interviews following the race, Cummings thanked many of those involved with the victory, including car owner Michael Boyle and even the Firestone company, which had provided his team with important racing supplies. In private, he thanked Charlie, as well. "He got a note from Cummings after the race," Roberta Wiggins remembered. "He told Charlie that he'd never forget what he did for him and said that Charlie was one of the greatest mechanics he'd ever known."

"It supersedes race," noted Richard Pierce. "And even in the early twentieth century, when race was much more prominent and a larger hurdle for these guys to overcome, it wasn't for Wiggins to go to Cummings and say, 'I can help you.' It was for Cummings to come to Wiggins, because of the social conventions of the day. . . . Cummings had to come to him, which made it OK. . . . Cummings was a professional who looked to make the most of his talent and his craft. Cummings understood that he was elevating the mastery of his craft with Wiggins's help, and that's all that really mattered."

Pierce continued, "The real athletes, the real champions, are the men and women who seek to elevate their greatness in any way possible—by shattering the social norms of the day, if needed—to make themselves smarter and more competitive. Judging by the competitive nature of both Wiggins and Cummings, I'm sure the two would have loved to have 'strapped it up' and gone head to head against one another in an official competition. Still, they came together in a mutual challenge to create a car that ran like lightning. Behind those garage doors, there was no color line, no race, and no barriers to overcome. That's what's at the heart of what made these great athletes truly great."

The association between the Colored Speedway Association and Michael Boyle was highly unusual. The amiable but aggressive union boss also headed the Boyle Valve Company, a Chicago piston manufacturing company that sponsored a number of racecars at Indianapolis and other auto racing events across the country.

Often sporting a bowler hat, a scowl, and the stub of a cigar clenched between his teeth, Michael Boyle was an unquestioned power broker in the city's political and social affairs. He earned the nickname "Umbrella Mike" because he was nearly always seen toting one over his shoulder. "Raised high, it signaled a greeting or a signal for his men to strike. Hanging partially open on the edge of a desk or bar, it was a convenient, discreet receptacle for tangible encomiums [from] supplicants for his favor."[5] Boyle spent much of his career dodging charges of extortion. He once was sentenced to twelve months in prison for antitrust violations before receiving a speedy pardon from President Woodrow Wilson. Chicago was known for its graft and corruption during the 1920s, and Boyle knew how to work the system. His union position reportedly paid him $50 a week, but he was able to amass a fortune in excess of $350,000—an achievement he attributed to "great thrift."[6]

Boyle's reign as business manager of Chicago's largest electrical union began in 1909 and lasted until his death in 1958. With more than a hundred thousand electrical workers under his direction, Umbrella Mike held the union, and the city, in his steely grasp for nearly a half-century. Chicago journalist Art Petacque noted that Boyle once wielded such power in the city that "in the days when Illinois executed felons in

Chicago union boss "Umbrella Mike" Boyle (*standing behind car*) was a
noted racecar owner and promoter who also helped support the
Colored Speedway Association circuit by supplying cars and money to
the organization. Courtesy Indianapolis Motor Speedway archives

the electric chair, after the governor refused to stay a doomed convict's
execution, the saying was: 'Only Mike Boyle can save him now.'"[7]

In negotiations with city government, Boyle was a pit bull. Only
twice during his tenure as the head of Local 134 did the city dare to
challenge him. And both times, Boyle made sure that it paid dearly for
its actions. The first time was on the evening of July 12, 1921. When
a meeting with city officials to negotiate a contract did not go as he
wished, Boyle ordered an immediate shutdown of all Chicago power
stations. As the sun set, 94,558 municipal streetlights blinked off, and
the city was suddenly plunged into darkness. Boyle, having returned to
his expansive, and well-illuminated, estate outside the city limits, sat
back and waited for a reaction from the city. For nearly twelve hours,

as local police ran frantically about the city with oil lanterns, the government attempted to persuade Boyle to call off the strike. Only after threats to prosecute him for manslaughter if any deaths occurred because of a stilled fire alarm box or disabled hospital did Boyle finally relent.

Chicago again felt Boyle's wrath on a bitterly cold day in January 1937. At the height of the Great Depression, government officials proposed withholding thirty-nine days of union workers' wages in an effort to ameliorate the city's financial woes. Boyle ordered thirty-eight of Chicago's fifty-five main drawbridges into the downtown area, known as "the Loop," to be raised simultaneously. Then he ordered a complete electrical shutdown downtown, which stranded thousands of Chicagoans there for hours during the late afternoon and early evening. The *Chicago Tribune* reported, "The giant bascule bridges were poised in midair like a row of upright elephants in the murky half light of the office buildings, as the city was suddenly bathed in blackness." As honking cars, clanging streetcars, and cursing pedestrians all clamored near the bridgeheads, Boyle reportedly told a colleague, "It's the city's funeral, not ours."[8]

The city and the press often called Umbrella Mike a dictator and "an author of 'whim strikes.'" But among union members, Boyle was a gregarious and deeply compassionate man and a "rough and ready fighter for the union cause."[9] Never was this more evident than in the case of Rufus Taylor, Chicago's first black electrical worker.

Taylor had once apprenticed himself to a white electrician and, through many hours of training, completed the necessary requirements to become a certified electrical worker. No electrical firm would hire the talented African American, however. So in 1918 he opened his own service shop to assist the construction industry on the south side of Chicago, where the city's black population continued to grow. The union, under Mike Boyle, was still in its infancy. Taylor and his fellow technicians faced sixteen-hour workdays. They were often paid no more than fifteen cents an hour. The working conditions were extremely hazardous. Nearly fifty percent of all electrical workers on the south side were seriously hurt or killed on the job.

In 1919, Taylor submitted his dues in hopes of becoming a member of Mike Boyle's Local 134. He was desperately seeking protection and assistance in his trade. Most union officers at that time would not have considered bringing a colored electrician into the IBEW fold. But Mike Boyle, who often called all the men under him "my boys," welcomed Taylor with open arms. Union support meant that prejudiced white contractors could no longer bully him into accepting substandard wages or force him to work long hours under dangerous conditions. With that support, Rufus Taylor was able to build a successful business for himself.

Perhaps it was this early encounter with Taylor that caused Mike Boyle to take an active interest in the Colored Speedway Association. His motives are not entirely clear. His relationships within the white racing community were doubtless a factor as well. Bill Cummings drove a Boyle Valve Special across the finish line to capture the championship at the 1934 Indianapolis 500-Mile Race. Wilbur Shaw paced a Boyle Valve Special to victory at Indy in 1939 and again in 1940. Both Cummings and Shaw, close friends of African-American drivers like Charlie Wiggins and Bobby Wallace, championed the cause of black auto racing. As well, backing the Gold and Glory Sweepstakes might have offered financial rewards to a wealthy car owner such as Boyle. With several top-quality Boyle Valve Specials racing against lesser makes and models in a black competition, the odds of winning the race, and thus a share of the prize money, were good. The opportunity to win some sizable side bets with local racketeers was also enticing.

Why a wealthy wheeler-dealer like "Umbrella Mike" Boyle would find himself entrenched in the actions of the Colored Speedway Association is unclear. What is clear is that, beginning in August 1926, Chicago IBEW support and Boyle's personal finances began to pour into the annual Gold and Glory Sweepstakes and other colored racing events throughout the Midwest. As well, Boyle Valve Special cars became a common sight on the starting line at many of these races. Chicago driver Bill Carson drove one of Boyle's machines in the 1926 and 1936 Gold and Glory Sweepstakes, and Wilbur "Wild Man" Gaines, another Windy City native, piloted a Boyle Valve Ford Special in the 1928 Gold and Glory classic. Gene Smith, a chauffeur with close ties to Bill Bottoms and Bill Jeffries, captured the 1930 Gold and Glory championship aboard one of Boyle's powerful racers.

Auto racing historian Joe Freeman noted, "I doubt that many black drivers cared about Boyle's background, other than having a sincere appreciation for his passion for racing and his willingness to lend a hand

and offer some of them a better ride. By the same token, I doubt that Boyle much cared whether it was a blacks-only race, a whites-only race, or whatever. It was probably seen as a good business deal, pure and simple. This is another example where the interest and passion for the sport supersede race. It was a win-win situation, benefiting both sides financially, while blurring the color line at the same time."

While color lines blurred within the racing community, many in local and state government in Indianapolis were working hard to ensure that segregation would remain a constant on Indiana's social and civic scene. Ku Klux Klan leader D. C. Stephenson was the political confidant of both Governor Ed Jackson and Indianapolis mayor John Duvall. Klan-backed politicians ran many committees within the Indiana general assembly. The Klan was the most powerful political force in the state. And yet all was not well among members of the organization that called itself "the Invisible Empire."

By the time Duvall took office in 1926, the Klan's power was waning. Stephenson worked diligently with Governor Jackson to push through some beefy contracts with the state highway commission. When rumors of graft and corruption in the new highway plan hit the press, the House Ways and Means Committee demanded an investigation. The contracts fell through, costing Stephenson and his hand-picked Klan contractors millions of dollars. Duvall's administration was also mired in scandal arising from Klan-backed initiatives. It appeared that while the Klan could get politicians elected with its incredible political machine, it was often far less able to implement legitimate legislation. During the years when Klan-backed candidates ran the city and state government, very few Klan initiatives were ever passed into law.

Then in March 1925, while attempting to chart a new course, the Klan received a devastating blow. Over the years, D. C. Stephenson had developed an underground reputation as a heavy drinker and womanizer who would often lash out in violent sexual behavior during his drunken rages. The KKK, the supposed bastion of purity and a flag waver for the temperance movement, lectured and threatened Stephenson about his abhorrent behavior, while at the same time covering up his actions in the press.

On March 16 a twenty-eight-year-old government worker, Madge Oberholtzer, went missing from her parents' home in Irvington, just east of downtown Indianapolis. Oberholtzer had recently taken a position as a secretary to Stephenson. She had a background in educational health and nutrition, and she was helping Stephenson edit a book he was writing on the subject. When the attractive, dark-haired girl was first reported missing, Stephenson insiders knew exactly where to look.

They did not have to search long. The following day, county prosecutors had already begun an investigation into Stephenson's affairs when one of the KKK leader's henchmen burst through the front door of the girl's home carrying Oberholtzer's limp, barely conscious body in his arms. He placed her on her bed and told a boarder in the home that she had been in an auto accident and needed immediate medical attention.

A doctor was summoned and immediately determined that she was the victim not of a car accident, but of rape. Her dress was ripped. Lacerations covered her breast, and her right cheek was bruised. She awoke just long enough to tell the physician that she had taken bichloride of mercury, a powerful poison, in hopes of killing herself. Ashamed that she had been raped, she no longer wished to live. Later she told the doctor of her harrowing experience with Stephenson: how she had been kidnapped and repeatedly raped, and how she slipped into a drugstore just long enough to buy the poison. The violent convulsions and fits of vomiting it caused frightened Stephenson into returning her to her home to avoid the scandal of having her die on his hands. The poison eventually caused Madge's kidneys to fail. She died on April 14, 1925.

Stephenson was tried for murder. During the trial, which received sensational headlines in the press for weeks, many Klan members began to question their loyalty to the KKK. Membership dropped drastically as thousands distanced themselves from the organization. Klan-backed politicians soon found their administrations in shambles. A Pulitzer Prize–winning series of reports in the *Indianapolis Times* in 1928 exposed the corruption surrounding the Ku Klux Klan, including bribes offered by Governor Jackson to state officers to encourage the appointment of Klan-backed candidates for office. Though he was indicted by a Marion County grand jury, Jackson escaped prosecution when the court discovered that the statute of limitations had expired. Jackson completed his term, then left politics.

Indianapolis mayor John Duvall was not as lucky as Jackson was. Accused of having traded jobs for votes during his election campaign, Duvall was convicted of violating the state corrupt practices act. He was sentenced to thirty days in jail and fined $1,000. The city council demanded his resignation, which he gave in October 1927. He never again sought political office.

Against the ropes and without its leader, the Klan attempted to recover its political influence in Indiana in the fall of 1926. The *Indianapolis Recorder* reported that nearly six thousand Klan members gathered outside a local church in an effort to win back the support of officers and members of the Marion County Voters League. Leading the rally was national Imperial Wizard Hiram Evans and many leaders of the Indiana Klan. But the rally produced little in the way of support. The Klan was losing its grip on Indiana.

The *Recorder* reported, "The Klan is fast losing its political prestige, and like a drowning man, is grasping at the last straw, the Marion County Voters League. If colored women and men vote in the primary, and vote to the man, the Klan will suffer bitter defeat that will eliminate them from further political activity and sinister influences."[10]

"The Klan, for all intents and purposes, was dead," remarked historian James Madison. "As a political and social organization, the Ku Klux Klan fizzled out and died. What did not die, however, were the segregationist attitudes that still continued to be a part of the state's social makeup. White-robed rallies were out, but the attitudes still haunted many towns around the state. The battle for racial, ethnic, and religious equality would now be fought on new, subtler battlegrounds. And in many ways, this kind of battle could be more dangerous than the overt racism shown by the Klan."

The lines of segregation were less clear. Catholics, Jews, African Americans, and foreigners faced many social landmines and often did not know where to tread. "Life on the road was always tough because we didn't know which towns were 'friendly' towns," remarked Al Warren. "On the weekends we'd tow our cars all over Indiana and the Midwest.

And most times, the toughest part was getting there and getting home. There were plenty of scary moments, and a lot of them weren't on the track."

Stephenson was in prison. His organization was in ruins. Many civil rights leaders in the state and region celebrated their victories. Initiatives such as the Colored Speedway Association had survived the deep racial divisions that plagued much of Indiana society. But segregation in motor sports still existed. Worse yet, instances of racial violence still erupted across the midwestern landscape.

One battle for racial equality was over. But the war had just begun.

6.

"A Darn Good Move on Us"

A thundering boom could be heard for more than a mile. The sky lit up in brilliant shades of emerald, navy, burgundy, and gold. Below, a large crowd oohed and aahed appreciatively. The fireworks show on the night preceding the 1929 Gold and Glory Sweepstakes was the largest and most impressive in the circuit's history. A mixed audience of both black and white fans from a twelve-state region gathered in the grandstand and on the grassy infield of the Indiana State Fairgrounds track to admire the splendor of the occasion.

The following morning thousands again gathered at the fairgrounds and gazed skyward at daring airplane stunts, including low-flying "loop-de-loops," daring dive bombs, and wing walking. A carnival atmosphere surrounded the fairgrounds. In years past, the annual Gold and Glory Sweepstakes had been held in August to coincide with black Indiana's Emancipation Day celebration. At the urging of Indianapolis city government officials, the Colored Speedway Association had moved the event to July 4 to coordinate with other Independence Day festivities throughout the city.

In the center of the infield at the one-mile dirt track, a twenty-five-piece brass band made up of local black musicians filled the air with bright, brash sounds, blending the new jazz with the traditional Sousa-like marches of the past. In the distance, the smell of grilled chicken and sweet corn lured hundreds of hungry patrons and caused large lines to form near the south end of the racetrack. General admission to the event was a dollar per person. All about the grounds, children grasped colorful balloons and gobbled cotton candy and ice cream. Young women in laced dresses and parasols gathered in the shade, talking and sipping tall glasses of tea and lemonade. Many young men found their way to the pit area, where they leaned in to watch as mechanics and drivers made last-minute adjustments to their racecars.

The organization of the race appeared smooth and effortless—quite a feat, considering the massive reorganization that had taken place within the Colored Speedway Association just two months earlier. After five years of hard work, most of the Association officials had stepped down from their posts. William "Pres" Rucker had resigned as president. Business manager Harry Dunnington was battling health problems and stepped down from his position as well. The Association's new officers included many of the most influential African Americans in Indianapolis. The new president, William H. Jackson, served as deputy township assessor. Charles J. Brown, the vice president, was a deputy in the Marion County auditor's office. Morris Taylor, the former athletic director of the Senate Avenue YMCA and a friend of Madam C. J. Walker, was the Association's official starter. Marcus Stewart, editor of the *Indianapolis Recorder*, also served with the organization, as did a handful of other wealthy black citizens of the city.

The chairman of the Colored Speedway Association was G. N. T. Gray, a man the *Chicago Defender* called "the big boss of the show."[1] When Gray was appointed, he reiterated the organization's mission to the *Indianapolis Recorder:* "For colored drivers to ever break into the American Automobile Association, they must show more speed and grit, coupled with a better knowledge of their cars and what they will or will not do."[2] A *Chicago Defender* column described Gray as "one of the few men who came to the city during the war period that had something and didn't try to 'hold everything.' He has been more than liberal in his support of the race and it is due largely [to] his effort that the race has been made the foremost event of its kind in the sport world. With an association composed of such men, the public can feel assured that they will receive the very highest entertainment."[3]

With the aerial stunt shows, fireworks, and brass bands wowing the crowd, Gray and the newly reorganized Colored Speedway Association did, in fact, seem to offer "the very highest entertainment," giving African Americans a chance to celebrate their heritage and culture. Helping to cultivate that sense of racial pride, a number of organizations set up booths and a speaker's platform near the southeast entrance of the fairgrounds. National representatives from the NAACP were there, as were officials from the national office of the Knights of Pythias, a black fraternal order. Each of these attracted hundreds of people and lent a sense of greater national importance to the Gold and Glory Sweepstakes.

In the middle of the hubbub was Roberta Wiggins, dressed in an elegant wide-brimmed hat and a light floral summer dress. She flitted about the booth where the Unique Social Club of Indianapolis raised funds for her organization by selling bright floral corsages. Roberta was the chairman of the Gold and Glory floral committee and took her job quite seriously. "She'd have had those ladies moving and active, that's for sure," Charlie's niece Mildred Overton laughed. "She was really in her element at those kinds of functions. She was there to socialize—to see and be seen. She lived for those moments."

Roberta's beauty matched her radiant personality. Her active role in city social clubs meant that her picture was often featured in the society pages of the *Indianapolis Recorder*. Photos of the graceful and shapely Mrs. Wiggins attracted a number of hopeful male suitors. Family and friends remembered that in her years as a successful model, she received many calls and letters from eager young admirers. "She very politely turned them away," Overton recalled. "She pledged her lifelong devotion to her husband." Throughout her lifetime, there was only one letter from a man other than Charlie with which she could not part. It was a three-page note in 1944 from a lonely U.S. serviceman. James Johnson, serving with an unnamed unit in the South Pacific, saw Roberta's picture in a copy of the *Recorder* his family sent him. He wrote,

Dearest Friend,

Your picture in the paper was most interesting, and being in a place where I am, it was more interesting still! I hope you don't mind me writing you asking you to send me a photo that I can keep in my wallet. . . . I hope you don't think I am being bold, but over here in the Southwest Pacific, where there is not any woman, nothing but coconuts and Japs, a photo of you could give me lots of inspiration. All the boys in my outfit want to write you. If only you knew what a letter or photo would mean to us here in the armed services, I know you would want to write everybody here. I know you will write, because you look like a nice person in your picture, and I know you will want to remember me and the boys in these tough times. Until we meet in mail,

Your Good Friend,

James Johnson

"With Aunt Roberta, there was always a little bit of ego, but a whole lot of compassion toward other people," Overton noted. "She was drawn to [people], and people seemed to be drawn to her."

Plenty of people were drawn to Roberta and the other women at the Unique Social Club booth on July 4, 1929, in the hours prior to the day's races. Perhaps the only place that matched such bustling activity was the drivers' pit area, where Roberta's husband, Charlie, also attracted a fair amount of attention. "There was just an excitement there, being around him during those big races," Al Warren remembered. "The local crowd loved him. The media always was around. Lots of us young fellas were running about, trying to help get him ready for the start. Then when he'd hop in that car and rev that big ol' engine, that thing just rumbled and went right through your heart. I get goose bumps today just thinking about it."

The total purse for the event was $2,500, the highest in black motor racing history. The $1,200 first prize helped attract a large number of entrants. In all, nearly seventy drivers entered cars in the time trials, a new national record on the colored circuit. Each was ready to challenge Charlie Wiggins, Bobby Wallace, Bill Jeffries, and the rest of the best colored racers in the world. In the past, each driver at the event had vied for one of only twenty qualifying positions for the hundred-mile main event. Because of increased interest, CSA officials had decided to increase the number of qualifiers from twenty to twenty-six.

Also buzzing about the pit area were a dozen sportswriters from leading African-American newspapers, including Sol Butler, sports editor for the *Chicago Bee;* Marcus Stewart, editor of the *Indianapolis Recorder;* J. E. Mitchell, from the *St. Louis Argus;* Willis Cole, from the *Louisville Leader;* Al Monroe, sports editor of the *Chicago Whip;* and William J. Robinson, of the *Detroit Independent.* Looking out beyond the pits to survey what he called "the vibrant canvas of humanity" around

Posters along Indiana Avenue and large newspaper advertisements, like this 1936 ad from the *Indianapolis Recorder,* generated excitement and energy within the African-American community for black auto racing's crown jewel, the Gold and Glory Sweepstakes. Courtesy *Indianapolis Recorder*

him, *Chicago Defender* journalist Frank Young pushed back the brim of his brown fedora hat to wipe his brow, then lit one of his trademark cigars and began to scribble words in his notebook with the flair of a circus ringmaster. "Primed and groomed to the last notch, stroked and rubbed endearingly, no less than is any thoroughbred on the eve of a supreme test, 26 babies of the greatest engineering brains in America repose ready to be wheeled out on the Fairgrounds speedway to prove by their showing that they can deliver the stuff that demands a place at the finish line."

Young continued, "All America must have turned its eyes and ears toward Indianapolis for this event, trying as it were to catch a fleeting glimpse of chocolate jockeys spurring their gas-snorting, rubber-shod speedway monsters to fame and fortune or to faintly hear the fascinating hum of racing motors. And this being no stretch of the writer's fertile imagination, for many states are represented among the gaily-painted chariots of steel and the assemblage of nervy, nervous, castor-fumed drivers on hand to flirt with death and danger in their quest for national fame and timely fortune."[4]

The *Indianapolis Recorder* echoed Young's enthusiasm. "If ever there was a town smitten with a love for gas and burning castor oil, Naptown is the burg. Men, women and children, preachers, deacons and hoi polloi all go in for watching the gas buggies race. The local 500-mile sweepstakes and this annual 100-mile grind for the colored championship of the world makes Indianapolis the hub of the auto racing universe."[5] Accompanying the *Recorder*'s coverage of the 1929 event was a full page of advertisements for, among others, Silver Flash Anti-Knock Gasoline, "used exclusively by all race drivers in the 100-mile championship auto race," and the Wangelin-Sharp Car Sales Company, featuring the Ford Cabriolet, "the official car" of the Gold and Glory Sweepstakes. In the ad for Wangelin-Sharp, African-American salesman Raleigh S. Coleman boasted that he had "already sold 51 new Fords since February." He promised, "I am the only one, Raleigh Coleman, that's to give you a square deal and personal service."[6]

Among the twenty-six qualifiers for the race were some familiar faces, such as Bill Jeffries in his Ford Frontenac, Charlie Wiggins aboard his Wiggins Special, and Bobby Wallace in a new test car loaned to him by Chevrolet Motor Company founder and racing enthusiast Arthur Chevrolet. Others drivers included Bill James, who had hammered and honed the bulky chassis of a Graham passenger car into a sleek racing design and retooled its engine to create a powerful V-8 racer. Edward Grice, a veteran of the Great War and a mechanic from Texas, was a three-time Gold and Glory participant who had once finished third. Grice entered a Fronty Ford with a V-8 engine. Another competitor was Barney Anderson, whom the *Indianapolis News* called a "heavy-footed, brown-skinned youth from Detroit."[7] Anderson entered a racer of his own make, an old Model A Ford that had been stripped down and then supercharged with a new racing engine and wheel base that allowed for greater traction on the dusty dirt surface. One driver, Wilbur Gaines, nearly missed the start of the race when his passenger car, with racer in tow, broke down en route from his home in Chicago to Indianapolis.

With a grand flourish, the official starter waved the green flag, the pace car, a World Champion Roosevelt Straight 8 Roadster, pulled off the track, and the race was under way. Amid the roaring crowd and a cloud of dust, Bill Jeffries, the previous year's Gold and Glory champion, pushed his car to a half-mile lead over the competition. Within seven laps, however, Barney Anderson and his old Model A overtook "Wild Bill" on the back straightaway.

One of the most exciting moments came early in the race, with Bobby Wallace of Indianapolis providing the thrills. Prior to the start of the race, Bill Jeffries had boasted that he was "the man to beat." Wallace had promised reporters and fans that he would "run Jeff a curve" and quiet the boisterous racer from Chicago. Seven laps into the race, Wallace's car had problems with its spark plugs. Quickly he darted into the pits. As crewmen worked frantically on his engine, Wallace watched the leaders, including Jeffries, very carefully and plotted his course of attack. He had fallen three long laps behind the pack by the time his crew fixed his car. With what the *Indianapolis News* called "a flair for pyro-technics," Wallace slammed on the accelerator and exploded back onto the track in a full-throttled effort to catch up to the leaders. Ripping around the one-mile oval at a blistering pace of more than seventy miles per hour, Wallace made up lap after lap on the field, including two laps on Jeffries, Anderson, and Charlie Wiggins, the three leaders at the time. By lap 54, Jeffries's car had sputtered and slowly crept into the pits, where it coughed up black smoke and died. At the time Wallace was in second place, having just overtaken Charlie and trailing leader Barney

Anderson by a lap and a half. As he passed Jeffries's pit area, witnesses reported that Wallace gave "Wild Bill" a smug wave.

Unfortunately for Wallace, his exuberance could not last. After the sixtieth lap, his car began to act sluggish, and he fell back into the pack. By lap 90 he was forced to pull into the pits for a second time, where his car stopped for good. His misfortune was Charlie Wiggins's gain. Charlie had kept a steady pace behind Wallace throughout the entire race, stopping only once for fuel and tires. When Wallace dropped out of the competition, the track opened for Charlie to make his move on Barney Anderson, who continued to lead the race. By the ninetieth lap, the Wiggins Special, which the *Recorder* called "a creation of Charlie's own brain and mechanical genius,"[8] had closed to within one lap of Anderson. But in the end, Anderson, who did not have to stop a single time for fuel or tires, was able to hold off the more experienced Charlie to capture the 1929 Gold and Glory championship by three minutes and seven seconds.

The *Indianapolis Recorder* reported, "Before the largest crowd of fans to ever witness the annual championship auto race, Barney Anderson, driving a Two Port Frontenac speed chariot, flashed across the finish line to receive the checkered flag and copped the $1,200 first prize at the Indiana State Fairgrounds speedway circuit." The paper noted that the final battle between Anderson and Charlie Wiggins "brought forth the finest examples of sportsmanship, nerve and determination ever witnessed here."[9] The *Chicago Defender* wrote of Anderson, "Barney drove one of the most beautiful races ever witnessed in this city, not stopping even once for oil, tires, gas or anything else he might have thought he needed on his wild ride. In the time trials, he was beaten by three heavy-foot masters, but in the main event, the thing that counted, he was not to be headed off, not to be passed, and not to be denied what he sought."[10]

Anderson's accomplishment was the high point of the 1929 Gold and Glory Sweepstakes. But the celebration at the speedway that day was marred by a fatal accident that occurred during the twenty-seventh lap of the race. Edward Grice, aboard his Fronty Ford, was navigating through a crowd of drivers at a speed nearing sixty-five miles per hour. Suddenly, as the drivers rounded the fourth turn, a strong wind swept across the track, kicking up a cloud of dust that the *Indianapolis Recorder* called "completely impenetrable." Attempting to speed through the dust storm, Grice gunned his engine, only to collide with William Walthall in a car of his own design.

The collision sent Grice's car twenty feet through the air, flipping over four times before it landed. Without a seatbelt or protection of any kind, Grice was thrown from the vehicle on the first turn. He landed amid the spectators in the bleachers near the grandstand. Hundreds of people scurried to the crash scene to help. Ambulance drivers took Grice's unconscious body to City Hospital, where he was listed in fair condition with a fractured skull and severe internal injuries. Friends and family held out hope for recovery. By the following day, however, Grice had failed to regain consciousness. In fact, he had taken a turn for the worse. At 10:00 P.M. on Sunday, July 8, Edward Grice, a thirty-six-year-old mechanic and father of two young children, died at City Hospital in Indianapolis. His was the only death ever recorded at the Gold and Glory Sweepstakes.

One race official told the *Indianapolis Recorder* that Grice was "a mighty fine fellow," and added, "his death is to be greatly regretted, as we found him always for fair play and true sportsmanship." Gold and Glory champion Barney Anderson noted, "Negro race drivers lost a true sportsman with the passing of Grice. He was a credit to the game." The *Recorder* eulogized, "It is said by former friends of Mr. Grice that he was from his early childhood decidedly of mechanical bent.... He constantly dreamed of piloting a machine at a dizzy pace while breathless and admiring spectators gazed in dazed amazement. All these juvenile, but admittedly ambitious visions of what he intended to do when he grew up and how, were inseparably associated with the glorious thought that some day he would receive the coveted victor's flag. On Thursday, July 4, with the tenacity of a determined fighter, Grice, undaunted by two previous futile attempts, tried again for the last time for evermore."[11]

"That fear of injury or death is one of those things that racecar drivers must always face," racing historian Joe Freeman said. "Especially in those days, the cars had a tendency to fly when anything hit those open wheels. Hitting another car or hitting a big bump in the road often meant that you went airborne. And with often little or no railing between you and the spectators, you could have a situation where a car would slide right off the track and come right into the crowd. It was always scary. It still is. But that's also part of the thrill, part of the excitement. It's part of what it meant to push yourself to the edge and back. These guys had to have a fair amount of courage to be able to continue to go at it week after week and be successful at it. The fact that most of them did it at all and survived was amazing in its own right. But there was always that fear lurking in the background. That's something drivers have to live with."

Former driver Joie Ray noted that to keep going as a race driver "you need a lot of experience and a lot of prayer. . . . Racing was very dangerous at that time. I can remember reading in the papers at the end of the season a list of fatalities for the year. It was always a pretty frightening thing. I'd wake up some nights thinking about it. It was scary, very scary. A lot of folks would wonder why I'd do it. Sometimes I'd wonder myself. But then that following weekend you'd get behind the wheel of your car and rev that engine. Then that adrenaline starts to flow, and you forget all about your fears. You push on that accelerator, and all you're thinking is 'Just win, baby.' At that point you're out to do the best you can. Speed is king, and that's all that matters. You have no fear, no fear at all."

The drivers and mechanics on the Gold and Glory circuit dared to run a dusty gauntlet, traveling from small town to small town, steering clear of large ruts, bumps, and unfriendly whites along the way. Times were often difficult for these intrepid sportsmen. Almost no hotel would host them. Almost no restaurant would serve them. Yet, with their racecars and hopes in tow, they left their regular jobs and their families behind to chase their dream of racing on the professional colored racing circuit. "Things weren't quite as bad here [in the Midwest] as they were down South, but it could get rough sometimes," Al Warren recalled. "We learned the routes that were the safest. You knew which roads and towns were friendly and which were not."

Some towns clearly were not friendly. The Ku Klux Klan might have faded from Indiana's social landscape, but segregationist attitudes were ever present in Hoosier towns such as Martinsville, Vincennes, Elwood, Kokomo, and other former Klan strongholds. "You wouldn't want to

Charlie Wiggins, aboard his "Black Cat" racer, prepares for a race in Dayton, Ohio. The Model T Ford Charlie used to haul his speedsters to the races is visible in the background. Courtesy Bruce Craig Photos

drive through some of those towns at night," Warren noted. "When you'd pull into a town like that, believe me, you'd know right away that you weren't welcome." When asked to elaborate, Warren said, "Sometimes it was stares. A time or two a lawman would come and ask to help you along, to get you moving back out of town as fast as you'd come in, that kind of thing. We'd hear stories about some towns. I don't know if they were all true, but you didn't want to test it. . . . Stories 'bout how some black fella would go through the town, then disappear. In one town they supposedly had a skull sitting on a shelf at a local bar. It was supposed to be the skull of the last colored man who came through the town . . . that kind of crap. That's why we'd try to figure out a route to take to different races—places where we could eat or stay the night—maybe in someone's home or barn, places like that. A lot of times, we'd sleep in the car, eat sandwiches we brought from home. That's how we got around."

"They didn't have interstate highways back then," noted former driver Sumner "Red" Oliver. "The roads were tough and really bumpy. We'd go to Iowa or Pennsylvania, and those trips were very, very long." Joe Freeman added, "It was a time of great experimentation in the automotive industry, not just for racecars, but for passenger cars, as well. A lot of these cars were not made for driving a long way on a hard, bumpy surface. Tires blew and engines overheated. Getting from town to town was often quite an adventure."

The Colored Speedway circuit was a semiprofessional league. All the drivers worked other jobs during the week and raced on weekends and holidays. Many African Americans earned lower wages than their white counterparts at local factories and shops. They worked long hours to earn a living during the week. Then they spent their weekend hours on the long winding roads that took them from town to town for racing events.

Others joined the drivers on their adventures. Frank A. "Fay" Young, sports editor for the *Chicago Defender,* spent one summer season traveling by car with the Gold and Glory drivers and their crews. He often kept a journal on these trips, scribbling various notes about his experiences. Some of those notes were printed in his weekly "Fay Says" columns. On one trek from Chicago to Indianapolis in 1924 he wrote, "Saturday morning, 6 o'clock, just outside of Hoopston, Illinois. Raining like the devil and the front tire of our car goes gaflooey, rim and all coming off. Raining pitchforks, and we make the change. Danville and some breakfast next. Commandeered the cook's stove in the kitchen to dry out. Call up Indianapolis colored Y.M.C.A. [on Senate Avenue] and they tell us the sky is dark, but it has not rained yet. . . .

"Off the asphalt and onto the dirt road. Indianapolis Route 33, eighteen miles out of Lebanon, Indiana. Another blowout and no spares left. Four miles to the nearest garage on the flat, which cuts the tire to a frazzle. Get fixed up, and after paying the man and thanking him, we notice his barn 'Kleage Realm, K.K.K.,' and we move on in a hurry—not scared, but just got a darn good move on us!

"More rain. Indianapolis at last, 12:45. Looks as though the race will be called off and we are kicking ourselves for not turning back 40 miles out as we started. Eats—something they called chicken and some good corn. Corn was fine, chicken needed a hacksaw to cut it. One-thirty, sun begins to shine. . . . Another blowout and we buy a new tire and get the old one fixed while we beat it to the track."

At the conclusion of the race Young and others who had journeyed from the Windy City decided to travel home together. Young's journal continued, "Now for the closing chapter. Back on Indiana Avenue, five hundred block. 'Noisy St. Louis' Kelley pilots us into an eat parlor, where we dispose of some ham and some hot tea. Quarter to eight, Chicago time. Wire the home office. Fill up the car with gasoline and follow Frank Smith's Packard out of town toward Chicago on the Jackson Highway. I said 'Follow.' Did you get me, Frank! Get to Lebanon, Indiana, after changing a tire that looks doubtful. Then a blowout and back to the doubtful tire. Put it on again. The Packard has 'gone to town.' We detour and keep rolling. Just as much dust this way as there was rain on Dixie Highway coming down. It's dark. We are hitting it up 55 and 60. Four hours later, signs. We get out, read them and cuss. Just 95 miles out of Indianapolis. Where have we been? I go to sleep on the back seat as we again head for Chicago. . . .

"Five miles outside of Hammond I wake up. Two o'clock has passed. We detour again and evidently get off the right road, because after riding another hour, we find ourselves going through Homewood. We are now 32 miles from home. Blue Island and then into Western Avenue into Halsted Street and back to the city. Gee! But it's good to have a home and last but not least, it was certainly great to see that race."[12]

Other journalists followed Young's lead and followed drivers from town to town, weekend after weekend. Often they would use their columns to advise African-American supporters coming to the race by car of safe routes into town. Most of the time, these directions were explicit. Other times, journalists described unfriendly towns with coded phrases, such as "dragon-eyed," or "hooded," both references to the Ku Klux Klan, or indicated a friendly restaurant with a phrase like "we experienced no 'back-lash' for our action."

Most African-American spectators were encouraged to travel to the Gold and Glory events by train. Oscar Schilling and Harry Earl, two of the original financiers of the inaugural Gold and Glory Sweepstakes and officials with the Cincinnati, Indianapolis and Western Railroad Company, often commissioned special train cars for blacks who wished to attend the races. Designated "coloreds only" compartments, these train cars included their own food service. The move proved highly successful for both parties. African Americans could travel and eat safely throughout their trip. And Schilling and Earl sold thousands of railway tickets and speedway tickets to their events.

Other African-American sportsmen during the 1920s and '30s were able to make similar accommodations to aid them in their travels from town to town. Negro National League baseball teams often chartered their own bus to get from site to site. Black basketball teams, such as the Harlem Globetrotters or the Harlem Renaissance, could, at times, ride a "coloreds only" train car. The Renaissance, or "Rens," as they were commonly known, eventually bought an old blue bus, gutted it, and revamped it with beds and a small refrigerator for long trips across the country.

Such was not the case for drivers and mechanics on the Gold and Glory circuit. Because they had to have their racecars in tow, they always had to travel the dusty roads in a passenger car, often alone. Indianapolis Motor Speedway historian Donald Davidson noted, "Nobody stayed in the Hyatt Regency or the Radisson in those days. Often drivers had to ask a farmer if [they] could sleep in a barn. And finding your way to the track was often challenging, as well. Directions sometimes were handed down through word of mouth only. Other times, you might have a small poster or card nailed to a telephone pole. That served as your marker to get to the event. Most of the tracks were out in the fields somewhere. Few were actually held in a heavily populated area. So navigating your way around the countryside with your racecar in tow was often a challenge."

For Charlie Wiggins, life on the road often meant driving the lead passenger car with either Roberta or an aspiring driver riding alongside. A "stooge," or apprentice, sat in and steered the racecar, which typically was tethered by rope to the car in front. Bumpy dirt roads, searing heat, and wind caused dust and rocks to be thrown from the car in front into the face of the unfortunate stooge. And when the storms came, the racecar offered neither a shield against flying mud nor shelter from pounding rain. "It was always a wild ride," Al Warren remembered. "Your whole body and your clothes would just be black when you finally got there. Most of the time, we couldn't stay in a hotel or house. So we'd have to sleep in the car for a day or two while we traveled. There was no place to clean up. And, man! I was a mess after some of those trips— smelling bad, looking bad, just awful."

Though he towed his racecar on many trips, there were times when Charlie handed the reins of his valued Wiggins Special to the only other person he trusted as much as himself to get the car out of a tricky situation. That person was his wife, Roberta. Historian Boniface Hardin explained, "Roberta was no mean driver herself. When the truck and trailer hit the road, Roberta was often at one wheel. In fact, on one occasion when several drivers refused to drive the truck down a treacherous hill in Cincinnati, Charles ordered that the wheel be turned over to Roberta, who would 'do it right.' And she did."[13]

Week in and week out, "coloreds only" races were featured in big cities and small towns throughout the Midwest. The Colored Speedway Association promoted popular events in fourteen cities in Michigan, Indiana, Iowa, Pennsylvania, Ohio, Kentucky, Wisconsin, and Illinois. All were preceded by the usual hype in the black press. One report from the *Indianapolis Recorder* trumpeted a race in Akron, Ohio: "Speed, speed, and then some speed is the boast of the several drivers, so much so that one needs anticipate bullet-like velocity almost from the starting bomb throughout the 100 laps until the checkered flag falls before the last dirt-covered, oil-dripping hero. . . . To see them in action, handled by colored officials and watched by a colored audience is a sight never to be forgotten. . . . All colored America is waiting for this event and the large delegations to attend from neighboring states lead the management to believe that so far as our race is concerned, this race will surpass in attendance the one just run, and rightly so, for it is our own." The article concluded, "History is being made along another line at these races; fame is gained for the winners and money put in their pockets; experience is acquired by the drivers. These help advance our cause and like in other lines, with experience, money and brains to back us, doors of the white man will not continue to swing closed against us."[14]

Such was the excitement and hype in the summer of 1930. A year earlier, race promoter and financier Harry Earl had worked with Colored Speedway Association officials to create a new "coloreds only" event at Walnut Gardens Speedway, twelve miles southwest of Indianapolis near the suburb of Mooresville. The Walnut Gardens Championship Auto Races would be held each year in mid-August, after the running of the annual Gold and Glory Sweepstakes on July 4. Each year's race would feature that season's Gold and Glory Sweepstakes champion, plus other top African-American drivers and their crews. The 1930 event was to be held on August 17. Quarter-page advertisements in the *Indianapolis Recorder* promoted an exciting event "featuring the country's most famous drivers, including Bobby Wallace, William 'Wild Bill' Buckner, Charlie Wiggins and Gene Smith of Chicago. Race fans are being urged to reach the scene of what promises to be one of the most sensational auto races." One ad promoted that the track would be oiled to keep down the dust.[15]

Luckily for Earl and his promoter, J. E. "Speed" Green, that year's annual Gold and Glory Sweepstakes had been a thriller. Chicago's Gene Smith, aboard a Boyle Valve Special, narrowly defeated Charlie Wiggins when Charlie's car ran out of gas on the ninety-fourth lap. At the time, Charlie had been leading Smith by half a mile, but he had had to use too much fuel in order to stay in front of the powerful Boyle car. Fans in Indianapolis were abuzz with talk about which town really produced the better drivers, Indianapolis or Chicago, a fiery rivalry that was often fanned in the press.

Earl and Green also used the rivalry to get more fans out to Walnut Gardens for the event. An article in the *Indianapolis Recorder* even showed a photo of Gene Smith in one edition, followed by a photo of Charlie Wiggins in the next. "Who will be the champion?" a subtitle asked.[16] On Wednesday, August 6, tickets went on sale, and local fans queued at the Colored Speedway Association headquarters for an hour to buy them. There was even talk of a daylong festival, complete with a parade and fireworks, similar to the celebrations that accompanied the Gold and Glory Sweepstakes.

But twenty-four hours after the tickets went on sale, plans for the celebration suddenly stopped.

African Americans in Indiana had battled time and again against the racism of Hoosier society. On August 7, 1930, the issue erupted in horrific ways that once again reminded black citizens throughout the state and country of the difficulties and dangers of being "colored" in America. On that day, a double lynching was reported in Grant County, Indiana, in the city of Marion, just sixty miles north of Indianapolis. Two African-American teens, Thomas Shipp and Abram Smith, were taken from the Grant County jail by a mob of angry whites. They were beaten relentlessly and hanged from the courthouse square as thousands of people watched.

A day earlier the two boys had been arrested for the murder of Claude Deeter and the alleged rape of Mary Ball. Deeter and Ball were a young Marion couple who were parked by the Mississinewa River in Grant County on the night of August 6 when Shipp and Smith tried to rob them. Deeter resisted, and a scuffle ensued. One of the boys hit Deeter over the head with a tree limb, giving him a fatal concussion. Ball, who ran for safety, later identified the boys. The Grant County sheriff's office picked them up late that night. The following morning, as word of Deeter's murder spread throughout the streets of Marion, white residents became increasingly outraged by their actions. The *Marion Chronicle* gave a detailed report and noted that two black teenagers were responsible for a white man's death. To intensify matters, Grant County sheriff Jacob Campbell, a former Ku Klux Klan member, hung Deeter's bloody shirt high atop the jail for every citizen to see.

By nightfall hundreds of Grant County residents had begun to gather outside the jail. Temperatures had soared to nearly a hundred degrees that day. Tensions throughout the city soared as well, as hot, angry citizens shouted and demanded to see the two boys. One Marion resident who was a teenager in 1930 remembered showing up for his job at a local roller-skating rink and being told by his boss that they were closing down the rink for the night. When he asked why, the manager said, "There's gonna be a lynching tonight."[17]

According to newspaper accounts, law enforcement agents offered little resistance as a crowd of fifteen hundred stormed the jail around midnight. They dragged the two boys into the streets. Outside many men, women, and children watched as mob leaders repeatedly beat the two. Then they were taken to the courthouse square, where they were hanged. Hundreds cheered, couples held hands, and curious onlookers gazed in amazement. Dozens posed gleefully for a photograph, a macabre "team picture" of the mob in celebration as their lifeless victims hung in the background. The mob demanded that the bodies of the two boys be left up throughout the night. "They would have them remain as evidence of their anger and as examples of white supremacy," reported the *Chicago Defender*. "The sun rose Friday on the mutilated remains of two boys."[18] A third teen, James Cameron, was also beaten for his involvement in the crime, but was spared lynching when mob members determined that he had nothing to do with Deeter's murder.

The following week, in a *Chicago Defender* editorial titled "Poor Indiana," Eugene N. Burdette lamented, "Indiana is more to be pitied than censured. For many years the law abiding, true American citizens of that state have had to contend with human reptiles, winding in and out through their community, poisoning the minds of the people against the recognized and accepted standards of law and order. An apparent ill effect of such teachings is seen in the recent lynchings. . . . We do not say that the guilty committers of crime should not be prosecuted, but we do say that we expect such prosecuting to be done through legal means—by lawful methods."[19] A sketch titled "The Crucifixion" accompanied the article. In it, two crosses stood erect in the background with the lifeless bodies of Shipp and Smith hanging from them. In the center was a large cross with the figure of Justice, with her scales, nailed to it like Christ. The large cross was labeled "Justice," with the word "Marion" spread across the ground below.

After the lynchings in Marion, the threat of a race riot from nearby black communities was very strong, as was the threat of more violence from white radicals who still lurked in the city. The Indiana National Guard patrolled the streets. Sixty miles south, the mood along Indiana Avenue in Indianapolis was subdued and mournful. Headlines announcing lynchings and other forms of racial violence in the South had blared across the pages of papers like the *Indianapolis Recorder* for years. But this crime was different. It had occurred right in their own backyard. These were families that several in Indianapolis knew—former neighbors and friends. Somehow carrying on with an auto racing celebration at Walnut Gardens no longer seemed important or proper.

On August 11, the day the funerals were held for the two Marion teenagers, a host of drivers, including Charlie Wiggins, Bobby Wallace, and Bill Buckner, called Harry Earl and withdrew their entries from the Walnut Gardens event. With so few drivers remaining on the roster and little promise of crowd support, Earl canceled the race. "It seemed too tough to go on at that point," one black Hoosier resident remembered. "We all knew something like that could happen in the South, but no one ever thought it would happen here."[20]

Burdette concluded his editorial with strong condemnation of the men and women of Marion who committed the crime against Shipp and Smith. "When mob members take matters in their hands in this manner, they are out of order and are violating the laws of the United States government. They are disregarding all respect for themselves, for their community, and for their state and nation. Other nations point to this country in disgust for allowing the repetitions of such narrow and emotional lawlessness. Mob members are themselves murderers, cowardly fugitives from justice, law violators having no respect for the nation and flag that hovers over them, and are enemies of these United States."[21]

The 1930 season was one of the Colored Speedway Association's most successful years, in terms of attendance, press coverage, fantastic races, and record-breaking speeds. Yet the league was struggling financially. The stock market crash the previous October at first seemed a temporary setback for the nation's economy. But soon businesses began to close, and people lost their jobs. It was becoming increasingly clear that this setback was anything but temporary.

In Indianapolis the African-American community was hit especially hard by the economic drought. Ten percent of the city's population was African American. Yet, during the Depression, they constituted nearly half of all citizens listed as unemployed. In 1931 the *Indianapolis Recorder* made an impassioned plea to fellow African Americans to help their brothers who were out of work: "The poor of this city, through no fault of their own, are in dire circumstances. A large number of them are crying for a few lumps of coal, a suit of warm clothing, a pair of shoes. And by all means they must be given shelter. All citizens must sacrifice to help those in need. What are you doing about it, Mr. Fortunate Citizen?"[22]

A prominent black physician, Dr. Benjamin Osborne, created a cooperative organization to help fight joblessness in black Indianapolis. According to Osborne, the goal of his group was to enable "the Indianapolis Negro to lift himself out of the mire of economic serfdom to a point of economic stability by producing and marketing some of the necessities of life, instead of remaining a dependent consumer factor."[23] He set up headquarters in the Walker Building and attracted a membership base of nearly a thousand colored citizens. Together, they grew, canned, and sold fruits and vegetables, made clothing, and built shelters for those suffering during the Depression.

In 1932 Indiana Democratic gubernatorial candidate Paul V. McNutt told a weary state, "A hungry man is never rational toward the life of the community or toward his own life. Therefore it is the business of government to make those adjustments which guarantee the right to live as a normal human being." When McNutt was elected that November, the *Recorder* declared that the new governor "gave colored citizens a new hope, a new ideal, a new determination to live."[24]

Going against the economic tide of the times was the club scene along Indiana Avenue, which burgeoned as others in the neighborhood's business district struggled. The repeal of Prohibition brought a new wave of social clubs to the Avenue, including the Sunset Terrace, the Cotton Club, Dee's Paradise Ballroom, and the Oriental Café. Nearly all of these clubs featured live music. Some of the larger venues played host to the biggest names in music. Race records were now being widely distributed. Names like Duke Ellington, Cab Calloway, Joe "King" Oliver, and Louis Armstrong were shining brightly on marquees from coast to coast. Each of these bands made numerous stops in Indianapolis. As well, many clubs promoted a "Battle of the Bands" competition, featuring some of the top local and regional names in early jazz and blues, including Leroy Carr and "Scrapper" Blackwell, a pair of talented musicians from Indianapolis who each garnered nationwide acclaim. The excitement of the club scene had a tendency to blur the color line in the city, as well. Young whites came out in large numbers to enjoy the rhythms of race music.

The merging of black and white increased in other areas of Hoosier culture, as well. Many of President Franklin Roosevelt's federal works programs, such as the Works Progress Administration and the Civilian Conservation Corps, employed thousands of black and white citizens.

In cities like Indianapolis, Chicago, and Cleveland, blacks and whites worked side by side. Work camp sites were seldom segregated. "Economics and society often separated blacks and whites in Indiana during the 1920s," noted historian Richard Pierce. "Suddenly everyone found themselves in the same boat, so to speak. In some instances, those attitudes changed."

The color line blurred in the world of auto racing as well. During the Depression, there was less money available for leisure activities. Auto racing, an expensive sport for drivers, team owners, and fans, was hit especially hard. As the nation's economy grew increasingly worse, many auto racing circuits throughout the country cut back on the number of events or shut down entirely. The Colored Speedway Association persevered, however, holding races in a number of midwestern cities, including Indianapolis, where the Gold and Glory Sweepstakes carried on a scaled-back, yet festive, black auto racing tradition. It survived through a great deal of teamwork between whites and blacks in the racing community.

A new management team had taken over at the Colored Speedway headquarters on the second floor of the Walker Building on Indiana Avenue. New Association member Freeman Ransom, business manager for the Walker Manufacturing Company and a founding member of the Negro National Business League, invited Howdy Wilcox, a top competitor at the Indianapolis 500-Mile Race, to serve as the promotional manager of the Colored Speedway circuit. Wilcox was one of the top drivers in the league at the time and a highly recognized figure in the world of auto racing. His personal endorsement of the colored circuit, along with his connections to wealthy white car owners at the Indianapolis Motor Speedway, helped give the African-American league a needed boost.

Joining Ransom and Wilcox were Joe Mitchell, proprietor of the Mitchellyn, one of the most popular dance halls on the Avenue, Dr. Benjamin Osborne, and *Indianapolis Recorder* editor Marcus Stewart. Just prior to the reorganization of the Colored Speedway Association, African-American drivers formed their own group to help promote greater training opportunities for blacks. Charlie Wiggins spearheaded the incorporation of the Colored Race Drivers Club, which was intended to "perpetuate the principles and interests of sportsmanship in

Freeman Ransom, noted Indianapolis attorney and business manager
for the Walker Manufacturing Company, sits in his Indiana Avenue
office. Among his many duties, Ransom oversaw the management of
the Colored Speedway Association in the early 1930s. Courtesy
Madam Walker Collection—Indiana Historical Society

race driving and other sports."[25] The new African-American drivers club
was widely embraced and endorsed by the top white drivers in the sport.

Blacks and whites came together on the track, as well. In addition to
a fifty- or hundred-mile main event, a Colored Speedway Association
affair often featured a special match race between top black competitors,
such as Charlie Wiggins or Bobby Wallace, and their leading white
counterparts, such as Harry MacQuinn, Bill Cummings, or Howdy
Wilcox. In 1931 and again in 1933, when the fee to rent the Indiana
State Fairgrounds was more than the Colored Speedway Association
could pay, white race promoters and old friends Oscar Schilling and

Howdy Wilcox, an accomplished driver at the Indianapolis 500-Mile Race, served as the promotional manager of the Colored Speedway Association in the early 1930s. His name lent considerable credibility to the black racing league. Courtesy Indianapolis Motor Speedway archives

Harry Earl allowed the league to hold the Gold and Glory Sweepstakes at Walnut Gardens Speedway. Contracts between the two white racing promoters and the Colored Speedway Association included a split of the gate receipts. The two charged the organization only one dollar to rent their facility for the day.

Also helping to buoy the league were the sensational driving performances of Charlie Wiggins. The man once known as "Wee Charlie" dominated the colored circuit throughout the early 1930s. He won the Gold and Glory championship for three straight years, in 1931, 1932, and 1933. In both 1931 and 1932, he nudged past Bobby Wallace to capture the checkered flag. In 1933, he beat out his own brother Lawrence, who had been racing part-time on the circuit since 1929. Charlie's success extended well beyond Indianapolis, as well. Chicago, Illinois; Winchester, Indiana; Akron, Ohio; Evansville, Indiana; Louisville, Kentucky; Madison, Wisconsin . . . race after race, Charlie Wiggins roared to victory, breaking many of his own colored dirt track speed records in the process.

Richard Pierce speculated on the passion that inspired him and kept him going race after race, city after city: "What really fuels a guy to go after his second or third or fourth championship when he's already beaten the other guys? What makes him come back and face that danger on the track again? How is he able to muster the courage and excitement to come back and try it one more time? It's not the competitors, though they might push him. It's not the fans, though they might inspire him. For Charlie, and other top athletes and competitors like him, the challenge comes from 'the Demon.' It's the Demon that pushes you beyond the traditional boundaries and creates new standards for yourself and the sport. And what is the Demon? The Demon is the perfect performance, that theoretical point at which you can get no better. All great athletes seek the perfect performance. And most know they'll never find it. But still they search. And to understand that mindset is to understand the psyche of someone like Charlie Wiggins: 'Can I make the car faster and stronger? Can I drive a better race?' Those are the insatiable questions that he seeks to answer. Does he need the fans? No. Does he need the hoopla? No. He needs the competition within himself, the ability to look beyond the danger and say, 'Today is the day I beat the Demon.'"

For nearly a decade, no one chased the Demon like Charlie Wiggins. But black racing's greatest driver was getting tired. Tapping into a sixth sense that many top sportsmen possess, he felt that his good fortune on the track was about to expire. After winning the 1933 Gold and Glory Sweepstakes, Charlie began to talk privately with Roberta about retiring from the sport. "He felt that he had had his time in the spotlight, and it was time to move on," Roberta remembered. "I think his heart was telling him it was time to stop." Still, his love for racing and his desire to help the league through tight economic times kept Charlie roaring around midwestern dirt tracks at speeds over eighty miles per hour for two more seasons.

By 1936, however, league business, friendships on the circuit, even the Demon seemed less and less important to Charlie. He had gone public with his concerns and wishes: Perhaps one more season or maybe two, but that was it. Charlie Wiggins would soon retire. A new breed of colored drivers, including his former protégés Leon "Al" Warren, Sumner "Red" Oliver, and Charles "Dynamite" Stewart, were getting better aboard bigger and faster cars. Charlie looked forward to ending his racing career with a few final thrills and challenges.

Little did he know that the 1936 Gold and Glory Sweepstakes would present him with the biggest challenge of his life.

7.

A Bad Premonition

During many low moments in the history of sports, shady characters have cast a pall on the spirit of sportsmanship. The 1919 World Series was baseball's low mark, when gamblers bribed eight members of the Chicago White Sox to throw games. The "Black Sox Scandal" rocked the sports world and left a lasting scar on the game of baseball. In basketball, the "Scandals of 1951" implicated dozens of top college players who had accepted bribes from gamblers to shave points in key national tournament games. Even colored auto racing had its own malignancy in 1935. And while the scoundrels involved received relatively little attention in the black press, their thievery in the midst of the Depression certainly crippled the sport and nearly destroyed it.

The 1935 Gold and Glory Sweepstakes at the Indiana State Fairgrounds had billed daredevil aerial stunt shows starring fifteen former flying aces from the Great War, motorcycle races, indoor midget car races at the fairgrounds coliseum the evening following the big competition, and unusual stunt shows. One of these sensational acts featured a motorcycle racer roaring at full speed through a wall of fire. Much of the pre-race hype focused on Charlie Wiggins, whom the *Indianapolis Recorder* called "the brown-skinned driver with nerves of steel," and his friend and rival Bobby Wallace, "a fearless driver noted for his thrilling finishes in races."[1] The ballyhoo was brash and colorful, just as it had been for the past eleven seasons.

The only difference between the 1935 Gold and Glory Sweepstakes and races held in previous years was that officials from the Colored Speedway Association did not stage this event. The press offered no explanation for the change, except to note that an unnamed racing outfit from Dayton, Ohio, would be orchestrating the hundred-mile racing event and all associated activities. Gone were some of the traditional names in the annual Indianapolis grind, such as "Wild Bill" Jeffries, who had hung up his leather helmet and goggles to work as a racing promoter in Chicago. Also gone were some of the familiar names within the Association, such as William "Pres" Rucker, the organization's founder, who had retired, and Harry Dunnington, the former business manager of the organization, who had succumbed to crippling health problems and died earlier that year. Gone as well was the support of many white drivers and promoters associated with the Indianapolis Motor Speedway.

Without these familiar faces, however, the Dayton crew managed to create an atmosphere similar to that of previous events on the Negro circuit. By keeping ticket prices low to accommodate patrons on tight budgets, the group was able to attract more than three thousand spectators, including racing fans from Chicago, Michigan, and Ohio, to the fairgrounds for the day's festivities.

Time trials were held early in the day on July 4, 1935, with twenty-four drivers qualifying. The main event would be run immediately following the air show, at 1:30 P.M. Among the qualifiers were Charlie Wiggins aboard his "23 Skidoo" Wiggins Special, Bobby Wallace in a four-cylinder Fronty Ford, and Charlie's brother Lawrence, who also drove a Fronty Ford. Other top drivers included two members of "Charlie's Gang." One was Charles "Dynamite" Stewart, piloting a Miller Schofield. He qualified second for the main event. The other was Andy Pryor, a young Indianapolis mechanic who had befriended Charlie the previous year. Pryor entered a "Hal Special" and qualified seventh in the time trials.

That afternoon, as the spectators enjoyed the thrills of the aerial stunt show, the drivers lined up near the track and made last-minute preparations for the race. Amid the hubbub, no one noticed that the promoters were not in their traditional position near the announcer's podium at the conclusion of the air show. Members of the Dayton promotion team were to bring the air show to a conclusion, introduce the Gold and Glory drivers, and officially start the race. But as the last plane passed overhead, the joyous applause in the grandstand soon turned to murmurs of curiosity, then shouts of confusion. The drivers looked up from their cockpits. Some left their cars and made their way to the podium to investigate.

No one was sure who discovered it first, but the reality of the situation came swiftly. It hit both the drivers and the spectators with a sudden, sickening blow. The *Indianapolis Recorder* mentioned problems with "last-minute details, which were incompleted [*sic*] at the eleventh hour." But the truth of the matter was that while everyone was distracted during the air show, the promoters skipped town with all the gate receipts. There was no prize money for the drivers, no profit to show for the day's festivities.

Indianapolis Motor Speedway historian Donald Davidson noted, "It was a very common thing in the 1920s and '30s to have unscrupulous promoters abscond with the funds during a race. Some drivers got wise to these scams after a while, however, and created a plan to stop them. While different races were going on, a driver who was not competing in a particular heat would stand outside the office door and watch to ensure that no one came running out the back door with a satchel in his hand. Occasionally that did happen, and there were cases in which drivers actually chased a promoter down the road to try to catch him and retrieve the money."

Unfortunately for the drivers and spectators attending the Gold and Glory Sweepstakes in 1935, no one was watching the back door of the office. The promoters—and the money—were gone. With no purse on offer, most of the drivers were unwilling to put their lives on the line in a hundred-mile dirt track competition. Some racers began to pull their cars back onto their trailers and prepare for a disappointing trip home. The press never reported the results of any races that day. However, family members of Charlie Wiggins, Andy Pryor, and Charles "Dynamite" Stewart all recall that an announcement was made to the crowd asking for voluntary donations to create a small purse for the winning driver. According to these accounts, most of the drivers agreed to square off in an abbreviated event, most likely a twenty-lap competition, in an effort to appease the crowd, each of whom had paid a one-dollar admission to watch the much-hyped Gold and Glory Sweepstakes.

"Auto racing was pretty raw in all aspects during that era," motor sports historian Joe Freeman said. "Races often were loosely organized events throughout the country. It was not like today, where you have structured racing bodies that govern the sport and all aspects of the promotion and financing. These were more like the old medicine show guys who would set up a 'fly-by-night' shop and sell a few bottles of snake oil, then slip out of town. They saw an opportunity for a scam. Unfortunately for many unsuspecting drivers who simply loved to drive and compete, they lost their entry fees, as well as the opportunity to win a purse that could help them pay for their trip to the track or pay for much-needed updates to their racecar. I suppose if there was a dark underbelly to the racing game in the early days, it would be the dishonest nature of many promoters in that day."

The spring rains poured relentlessly outside the Walker Coffee Pot on April 19, 1936. Inside, twenty-four of the African-American community's leaders shook their damp umbrellas and overcoats and made their way through the crowded eatery to a back room on the ground floor of the Madam Walker Center on Indiana Avenue. Several gathered around a wood stove, trying to dry out and warm up. Near the front of the room, Henry Richardson topped off his cup of coffee, drew in a long sip, cleared his throat, and asked everyone in the room to gather around. The meeting of the newly organized Gold and Glory executive committee was about to begin.

Richardson was a powerful voice in the black community. Indeed, he was a powerful voice in Indianapolis. He had once been appointed a judge in the Marion County Superior Court, the first African American to hold such a post. He was also one of the first African Americans to be elected to the state legislature during the twentieth century. He was an ardent civil rights activist who supported many causes around the state. On this day his cause was the future of black motor sports across the state and country. The 1935 Gold and Glory Sweepstakes had been a disastrous blow to the sport. The Colored Speedway Association, the backbone of organized racing for Negro drivers for more than a decade, was practically bankrupt, the result of mismanagement, a lack of leadership in 1934 and 1935, and tight economic times. Richardson wanted to pull the sport out of the mire, clean it up, and put it back on display as a dazzling example of black entrepreneurship. To do so in the midst of the Great Depression, even as other auto racing circuits in the country were fizzling and fading, would make a powerful social statement and put some of the glory back into the Gold and Glory Sweepstakes.

Celebrated attorney, legislator, and civil rights activist Henry Richardson, pictured here with his secretary and a female client, served as chairman of the Colored Speedway Association in 1936. Courtesy *Indianapolis Recorder* Collection—Indiana Historical Society

It was clear from the outset that Richardson meant business. He asked for and received support from Indiana lieutenant governor M. Clifford Townsend, as well as Vernon L. Anderson, a leading African-American official in the prosecutor's office. Richardson also tapped African-American leaders in neighboring Indiana cities, such as Muncie, Terre Haute, and Richmond. He brought back many early supporters of the Colored Speedway Association, including former Association officer Freeman B. Ransom. The white racing community was back, as well, including old friends Howdy Wilcox, Harry MacQuinn, Bill Cummings, and car owners such as Michael Boyle and Arthur Chevrolet, who agreed to supply cars and cash to the group. Financier and promoter Harry Earl had pledged by wire to support the cause. The Richardson political machine was hard at work to generate money and organizational support to pump new life into the ailing Colored Speedway Association.

Richardson next turned back the clock twelve years, asking William Rucker to return to the helm as president. The sixty-seven-year-old Rucker had retired from the sport in 1929, having tired of the ceaseless pressures of managing a national auto racing circuit. In the early days of the Colored Speedway Association, Rucker had relied heavily on the savvy business practices of the late Harry Dunnington. In need of these important services once again, he now asked Eugene Armstrong, a successful business executive and political advisor, to act as vice president of the Association. Armstrong agreed. The Colored Speedway Association was back in business and began work right away to organize the 1936 Gold and Glory Sweepstakes, to be held on September 20.

The executive committee next worked to secure top driving talent to attract spectators to the event. At the top of their list were former colored circuit champions Charlie Wiggins, Bobby Wallace, Bill James, and Bill Carson. As well, a number of Charlie's protégés received invitations, including Charles "Dynamite" Stewart, Leon "Al" Warren, and Sumner "Red" Oliver. The *Indianapolis Recorder* rejoiced. "Annual Gold and Glory Sweepstakes to Be Renewed," the headline blared. "Hoosiers have been gripped with the 'race fever,' as advance tickets to the Gold and Glory Sweepstakes race to be held here September 20 are moving at a fast clip. . . . Fan interest in the big gasoline classic will be centered around Charlie Wiggins and other local drivers who will be contesting

Car owners Louis Chevrolet (*with hat on*) and his brother Arthur (*in vest, to Louis's right*) tested out new racing engines and parts with driver Bobby Wallace during the Gold and Glory Sweepstakes. Courtesy Indianapolis Motor Speedway archives

against a horde of out-of-town entrants who are out to win some of the pot of gold that awaits those who finish in the money. The top names in sports and society will be rubbing elbows here from all sections of Indiana, Ohio, Illinois, and Michigan. The race will be to the Negro what the Memorial Day race is to the white community, or what the Kentucky Derby is to Louisville, a sporting attraction which will live for years and years to come." Freeman Ransom told the press, "Colored drivers could and should be allowed opportunity to display their skill and courage, as well as to have the chance for winning prizes. As a broad aim of our group, we [envision] colored drivers in the 500-mile classic."[2]

Music promoter Matthew Dickerson was to stage a Gold and Glory gala ball at Tomlinson Hall the night of the race. Dickerson was a master promoter and booking agent who often arranged to bring the biggest names in music, such as Louis Armstrong, Chick Webb, and Duke Ellington, to Indianapolis. The Gold and Glory Ball would be another masterstroke for the ingenious promoter. The *Recorder* reported that Dickerson's gala would feature a battle of the bands between "the well-known Clarence Paige and his aggregation of musicians hailing from Cincinnati and the nationally famous Windy City dance band headed by the inimitable maestro Erskine Tate of the Savoy Ballroom." The ball promised "top entertainment from 9 'til Morn, which will introduce the peculiar rhythm and style of 'swing' that has never before invaded Naptown."[3] More than three thousand tickets were sold for the dance the first week they were on sale.

Politics also figured prominently in the festivities. The Democratic Party was firmly entrenched in the African-American community less than a decade after the fall of the Ku Klux Klan in Indiana. Political hopefuls, including Clifford Townsend, the Democratic candidate for governor, and Gold and Glory organizer Henry Richardson, himself an incumbent candidate for the state legislature, saw great potential in reaching eight to ten thousand race fans and registered voters. Much of the pre-race celebration would become a flag-waving political rally in central Indiana.

By August anticipation was beginning to build for the big event. *Indianapolis Recorder* sports columnist Lee A. Johnson, in his weekly "Shooting the Works" column, noted, "Next month at the Indiana State Fairgrounds, another sporting event returns, an event which may live to be one of the greatest of Negro affairs in a sport which has made Indianapolis internationally popular. When we speak of automobile races, the mind automatically recalls the 500–Mile Races at the Speedway. Now we are beginning to witness our own speed classics with ebony pilots shooting around the turns at breakneck speed for fame and glory. A crowd of 25,000 fans is expected to witness the event, which will put this city on the map of sportsmen who follow the big attractions."[4] Johnson may have been a bit overzealous in his estimate of the race's possible attendance. Three weeks before the event nearly eight thousand tickets had been sold to fans throughout an eight-state region. It was hardly the twenty-five thousand Johnson boasted, but it was still an impressive total, particularly in the midst of the Great Depression.

The "rebirth" of the Gold and Glory Sweepstakes was being billed as the "Ebony Classic." The total purse was $3,000, with $1,000 earmarked for the victor. Bobby Wallace was the first to register, in a Dreyer Special that had seen action in many all-white AAA-sanctioned races. Chicago's Bill Carson, whom the *Chicago Defender* called "one of the cleverest drivers on dirt tracks and the chief rival of all on the circuit,"[5] registered with his powerful V-8 Boyle Valve Special. Al Warren entered a DeSoto 6 Special. "Dynamite" Stewart signed up with a Schofield Special. Red Oliver entered a car called "Jinx," a retooled eight-cylinder Studebaker Special that had been in a frightening accident at the Indianapolis 500-Mile Race in 1935. Former Gold and Glory champion Bill James entered a midget car, a Stewart Radio Special, the first of the tiny racing machines ever registered in the yearly African-American racing spectacle. In all, thirty-seven drivers entered their cars for the event, each hoping to secure one of twenty-three qualifying spots for the race.

Race promoters reasoned that this year's race would be particularly sensational. Vernon Anderson explained to the *Recorder*, "First, faster cars are entered in the race; second, more seasoned drivers will be at the helm; to qualify, drivers must attain a top speed of at least 80 miles per hour for ten laps of the mile track before qualifying; and last, all cars are high geared for speed." The sports reporter for the *Recorder* expanded on Anderson's remarks, adding, "Many [who] have asked themselves the question as to whether our drivers can really pilot a car in the big Memorial Day races handled at the Speedway annually can come and see for themselves. . . . Sponsored by the Gold and Glory Racing association, the automobile race here Sunday is to be held in the hope of making it similar in popularity and public acceptance to the Indianapolis Motor Speedway 500 Mile Race."

The article continued, "Drivers of our race are barred from participation in all AAA races. . . . Howdy Wilcox, famed for his showing in past Memorial Day races, announced that he will go to the battle line for our boys in the bigger racing game if we come out and support them in the Gold and Glory race. . . . Your own interest may cause the promoters to allow Negro pilots to enter the races for big money. If you support your own drivers, that will be reason enough, for they want that type of backing for every driver in their classic."[6]

Attention clearly centered on Charlie Wiggins. The September 12 edition of the *Indianapolis Recorder* featured a banner headline proclaiming, "Wiggins to Pilot Car in Race" and included a photo of Charlie aboard his familiar Wiggins Special with a special Roof racing head mounted on the engine for greater speed and performance. The photo caption read, "Charles Wiggins, ranked as a 'Class A' pilot on the dirt track and winner of several championships, is entered in the Gold and Glory Sweepstakes races at the Indiana State Fairgrounds on September 20. Wiggins, a local driver, is figured upon by local sportsmen as the one who will finish well up in the money on his past record the last few years." Another article noted, "[B]lack and white drivers agree that Wiggins is one of the best race drivers Indianapolis has ever produced."[7]

Charlie was never one to believe in the hype. "He didn't care none for the attention," remembered Red Oliver. "If it was good for auto racing, then it was good for Charlie." Al Warren recalled, "Racing was just who he was. It was what he was all about. There were guys that talked the talk, but Charlie walked the walk. He let his driving do the talking. Others made much more noise over his accomplishments than he ever did."

For ten years the Negro Speed King had been burning up dirt tracks throughout the Midwest with unparalleled success. Now approaching the twilight of his career, he looked forward to a few final races against some of his best friends and greatest rivals. Bill Carson, Bobby Wallace, Bill James, Red Oliver, Al Warren—the nation's top African-American drivers and mechanics again made their annual pilgrimage to Indianapolis in hopes of dethroning Charlie Wiggins, the four-time Gold and Glory champion. As race day dawned, Charlie awoke early and pulled on his white mechanic's overalls. The sun was just beginning to rise as he headed to his garage and began to hitch his car to the trailer. He grabbed his leather helmet and goggles. It was time to go to work.

When Charlie and Roberta Wiggins arrived at the fairgrounds, more than eight thousand admiring spectators, a crowd the *Indianapolis Recorder* called "a gaily attired mixed crowd of whites and blacks,"[8] greeted them. Charlie's wife vividly remembered the scene. "I'll never forget that day as long as I live. Charlie and I stood near the track before the race and watched all those people walking about. It was quite a sight, and I was very excited. But then, I can't quite explain it, but I got this awful chill in my body. It was strange. I looked at Charlie, and he was all serious-looking. I could tell he felt it too."

Historian and Wiggins family friend Boniface Hardin noted, "At

Charlie Wiggins just prior to the start of the 1936 Gold and Glory Sweepstakes, a race marred by a tragic thirteen-car pileup that threatened his life. Courtesy Mrs. Mildred Overton

the beginning of the 1936 race, Roberta saw 'Pres' Rucker in a crowd of dignitaries and told him that she didn't feel good, that she felt like something was going to happen. There wasn't anything she knew that would cause this feeling to occur, but she felt it and knew it to be true. And worse yet, perhaps, she knew that Charlie had a sense of trepidation about the race."

Storm clouds rumbled overhead as the pre-race political rally concluded around noon on that warm Sunday. As the drivers pulled their racecars onto the track to begin their qualification heats, thunderclouds opened up, and a small, late-summer shower passed over the crowd. The rain caused a one-hour delay in the start of the time trials. Race officials began to look at their watches with great concern. A "blue law" was in effect for the region. This law required that all business operations cease at 6:00 P.M. on Sundays. The rain delay, followed by the time trials, would leave little time to run the actual race.

For races on paved surfaces, the track requires little preparation before a race begins. Prior to dirt track events, however, it is customary for officials to spend an hour watering and oiling the track in an effort to keep down the dust and create a safer surface for the drivers. As the rainstorm eased on September 20, 1936, race officials acted in great haste to line up drivers for the time trials. They had no time to lose. At 1:00, only five hours before the Sunday curfew, officials made a critical judgment: the water from the storm would need to serve as the only treatment of the track prior to the race. There was no time to apply the proper water and oil treatment.

In the qualification heats, Charlie Wiggins earned the pole position for the Gold and Glory Sweepstakes. "Dynamite" Stewart and Andy Pryor also earned spots near the front of the pack. What drew the drivers' greatest attention, however, was a car in the middle of the pack. Bill James's car was the first midget racer in the Negro racing circuit. Many of the Gold and Glory participants, including Carson and Charlie Wiggins, began to protest to race officials that the midget, a small, lightweight speedster, was unsafe in a competition with larger and more powerful V-8 model cars. Most argued that the smaller car would be more difficult to see on the dusty surface. A shouting match with officials ensued for the next two hours. Charlie realized he was arguing in vain. Rucker and other Association members were clearly set on their decision to allow the midget car into the competition. While other drivers and mechanics continued their heated debate, Charlie returned to his car, propped himself on the hood, and looked out over the track. He had a look of quiet concern on his face.

Roberta remembered, "A lady next to me asked if Charlie was bothered by the folks arguing. But he wasn't looking at them. He was looking at the track. It was drying out, you see. And the dryer it gets, the more dangerous it gets. . . . At one point while we waited, Charlie came over to me. He had had a bad premonition. He looked out over the track, shook his head and told me, 'Somebody's gonna get hurt today.' I cried and begged him not to go out there. But he just held me close and said, 'You can't ever be afraid. You have to face it. No, you can't ever be afraid.'"

Shortly after leaving his wife near the grandstand, Charlie saw Red Oliver and expressed the same concern to him. "Charlie told me that the track was in such bad condition that someone surely would get hurt."[9]

Finally, "Pres" Rucker pulled a pocket watch from his vest and looked at the time. Three-thirty. Time was running out on the rebirth of his grand national celebration. A decision had to be made: the midget racer was in. No time to water the track. The race would begin in thirty minutes. Drivers leaped into their cockpits. Engines revved. Howdy Wilcox grabbed the green flag and waved it furiously. The time was 4:10 P.M. The race was on. Dust clouds billowed wildly as drivers rounded the first turn. Red Oliver remembered, "It was so dusty you couldn't see ten feet in front of you." In the grandstand, Roberta Wiggins buried her face in her hands. She could not bear to watch.

It took only about sixty seconds for Charlie's "bad premonition" to turn into reality. As the cars rounded the fourth turn to complete the second lap of the race, one of the cars near the lead began to skid out of control. Bill James's midget racer instantly collided with the car, killing James's engine. The midget car sat motionless in the middle of the track amid giant clouds of dust. James watched helplessly as the pack closed in around him.

The first driver to plow into the dust cloud was Charlie Wiggins, who had already built his speed to nearly eighty miles per hour. Unable to see James, he slammed directly into the tiny racer. The force threw Charlie from his car ten feet through the air. He rolled over near the infield, only to see his own car airborne above his body. The car came down hard on Charlie's right leg. The momentum of the vehicle pushed his body along the ground until the car crashed into the inside railing, pinning him between the front grill of the car and a splintered wood rail.

Searing pain shot through Charlie's leg. He had little time to react. He made a few desperate attempts to pull himself free from the wreckage. The next driver to enter the fiery scene was Al Warren. "I saw one of the boys on the infield trying to flag me down to stop. So I tried to stop, but my car hit somebody. I couldn't tell who it was because of the dust. All of a sudden I heard Charlie yelling, 'Take it off my leg! Take it off my leg!' I looked around, but I couldn't see anything. So I jumped out of my cockpit. I was stuck in there, and I'm not sure how I got out of the car so fast. Then I followed Charlie's voice until I saw him stranded

The *Indianapolis Recorder* called the thirteen-car accident at the 1936
Gold and Glory Sweepstakes a "mountain of rending, distorted metal
and buried men." Here drivers, mechanics, and firemen work to put out
a blaze in one of the wrecked vehicles. Courtesy Mrs. Mildred Overton

there. It was a terrible sight. Blood was everywhere. I grabbed under his
arms and started to pull him out. It was then that I heard this really loud
roar, and then I realized, 'Oh my God! The other cars!' I tried to pull
Charlie out, but someone else hit the back of his car, and it threw me
clear into the infield. I looked back, and all I saw was Charlie's body
flying through the air. My God, what a horrible sight!"

Six, then ten, then thirteen cars skidded out of control and slammed
into the swelling inferno. The *Indianapolis Recorder* described cars "melt-
ing into a mountain of rending, distorted metal and buried men." Red
Oliver was the seventh driver into the wreck. He avoided the wreckage
by running his car into the outer fence railing. "I heard the crowd

screaming, and then I heard it . . . Bam! Someone yelled, 'There's a wreck on the far end.' I couldn't stop in time, but I was able to get out of the way. I looked over and saw one boy run right into Charlie. It crushed Charlie's leg. Oh, my! It was terrible."

Cars were strewn about the infield and outfield. Many had burst into flames. The thirteen-car pileup caused race officials, ambulance workers, and distraught fans to pour onto the track in a desperate attempt to pull bodies from the wreckage. Roberta Wiggins screamed in horror as she dashed across the infield. As she ran, she heard a voice screaming "He's dead. Charlie's dead." The words rippled throughout the crowd in an instant. Panic-stricken, Roberta darted about in the smoke and burning oil fumes until the grief and the toxic odor brought her to her knees. She felt sick, dizzy, and disoriented. "My God! My Charlie. My God!" she screamed.

A few feet away from Roberta, Bobby Wallace, with blood streaming from his forehead, led a charge by several other drivers and emergency workers to find Charlie's body in the twisted heap. Their search lasted no more than a minute or two. There, near the infield of the fourth turn, lay the limp, semiconscious body of the Negro Speed King. Al Warren remembered that Charlie's body looked as though it had been dipped in blood from the waist down. He was still alive. Each breath was strained in the thick dusty air. Warren yelled for Roberta, who stumbled through the infield grass, then fell at Charlie's side. She clutched what was left of his bloodstained, dust-scarred mechanic's outfit. She cried out his name over and over. Dazed, Charlie whispered to his wife to remove ninety dollars in cash from his front right pocket and take care of it. Roberta unzipped the pocket and reached in, only to find to her shock that the money had disappeared. Charlie faded back out of consciousness as two emergency workers lifted the racing great onto a stretcher. One driver escorted Roberta into the ambulance. A paramedic tied a makeshift tourniquet around Charlie's battered right leg and attempted to stop the bleeding. Roberta held Charlie's head and caressed her husband's brow. She could only remember the paramedic muttering to himself, "Too much blood. . . . We've lost too much blood."

Within minutes the ambulance doors burst open, and Charlie was being wheeled down the hall of the Jim Crow wing of Indianapolis City Hospital. As they took him into the emergency room, Roberta stood in the hallway with tears streaming down her cheeks and Charlie's blood dripped down her blouse. A young doctor with a grim expression on his face dashed down the hall to the emergency room. On his way, he accidentally bumped into Roberta. He looked back at her, then pointed to an old wooden chair positioned in the middle of the hall. "Wait here," he commanded. Then he slipped through the large wooden doors. She collapsed in the chair. The shock and confusion were overwhelming. Roberta Wiggins sat motionless and waited to hear of her husband's fate.

It had been one hour since the accident, and the smoke and dust had finally begun to settle at the Indiana State Fairgrounds. Only ten cars remained from the twenty-three that had started the race. Bobby Wallace, Chicago driver Wilbur Gaines, Cleveland speedster Robert LaSallica, Garland Brooks from Terre Haute, and local driver Andy Pryor were all sent by ambulance to City Hospital with minor injuries. All were released within a few hours. Al Warren, who was not injured in the accident, was not able to salvage his car and had to withdraw from the competition. Red Oliver's racer had a bent front axle but was still operational. Chicago's Bill Carson had a dented frame on his racecar, but his engine continued to run perfectly. "Dynamite" Stewart was one of only five drivers to avoid the tragic mishap altogether. "Pres" Rucker and other race officials decided to gather the remaining drivers and run a shortened event, a fifty-mile derby, in order to complete the race and beat the Sunday "blue law."

Forty laps into the fifty-lap affair, Carson held a slender lead over Red Oliver, "Dynamite" Stewart, and two Indianapolis rookies, Johnny Wand and Henry Rogers. Oliver was gaining fast by the forty-seventh mile, and the crowd began to cheer. Rucker glanced at his watch. It was six o'clock. A member of the Marion County sheriff's department approached the head of the Colored Speedway Association and asked Rucker to wave the checkered flag and end the race. The curfew was now in effect. Rucker begged the officer to allow the drivers to complete the final three laps of the race. But the sheriff was insistent. The race had to end. Now.

Carson and Oliver were almost neck and neck when Rucker made his way to the finish line and waved the flag. Carson was leading Oliver by a half-car length on the back straightaway. The drivers, who did not see Rucker's signal at first, continued to jockey for the lead. As they rounded the fourth turn, Oliver, in his sturdy Studebaker, surged ahead of Carson's Boyle Valve Special. As both crossed the finish line, Oliver took the checkered flag, roaring to an apparent one-second victory over his Windy City rival. Oliver leapt from the cockpit and, with giddy enthusiasm, began to hug members of his crew. But his celebration was premature. Rucker and other race officials abruptly deflated Oliver's exuberance. They informed him and the rest of the crowd that the race was officially over at the point when Rucker first waved the flag, while Oliver and Carson were still battling on the back straightaway. Carson had won the race by less than one second. Despite an ardent protest by Red Oliver and his Ohio crew, Bill Carson was awarded the $1,000 first prize in the 1936 Gold and Glory Sweepstakes. Oliver was forced to settle for second-place honors and a $400 check. Johnny Wand finished third, followed by Henry Rogers and Charles "Dynamite" Stewart.

Immediately following the event, drivers, crew members, officials, and fans raced into downtown Indianapolis to Tomlinson Hall, where the food was hot and the music was hotter. Each hoped to procure a good table for the Gold and Glory gala ball. The dance attracted nearly three thousand patrons. Each sought to shake off the dust and the bad memories of the horrible incident earlier in the day. Soon Clarence Paige and Erskine Tate filled the night air with the sounds of swing. Vernon Anderson and William Rucker presented trophies and prize money to the top three drivers at a ceremony prior to the big show. They also announced that the remainder of the purse, nearly $1,500 total, would be divided equally among the rest of the drivers, including the thirteen involved in the accident near the start of the race.

Several of the drivers who suffered minor injuries in the wreck were in attendance at the ball that night. A little more than an hour after the festivities began, Andy Pryor, who had suffered a dislocated shoulder, arrived in a new suit with his arm in a sling. Shortly after Pryor's entrance, Bobby Wallace, his head bandaged for a concussion, entered the hall. Both Pryor and Wallace received a warm reception from the

Charlie's brother, Lawrence Wiggins, posed beside a crippled racer following the 1936 Gold and Glory Sweepstakes. Courtesy Mrs. Mildred Overton

crowd as they made their way across the dance floor to a table near the bandstand.

Slight murmurs began to ripple through the crowd: What had become of Charlie Wiggins? Many heard a rumor that he had died on the track. Others heard that he had suffered severe blood loss and slipped into a coma. All anyone knew for sure was that the Negro Speed King was listed in critical condition at City Hospital. There was no word on his prognosis. After a while the music and dancing overtook the whispers of concern. Still, many questions circulated throughout the hall, with no answers to be found.

Charlie's brother Lawrence stayed with Roberta for six hours. At one point he brought her some hot coffee. Another time he brought hot soup. Both times she refused to drink it. At 11:00 P.M. he offered to call a taxi to take her home. Clearly Roberta was exhausted. He offered to take her place in the wooden chair outside the emergency room. He promised to phone her with any news on Charlie's condition. But again she refused. At Roberta's urging Lawrence agreed to leave for a few hours' rest and return first thing in the morning. He held his sister-in-law tight, prayed, and then gave her one last embrace. Then Lawrence turned to leave. Roberta looked down the hall and into the bright fluorescent lights. She caught a glimpse of Lawrence's silhouette slumping as he shuffled toward the exit.

She was now sitting alone, just as she had done when emergency workers first brought Charlie and her into the hospital earlier that afternoon. When she closed her eyes, she could replay the scenes in her mind in great detail:

"Get out of the way! Get out of the way!" one large man in a felt cap yelled from the infield.

Roberta recalled seeing fire rising from the twisted chassis that was Charlie's car. Two mechanics grabbed large blankets and threw them over the burning engine in an attempt to smother the flames.

Roberta remembered more voices rising above the pandemonium: "He's under the car," one driver shouted. "A doctor. Where's the god-damned doctor?" another cried.

Images continued to flash through Roberta's mind: Charlie's racer was flipped on its side. His dented wheelbase pierced the thick, smoky air. The tires were gone. One tire rim, now bent into an oblong shape, continued to spin slowly. The back end of the chassis was completely crushed. The hood remained closed, but flames lapped up over the gaps on either side of the car, spiraling skyward into the dark, smoke-filled air.

It was then that she remembered seeing her husband near the infield.

"It's Wiggins," she heard someone say. "It's Charlie. Get the ambulance here." "Is he dead?" a woman asked. Others made comments. Some yelled instructions to her. Little of it made any sense to her at the time.

She recollected the sound of the sirens. Two paramedics ran over to pick up Charlie's limp body. "You need to let him go, ma'am," one of them commanded. "Please let me take him to the hospital. Ma'am, you need to let him go." His eye caught hers and Roberta snapped back into full awareness. She nodded and climbed aboard the emergency vehicle. Just as she stepped into the back of the ambulance, Roberta took one last look at the horrific sight. "It looked like dying soldiers on a battlefield," she recalled.

Within a few seconds Roberta and Charlie were whisked away in the ambulance, bound for Indianapolis City Hospital. When they arrived the driver did not pull into the most immediate and accessible entrance to the facility. Hospital regulations demanded that the ambulance pull around to the side doors that led to the "coloreds only" or "Jim Crow" wing of the building. Inside, young doctors using outdated equipment struggled to serve the city's seventy thousand black residents in a small, seventy-bed facility. Only one surgeon was on call when Charlie Wiggins was brought in to the hospital.

The narrow hallway was floored with black and white tiles that reflected the harsh, blue-white fluorescent lights above. The area was cold and antiseptic. Only two pieces of furniture interrupted the seemingly never-ending rows of checkered tiles: the worn wooden chair in which Roberta sat and a weathered clock that hung on one of the white walls at the end of the hall. The clock's pendulum swayed with its own slow, steady tempo. The sound melted into the drone of activity up and down the ward. Periodically Roberta could hear the clock's chimes. The ringing momentarily brought her out of her trance and painfully awakened her to her surroundings once again.

The clock struck twelve times. It had been nearly eight hours since the accident. All the other drivers injured in the thirteen-car pileup had been released with apparent minor injuries. Only Charlie remained in critical condition. Roberta strained to hear any word through the thick wooden doors that led into the emergency room. The air was stuffy and warm. The surgeon and his team had not taken a single break all evening.

Finally, shortly after midnight, a young intern stepped out from behind the doors for a moment of fresh air. He spoke with Mrs. Wiggins.

Roberta trembled. "How's my Charlie?" she asked the young man. Sweat glistened on his face. He shrugged his shoulders and shook his head. It was still too early to tell. Charlie's right leg was severely damaged in the wreck. It had hemorrhaged, causing him to lose a dangerous amount of blood. Only a few units of his blood type were left. The intern asked Roberta if there were any family members or friends nearby who could donate blood. For the first time since she arrived at the hospital, Roberta stood up from the chair and made her way to a telephone down the hall. She was about to summon the cavalry. Help would soon be on the way.

It was 12:20 A.M., and inside the main auditorium at Tomlinson Hall, the Clarence Paige Orchestra was about to take the stage for the second set in the "Battle of the Bands" competition. A ticket taker in the lobby continued to usher a fair queue of late-night partygoers into the dance hall. Suddenly the lobby phone rang. A tired, distraught voice on the other end of the line asked to speak to Mr. William Rucker immediately.

Rucker had been sitting at a front table near the stage with other Gold and Glory Sweepstakes dignitaries, including financial backers, regional NAACP representatives, and state political candidates. All shared rounds of cigars and whisky and listened as Rucker began to speak of plans for the organization of several Gold and Glory clubs throughout the Midwest. Already under way was the incorporation of two new black motor sports leagues in Dayton, Ohio, and Louisville, Kentucky.

As Rucker continued to unveil his vision for the future of black auto racing, the headwaiter interrupted to notify him of an urgent phone call in the lobby. Rucker excused himself. He picked up the line and listened carefully to the quavering voice on the other end. He attempted to calm Roberta Wiggins, and then hung up the phone and went to work. He dashed to the front of the stage and made an announcement to the crowd: Charlie Wiggins, the Negro Speed King, was in critical condition and in desperate need of blood. Volunteer blood donors were needed at City Hospital right away.

Charlie's friend and chief rival Bobby Wallace still had a bandage on his head and a patch over one eye from his own injuries suffered in the same accident earlier that day. And yet the intrepid racing veteran was the first to leave the dance to help Charlie. He and several of his friends, including Gold and Glory promotion officer Cecil Powell and former driver Hugo Barnes, piled into Wallace's giant Stutz Bearcat and made their way to the hospital. Others who arrived at the emergency ward included black businessmen Amos Hartwell, Emmett Barnes, E. H. Alexander, Alfred Davis, and Elvis Ensley. Many white drivers, promoters, and fans also volunteered to help their hero. They included Joe Baker and Cecil Kerrico, as well as brothers Ed and Steve Baker, who had both spent time training in Charlie's garage.

What greeted them at the hospital was disturbing. Roberta, normally elegant and attractive, appeared gaunt and disheveled. Wearily she pointed to an intern, who ushered the men into a sterile area to be tested for blood compatibility. Those who were a match were escorted directly into the surgery area. A thin curtain separated each of the donors from the medical staff, who continued to work furiously on wounds to Charlie's right leg and right eye. Pools of blood stood at the base of the operating table. One witness noted that the mood in the room was "horribly tense."

As each exited the surgery room, he was greeted by Roberta, who asked for any word, any sign of progress. Most tried to reassure her, but the grim expressions on their faces no doubt gave away the truth of the matter. The loss of blood was most likely too great. Chances of survival were slim. "I had no more tears left to cry," Roberta remembered. "I felt my legs give out under me. Someone, I'm not sure who, must have caught me and put me back in the chair. They gave me a glass of water and a cold cloth for my head. But I just couldn't think straight. As far as I was concerned, life was over."

By 1:30 A.M. everyone had left except Bobby Wallace, Hugo Barnes, and Charlie's brother Lawrence. "Those drivers were a fraternity . . . very, very tight," Roberta remembered. All three decided to stay with Roberta until she finally heard word on Charlie's condition. They did not have to wait much longer. At 2:00 A.M., nearly ten hours after the wreck and after more than eight hours in surgery, the doctor emerged, soaked in sweat. He stood before Roberta Wiggins and delivered the news she had been waiting for all night long. Charlie would live. But the wreck had so severely damaged his right leg that it had had to be amputated. As well, a shard of metal had ripped through his right optic nerve. Charlie would no longer be able to see through that eye. The news of the loss of Charlie's leg and eye plunged Roberta into even greater despair. But the news that he would survive slightly buoyed her spirit and gave her a glimmer of hope for the long term.

"They finally allowed me to go see him" the following morning, Roberta recalled. "I held Charlie tight. He seldom cried, but that day, we sat holding each other, and we cried and cried. Racing meant so much to Charlie. And now we knew that his racing career was over." After more than a week of recovery, Roberta wheeled Charlie out of City Hospital in a battered wooden wheelchair. Several well-wishers were on hand to welcome him as he left the hospital. But the cheerful smile that normally greeted them was gone. In one horrible instant on September 20, 1936, Charlie Wiggins had been stripped of an important part of his identity. "Racing was his life," his niece Mildred Overton recalled. "And even though he bounced back to enjoy a successful life after the accident, I think there was always a part of him he felt was missing. Charlie, the man, may have survived, but Charlie, the 'Negro Speed King,' was dead."

Charlie spent almost a month at home recuperating. Then, with the same indomitable spirit and ceaseless perseverance that defined his character, he went back to work in his garage. He first fashioned a wooden leg for himself in his wood shop. He next carved a series of canes with different curvatures to allow him to lean into the bodies of a variety of car makes and models while standing. According to Roberta, Charlie had his shop back up and running at full capacity within six months of the accident.

Historian Richard Pierce commented, "Wiggins, without a doubt, was as hard as his racecars. I mean, what is it that makes a true hero? Is it the guy who hits the most home runs or runs the fastest laps? Or is it the guy who, with the faith of thousands riding on his shoulders, gets knocked flat on his back, then has the guts to get back up, dust himself off, and go back at it with supreme confidence in his abilities and in himself? If that's not Wiggins, I don't know who it is. Social obstacles, racial obstacles, and now physical obstacles. He's bound and determined that nothing—absolutely nothing—will slow him down. He was simply as hard as his racecars."

His racing career was over. But the accident in 1936 did little else to slow him down. For the next four decades, Charlie continued to work in his garage, repairing racecars and training new drivers and mechanics. Top racing teams at the Indianapolis Motor Speedway commonly used Charlie's special fuel mixtures and elements of his four-cylinder chassis design. His ideas for a more fuel-efficient engine system helped many drivers, both black and white, compete for top prizes in motor sports events throughout the country. On test tracks he continued to offer solid driving advice, and he mentored many successful young drivers during the Depression era, including five of the top ten Indy 500 drivers during the 1930s.

As well, Charlie encouraged Al Warren to study for his pilot's exam. Warren became one of the first licensed African-American pilots in Indiana. Charlie continued to cultivate the racing career of Sumner "Red" Oliver. Red competed on the outlaw circuit through the 1950s before becoming a racing mechanic. He eventually became the first African-American to be officially hired as a mechanic by the Indianapolis Motor Speedway when he joined George Bignotti, Jackie Howerton, and the Patrick Racing Team in 1973. Charles "Dynamite" Stewart, another of Charlie's protégés, also enjoyed a successful racing career on the outlaw circuit. He paved the way for African-American driver Joie Ray, who shattered the AAA color barrier in motor sports in 1946.

The news of Charlie's career-ending injury was a staggering blow to the Colored Speedway Association. In the midst of the Great Depression, without the black racing league's biggest drawing card, "Pres" Rucker and his fellow Negro racing executives knew it would be difficult to attract new spectators to the sport. Then, two weeks after Charlie's release from the hospital, the Association received more bad news.

Bobby Wallace, who had suffered a concussion in the accident, began to complain to family members of severe headaches and dizziness. Things seemed fuzzy to him. He struggled with bouts of sickness, depression, and double vision.

Clearly Wallace could not drive a racecar in such a condition. He returned to the doctor and asked to have further tests conducted. What the doctor found stunned Wallace and drove a knife through the heart of the Colored Speedway Association. Bobby had a skull fracture so severe that physicians demanded he be admitted at once to the hospital. Somehow, in the hubbub of the race tragedy, the severity of his injury had slipped past doctors without detection. Emergency surgery was needed to his right front brow. A metal plate was screwed into his skull to prevent further cracking. Wallace had been unknowingly close to death. Any sudden complications might have resulted in a massive brain hemorrhage. Doctors told Wallace he was lucky to be alive. They also informed him that his racing career was over.

Within two weeks the Colored Speedway Association had lost its top two drivers: first Charlie and then Wallace. The circuit was in the midst of promoting its new organizations in Dayton, Ohio, and Louisville, Kentucky. They had planned a premiere racing event in Dayton in the spring of 1937. But "Pres" Rucker and other officials in Indianapolis knew that a league without heroes like Charlie and Wallace would be a tough sell to African-American families on a tight budget. Rucker had helped stage two final races at the end of the 1936 season that only attracted eight hundred spectators in total. The organization could not cover its current expenses. Certainly it could not afford to launch new racing leagues in Dayton and Louisville. Late in October 1936 Rucker postponed the Dayton debut indefinitely. There was no mention of a launch in Louisville at all. One month later the organization was bankrupt. The Indiana Avenue offices of the Colored Speedway Association closed for the last time in November 1936.

"It was the end of an era," Rucker's grandson, Paul Bateman, reflected. "My grandfather had always dreamed of creating a league that would eventually allow African Americans to compete at the Indianapolis 500. Who knows what might have happened had the financial times not been what they were. We might have had a situation like baseball's Negro Leagues. Black athletes might have been able to enter the sport en masse and had a tremendous impact on auto racing. They were so close. They were ten years too early. They just missed their time."

For twelve years the Colored Speedway Association had survived immense social and racial pressures to create new opportunities for African Americans in the realm of sports. Only during the worst economic times in the nation's history did the organization finally buckle and collapse. Still, the Gold and Glory Sweepstakes and other top African-American auto races represented an opportunity for blacks to excel in motor sports and stake their claim to an important part of America's social history. "It was a part of the cultural renaissance of the era," historian Joe Freeman noted. "Racing was an important part of 1920s and '30s culture in America. The Gold and Glory Sweepstakes was black America's way of participating in that cultural phenomenon. The fact that black drivers and mechanics accomplished this amid great social unrest, yet still earned the respect of their white brethren in the world of motor sports, says a great deal about these men as mechanics, as drivers, and as human beings. Their names may be forgotten today, but their accomplishments were truly heroic."

"When you understand that this is not a story about auto racing, then you truly understand the story of the Gold and Glory Sweepstakes," historian Richard Pierce summarized. "It's the story of men who were on a stage—a social stage—chasing their dreams under the harsh glow of the spotlight. Watching them was a black community that looked to them as trailblazers. To them, these guys were their representatives—the best and brightest in their community. Also watching them was a divided white community. Some whites wanted them to succeed and supported them in their efforts. Others only wished for their failure and even plotted their demise. When you combine all of these factors in a setting that included a black social renaissance, the rise of intense racial segregation, and the economic pressures of the Great Depression, you have an incredibly complex and dynamic set of social phenomena that make this racing event highly significant and powerful."

Al Warren reflected, "People said we were heroes. I never really thought it was that big a deal. We just loved racing, and we'd do practically anything to chase our dreams. That's really all there was to it. Yeah, we had to face some tough times. But we had a lot of good people helping us, too. I guess if you love something enough and believe in it enough, you're willing to take the risks. We just wanted to be racecar drivers. That was our goal. We believed in it, and we did it."

Before Jackie Robinson, before Joe Louis, before Jesse Owens, the men of the Gold and Glory Sweepstakes won much more than trophies and prize money. They garnered respect and achieved an initial victory in the fight for civil rights. Historian Boniface Hardin commented, "The Gold and Glory Sweepstakes was a significant social event, and it was a great honor to be a part of it. In that day and age, the people who won these races were truly heroes in our community. That's why their story is one that represents courage and one that celebrates the best of the human spirit."

Epilogue

These Men of Grease and Grit

In March 1975, *Indianapolis News* reporter Reginald Bishop paid a visit to a large two-story house on Indianapolis Avenue on the city's near west side. He had heard remarkable stories about the man who lived in the house—a man many old-timers in the black district called the greatest colored racer in the history of motor sports. The man who greeted Bishop that day hardly appeared to be a rugged sports icon of the early twentieth century. He was a quiet, slightly built seventy-seven-year-old man with a glass eye and a wooden leg. He hobbled to the door and stepped onto the porch. As he shook Bishop's hand, he flashed a broad smile, which was the only thing that resembled the photos Bishop had seen of the man during his heyday in the 1920s. "I'm glad you're here," he stated in a friendly voice. "My name is Charlie Wiggins."

For the next three hours, Bishop sat mesmerized as the slender, soft-spoken man wove one rich, colorful story after another: bootleggers, the Ku Klux Klan, "Charlie's Gang," John Dillinger, fast cars, and the accident that nearly cost him his life. Throughout the afternoon, Charlie painted a vivid portrait of a full, rich life that, over the course of the past fifty years, had faded into obscurity. Bishop left Charlie's home with a newfound appreciation for the former Indianapolis mechanic. "Charles Wiggins, 77, is a special person—a rare breed," Bishop wrote on March 21. "Being black and in the automobile business 50 years ago was not easy, but after listening to Wiggins, one gets the impression one never loses his love of the sport."[1]

Bishop was one of only two journalists to have the opportunity and forethought to record a firsthand account of Charlie Wiggins's story. The other writer to chronicle Charlie's life was not a newspaperman, but rather a family friend, Boniface Hardin. A Benedictine priest and local historian, Hardin spent much of the 1970s documenting various aspects of Indianapolis's African-American heritage as editor of *The Afro-American Journal*. In 1975 Hardin spent three weeks chronicling the adventures of Charlie Wiggins and other drivers associated with the Gold and Glory Sweepstakes. He remembered his frequent encounters with Charlie and Roberta: "When you sat in their presence, you felt the glow from both of them. You had this constant sense that it wasn't just Charlie out there experiencing all these things. Roberta was very much a part of her husband's accomplishments. . . . They were a proud couple that had been through a lot together. They were weathered and tough, a picture of quiet strength."

Hardin published a six-page article in his magazine that celebrated the accomplishments of Charlie Wiggins and the other drivers and promoters of the Gold and Glory Sweepstakes.[2] He later became the president of Martin University in Indianapolis. In addition to his re-sponsibilities as a university official, he continues to crusade for the preservation of African-American history in the region. The story of Charlie Wiggins and the Gold and Glory Sweepstakes is one of his favorite examples of a lost heritage in America's black culture. "Charlie was extraordinary, because he did not allow the social conventions of the day to limit him or define him in any way. That is a significant state-ment, considering the segregationist attitudes that encompassed mid-western cultural life at the time when Charlie practiced and perfected his craft. He was smart, and he was tough. Auto racing was his way of claiming his own identity. The social forces of the day wanted to take that identity away from him, but his personal will and his exceptional

The loss of his right leg ended Charlie Wiggins's racing career. Pictured here with a wooden leg he fashioned himself on a lathe in his workshop, Charlie continued to fight for racial equality in motor sports until his death in March 1979. Courtesy Mrs. Mildred Overton

skills allowed him to hold his ground and create new opportunities for himself and others."

Hardin continued, "The road to social equality—the road to *true* civil rights—was and is a long and winding one. We have traveled down that road one small step at a time. At the turn of the century, Paul Laurence Dunbar led the way with his poetry. Madam Walker guided us with her leadership in the boardroom. Rosa Parks did it on the bus. And Charlie Wiggins did it on a racetrack. In an auto racing town like Indianapolis, Wiggins found a way to win a war for social justice that had a far-reaching impact on the city and on motor sports across the country during the era. It was not only *his* victory, but a victory for *all* who valued social justice in America."

Charlie continued to work as a mechanic and trainer for racecar drivers until his death in March 1979 at the age of eighty-one. Roberta passed away in 1998. Until the day of his death, Charlie crusaded for increased rights for African Americans in auto racing. Throughout his life, he was plagued by recurring illnesses brought on by infections in his wounded leg. Mounting medical costs left Charlie and Roberta nearly penniless at the time of his death. They were buried in unmarked graves at Crown Hill Cemetery in Indianapolis.

In July 1926 Frank A. "Fay" Young, the colorful writer and sports editor for the *Chicago Defender,* pondered the legacy of Charlie and other African-American drivers, mechanics, and promoters in a special editorial titled "Racing for Gold and Glory." He wrote, "Of what will younger generations speak when they talk of the accomplishments of these great colored racers? Will it be that with heart and heavy foot, they might become the fastest in the land? Or will it be that they did something far greater? For these men of grease and grit are a celebration of all that is grand for our Race. Let us hope that our children speak of the latter. For it is in this moment that we have achieved true greatness."[3]

The legacy that remains of Charlie Wiggins and the Gold and Glory Sweepstakes is faint, like a last ray of golden sunlight that lingers on the horizon after a brilliant sunset. Almost seventy years after the last running of the annual Colored Speedway Association event, all but a few of the surviving drivers and mechanics of the time remembered encounters with men such as Charlie Wiggins, Bobby Wallace, and Sumner "Red" Oliver. The lasting economic turbulence of the 1930s prevented racing officials in the African-American community from cultivating a new breed of drivers who could help push for integration in the years immediately following World War II, when athletes like Jackie Robinson were making such incredible social and cultural inroads in the world of sports.

"Auto racing was an expensive sport then, just as it is today," motor

Chicago Defender journalist Frank A. "Fay" Young once called Charlie
Wiggins and all drivers of the Gold and Glory Sweepstakes "men of
grease and grit" who represented "all that is grand for our Race."
Courtesy Mrs. Mildred Overton

sports historian Joe Freeman reflected. "Most people did not have the
opportunity to hop behind the wheel of a top-notch racecar and get the
training needed to compete on a speedway circuit. The Great Depression caused the sport to fizzle out, especially on the black circuit. After
the war, when time and money were being filtered back into the sport
again, there was no new crop of black drivers ready to take over the reins
of the organization and compete nationally. . . . By 1947 baseball was
integrated. Other sports followed suit. But African Americans now
lacked the overall resources they once had to make a powerful impact on
the sport. The drivers and mechanics of the Gold and Glory Sweepstakes represented the pinnacle of black auto racing. Unfortunately they
were ten years ahead of their time."

The social influence of this unfortunate economic heritage could be felt for decades to come. For almost seventy years after the final running of the Gold and Glory Sweepstakes, very few African-American drivers and mechanics trained and competed in organized auto racing events around the world. In the year 2000 officials from the Indy Racing League, the Championship Auto Racing Teams (CART), and NASCAR announced increased efforts to improve financial resources and training for young African-American drivers and mechanics who wished to enter the auto racing industry. But in a sport that continues to require multimillion-dollar sponsorships in order to succeed, the road to social justice remains, as Boniface Hardin put it, "long and winding."

However, Joe Freeman believes that this situation in no way lessens the historical significance of the Gold and Glory Sweepstakes. "It represented a cultural renaissance that was an important part of black culture

Charlie's legacy finally reached the hallowed Brickyard of the Indianapolis Motor Speedway when, in 1973, Sumner "Red" Oliver, one of his protégés, joined the Patrick Racing Team as the first African-American mechanic in Indy 500 history. Courtesy Mrs. Mildred Overton

during the 1920s and '30s. The Gold and Glory Sweepstakes was Indianapolis's contribution to this national celebration of black pride. . . . Charlie Wiggins, in particular, really did break some ground. The fact that he was well known and visited by important drivers and mechanics, both black and white, meant that he made, in his own way, an important and dignified statement of integrity about the black population and its place within auto racing and in society as a whole."

Historian Richard Pierce reflected, "Charlie was more than a driver, more than a mechanic. He was an icon. He represented victory for all African Americans in our community. He was the best that we could be, just like Joe Louis or Jackie Robinson was the best that we could be. It was a time when heroes were desperately needed in the black community. And Charlie was a hero."

Appendix: Gold & Glory Sweepstakes Participants

There are no surviving official racing records documenting the drivers and cars registered in the Gold and Glory Sweepstakes during its run from 1924 through 1936. The best records available are found in microfilm copies of three leading African-American newspapers: the *Indianapolis Freeman,* the *Chicago Defender,* and the *Indianapolis Record-er.* Information from these three publications was syndicated and distributed to other leading black newspapers throughout the country. The following list of drivers, cars, and racing details is taken primarily from these sources. In some cases, little is known of the results of the race, other than the name of the winning driver and the model of his car.

August 2, 1924—Indiana State Fairgrounds, Indianapolis, Indiana

Winner: Malcolm Hannon—Barber-Warnock Ford Special—Avg. Speed = 63.5 mph
Second place: John Simmons—Fronty Ford

Entrant	City	Car (Type)
Hugo Barnes	Indianapolis, IN	R. and B. Special (4-cylinder)
Oscar Black	Indianapolis, IN	Fronty Ford (4-cylinder)
William Buckner	Indianapolis, IN	Duesenberg Special (4-cylinder)
Ben Carter	Indianapolis, IN	Sneider Special
Lawrence Dawson	Indianapolis, IN	Fronty Ford (4-cylinder)
William Edwards	Indianapolis, IN	Fleming Special (4-cylinder)
William Green	Indianapolis, IN	Buick-Green Special (4-cylinder)
Malcolm Hannon	Indianapolis, IN	Barber-Warnock Ford (4-cylinder)
Charles Hill	Kokomo, IN	Fronty Ford (4-cylinder)

Entrant	City	Car (Type)
William Hyde	Indianapolis, IN	B. and E. Special (4-cylinder)
Clifford Jackson	Chicago, IL	Dover Special (4-cylinder)
Oscar Jackson	Indianapolis, IN	Overland Special (4-cylinder)
Jessie James	Indianapolis, IN	Fronty Ford (4-cylinder)
Bill James	Indianapolis, IN	Woodnut Special (4-cylinder)
Bill Jeffries	Chicago, IL	Fronty Ford (4-cylinder)
George E. Jones	Indianapolis, IN	Huff Special (4-cylinder)
Luke Lewis	Indianapolis, IN	Lewis Special (4-cylinder)
George McMillen	Indianapolis, IN	Chevrolet Special (4-cylinder)
"Cowboy" Moore	Chicago, IL	Dreamland Duesenberg Special (4-cylinder)
Herbert A. Pipes	Indianapolis, IN	Fronty Ford (4-cylinder)
A. J. Russell	Chicago, IL	Rajo Special (4-cylinder)
Jack Sargent	St. Louis, MO	Shield Special (6-cylinder)
John Simmons	Indianapolis, IN	Fronty Ford (4-cylinder)
William Smith	Indianapolis, IN	J. and H. Special (6-cylinder)
William Walthall	Chicago, IL	Marmon Defender Special (6-cylinder)
Eustice Williams	Indianapolis, IN	R. and B. Special (4-cylinder)
Mason Williams	Indianapolis, IN	"Partner" Duesenberg (4-cylinder)
Charles Woods	Indianapolis, IN	Ghost Special (4-cylinder)

August 8, 1925—Indiana State Fairgrounds, Indianapolis, Indiana

Winner: Bobby Wallace—"Trey of Hearts" Special—Avg. Speed = 64.9 mph
Second place: Bill Carson—Lyons Special

Entrant	City	Car (Type)
Hugo Barnes	Indianapolis, IN	R. and B. Special

Entrant	City	Car (Type)
Louis Bennett	Indianapolis, IN	Erich Special
Ulysses Brents	Indianapolis, IN	S. and B. Special
William Buckner	Indianapolis, IN	Canadian (Duesenberg) Special
F. A. Buford	Chicago, IL	Rajo Special
Bill Carson	Chicago, IL	Lyons Special
William Greene	Indianapolis, IN	McLean Duesenberg Special
Malcolm Hannon	Indianapolis, IN	Fronty Ford
Charles Harper	Chicago, IL	Harper Special
Bill Jeffries	Chicago, IL	Fronty Ford
Joe Lewis	Columbus, OH	Chevrolet Special
Richard Perkins	North Manchester, IN	Fronty Ford
Jack Sargent	St. Louis, MO	Fronty Ford
John Simmons	Indianapolis, IN	Schneider Special
Ernest Stevens	Chicago, IL	La Resta Special
W. H. Valentine	Indianapolis, IN	"Partner" Duesenberg Special
Bobby Wallace	Indianapolis, IN	"Trey of Hearts" Special
"Doc" White	Keokuk, IA	Buick Special
Charlie Wiggins	Indianapolis, IN	Wiggins Special
W. W. Woods	North Manchester, IN	Foster Special

August 7, 1926—Indiana State Fairgrounds, Indianapolis, Indiana

Winner: Charlie Wiggins—Wiggins Special—Avg. Speed = 66.7 mph
Second place: Ben Carter—Fronty Ford

Entrant	City	Car (Type)
Barney Anderson	Detroit, MI	S. and A. Special
Hugo Barnes	Indianapolis, IN	Butcher Special
Bill Bottoms	Chicago, IL	Frontenac Special
William Buckner	Indianapolis, IN	Buckner (Duesenberg) Special
Sam Buford	Chicago, IL	Fronty Ford
Bill Carson	Chicago, IL	Boyle Valve Special
Ben Carter	Indianapolis, IN	Fronty Ford
Lawrence Dawson	Indianapolis, IN	Fronty Ford
Eddie Dice	Chicago, IL	Fronty Ford
Russell Garrett	Boston, MA	Garrett Special

Entrant	City	Car (Type)
Malcolm Hannon	Indianapolis, IN	Bowers Special
Bill Jeffries	Chicago, IL	Fronty Ford
Bill Johnson	Chicago, IL	Frontenac
George Palmer	Columbus, OH	Hudson Special
Robert Porter	New York City, NY	Hoff Special
Ernie Stevens	Chicago, IL	Stevens Special
W. H. Valentine	Indianapolis, IN	"Partner" Duesenberg Special
Bobby Wallace	Indianapolis, IN	Fronty Ford
Doc White	Keokuk, IA	Buick Special
Charlie Wiggins	Indianapolis, IN	Wiggins Special
W. W. Woods	North Manchester, IN	Foster Special

July 4, 1927—Indiana State Fairgrounds, Indianapolis, Indiana

Winner: Bill James—Graham Fronty Ford Special—Avg. Speed = 56.72 mph
Second place: Bill Jeffries—Fronty Ford

Entrant	City	Car (Type)
Bill Carson	Chicago, IL	Lyons Special
W. C. Green	Indianapolis, IN	Fronty Ford
Eddie Grice	Dallas, TX	Fronty Ford
Malcolm Hannon	Indianapolis, IN	Hannon Special
William Hannon	Chicago, IL	Fronty Ford
Bill James	Indianapolis, IN	Graham Fronty Ford Special
Bill Jeffries	Chicago, IL	Fronty Ford
Rodney Morris	Washington Court House, OH	Morris Special
Brooks Patterson	Indianapolis, IN	Fronty Ford
Gene Smith	Chicago, IL	Boyle Valve Special
Bobby Wallace	Indianapolis, IN	Chevrolet Special
"Toots" Washington	Pittsburgh, PA	Schofield Special
Ben West	Indianapolis, IN	West Special
Doc White	Keokuk, IA	Challenge Special
Charlie Wiggins	Indianapolis, IN	Wiggins Special

July 4, 1928—Indiana State Fairgrounds, Indianapolis, Indiana

Winner: Bill Jeffries—Fronty Ford
Second place: Rodney Morris—M & M Special

Entrant	City	Car (Type)
Sherman Bland	Indianapolis, IN	Ford Special
"Bugger" Burns	Washington Court House, OH	Fronty Ford
Carl Burnside	Tulsa, OK	Tulsa Special
Carl Foster	Chicago, IL	Foster Special
Wilbur Gaines	Chicago, IL	Boyle Valve Ford Special
Bob Green	Indianapolis, IN	Green Streak
Malcolm Hannon	Indianapolis, IN	Hannon Special
Bill James	Indianapolis, IN	Graham Special
Bill Jeffries	Chicago, IL	Fronty Ford
Johnny Jordan	Chicago, IL	Fronty Ford
Rodney Morris	Washington Court House, OH	M & M Special
Martin Rhodes	Indianapolis, IN	Rhodes Racing Special
Clarence Schofield	Chicago, IL	Schofield Special
Gene Smith	Chicago, IL	Boyle Valve Special
Tim Strothers	Indianapolis, IN	Whippet Special
Harry Taylor	Indianapolis, IN	Triumph 4 Special
Bobby Wallace	Indianapolis, IN	M. B. Special
Norman Washington	Indianapolis, IN	Washington 4 Special
"Toots" Washington	Pittsburgh, PA	P. C. Special
Doc White	Keokuk, IA	Challenge Special
Charlie Wiggins	Indianapolis, IN	Wiggins Super Special
James Williams	Chicago, IL	Mystery 4 Special

July 4, 1929—Indiana State Fairgrounds, Indianapolis, Indiana

Winner: Barney Anderson—Model A Ford—Avg. Speed = 67.22 mph
Second place: Charlie Wiggins—Wiggins Special

Entrant	City	Car (Type)
Barney Anderson	Detroit, MI	Model A Ford
Garland Brooks	Terre Haute, IN	Miss Terre Haute Special
"Bugger" Burns	Washington Court House, OH	Rajo Ford Special

Entrant	City	Car (Type)
Bill Carson	Chicago, IL	Essex Special
Lawrence Dawson	Indianapolis, IN	Duesenberg
Wilbur Gaines	Chicago, IL	Frontenac
Ed Grice*	Dallas, TX	Fronty Ford
Charles Hill	Windfall, IN	Goodyear Special
Bill James	Indianapolis, IN	Graham Special
Bill Jeffries	Chicago, IL	Fronty Ford
D. Montague	Detroit, MI	Spencer Special B.V.S.
Rodney Morris	Washington Court House, OH	Rajo Special
Brooks Patterson	Indianapolis, IN	Fronty Ford
H. Robertson	Terre Haute, IN	Frontenac
W. Russ	Philadelphia, PA	Russ Special
Jack "Long Shot" Sargent	St. Louis, MO	*Indianapolis Recorder* Special
Billy Schaffer	Chicago, IL	Duesenberg Special
Gene Smith	Chicago, IL	Elgin Piston Pin Special
M. Threlkeld	Chicago, IL	Fronty Ford
Bobby Wallace	Indianapolis, IN	Chevrolet Special
William Walthall	Chicago, IL	Walthall Special
"Toots" Washington	Pittsburgh, PA	Clearing House Special
Charlie Wiggins	Indianapolis, IN	Wiggins Special
Lawrence Wiggins	Indianapolis, IN	Gilley Special

* Ed Grice was killed in an accident in lap 27. He was the only fatality ever listed in the Gold and Glory Sweepstakes.

July 4, 1930—Indiana State Fairgrounds, Indianapolis, Indiana

Winner: Gene Smith—Boyle Valve Special—Avg. Speed = 60.0 mph
Second place: Hugo Barnes—Graham Special

Entrant	City	Car (Type)
Barney Anderson	Detroit, MI	Model A Ford
Roy Artist	Indianapolis, IN	Schofield Special
Hugo Barnes	Indianapolis, IN	Graham Special
William Blackman	Chicago, IL	Duesenberg Special
Garland Brooks	Terre Haute, IN	Fronty Ford
"Bugger" Burns	Washington Court House, OH	Ford Special

Entrant	City	Car (Type)
Bill Carson	Chicago, IL	Fronty Ford
Bill Cunningham	Chicago, IL	Fronty Ford
Spencer Freeman	Detroit, MI	Duesenberg
Wilbur Gaines	Chicago, IL	Frontenac
Bill James	Indianapolis, IN	Graham Special
Bill Jeffries	Chicago, IL	Fronty Ford
Rodney Morris	Washington Court House, OH	Rajo Special
Harvey Robinson	Terre Haute, IN	Fronty Ford
Jack "Long Shot" Sargent	St. Louis, MO	Fronty Ford
Gene Smith	Chicago, IL	Boyle Valve Special
Dave Terry	Detroit, MI	Roof Special
Bobby Wallace	Indianapolis, IN	Chevrolet Special
William Walthall	Chicago, IL	Walthall Special
"Toots" Washington	Pittsburgh, PA	Clearing House Special
Doc White	Keokuk, IA	Buick Special
Charlie Wiggins	Indianapolis, IN	Wiggins Special

July 4, 1931—Walnut Gardens Speedway, Mooresville, Indiana

Walnut Gardens Speedway owner Harry Earl, one of the original financiers of the Colored Speedway Association, hosted the Gold and Glory Sweepstakes in 1931 when the cost of renting the Indiana State Fairgrounds's one-mile track became too high during the Great Depression. Earl charged the CSA only one dollar to rent the speedway for the day. The 1931 race was shortened from one hundred miles to fifty miles. Only a partial list of drivers was given in the press, but the *Indianapolis Recorder* reported that competitors from an eight-state region were entered in the race.

Charlie Wiggins, driving his famed Wiggins Special, captured the Gold and Glory championship with an average speed of 58.2 miles per hour. Bobby Wallace finished in second place. In addition to the known drivers listed below, seventeen others competed in the race, according to the *Chicago Defender*.

Entrant	City	Car (Type)
Barney Anderson	Detroit, MI	Frontenac
William Buckner	Indianapolis, IN	Snortin' Special
Bill Carson	Chicago, IL	Fronty Ford
Wilbur Gaines	Chicago, IL	Frontenac
Bill Jeffries	Chicago, IL	Fronty Ford
Johnnie Jordan	Fort Wayne, IN	Fronty Ford
Gene Smith	Chicago, IL	Boyle Valve Special
Bobby Wallace	Indianapolis, IN	Chevrolet Special
Charlie Wiggins	Indianapolis, IN	Wiggins Special
Lawrence Wiggins	Indianapolis, IN	Fronty Ford Special
Bob Wilcox	Fort Wayne, IN	Duesenberg

September 24, 1932—Indiana State Fairgrounds, Indianapolis, Indiana

The Gold and Glory Sweepstakes returned to the Fairgrounds track in 1932. It was the height of the Great Depression, and only six hundred spectators were willing to pay the relatively steep admission price of two dollars per person. With so few paying customers, the promoters could not afford to offer drivers the promised purse of $2,000. Several irate drivers began to shout and even threaten the promoters. A shoving match ensued. The small gathering of fans booed loudly.

Several drivers, including Charlie Wiggins and Bobby Wallace, attempted to restore order to the scene. More than ninety minutes after the race was scheduled to begin, the drivers and promoters came to an agreement. They would hold an abbreviated match, a twenty-mile "winner-take-all" competition. Charlie Wiggins, who attained a remarkable 80.4 miles per hour in the preliminary heats to capture the pole position, defended his Gold and Glory title by holding off Bobby Wallace by four car lengths. Charlie's winning time was 17:05, or about 70.2 miles per hour.

Entrant	City	Car (Type)
Hudson Andrews	Akron, OH	Schofield Special
Roy Artist	Indianapolis, IN	Artist Special
Roger Bailey	Indianapolis, IN	Fronty Ford
Hugo Barnes	Chicago, IL	Strumil Special

Entrant	City	Car (Type)
William Blackman	Chicago, IL	All Parts Special
D. A. Brooks	Terre Haute, IN	Fronty Ford
William Buckner	Indianapolis, IN	Fronty Ford
S. A. Buford	Coal City, IL	*unknown*
Paul Butler	Indianapolis, IN	Fronty Ford
Bill Carson	Chicago, IL	Strumil Special
Gill Cunningham	Chicago, IL	Cunningham Special
Lawrence Dawson	Indianapolis, IN	Fronty Ford
Grant DeHaven	Los Angeles, CA	*unknown*
J. C. Douglass	Columbus, OH	Rajo Special
Andrew Ford	Indianapolis, IN	Chevrolet
Hollis Ford	Indianapolis, IN	Chevrolet
Malcolm Hannon	New York City, NY	Graham Special
Bill Jeffries	Chicago, IL	Strumil Special
Johnnie Jordan	Fort Wayne, IN	Fronty Ford
Thomas Norman	Indianapolis, IN	Norman Special
Bernard Reed	Richmond, IN	*unknown*
Henry Rogers	Indianapolis, IN	Duesenberg
Gene Smith	Chicago, IL	Strumil Special
Bobby Wallace	Indianapolis, IN	Fronty Ford
William Walthall	Chicago, IL	Walthall Special
Charlie Wiggins	Indianapolis, IN	Wiggins Special
Lawrence Wiggins	Indianapolis, IN	Fronty Ford

August 21, 1933—Walnut Gardens Speedway, Mooresville, Indiana

With the country struggling through the economic turbulence of the Great Depression, most auto racing events throughout the country were suspended. Again this year, the Colored Speedway Association could not afford to rent the Indiana State Fairgrounds facilities. But once again the Association received some unexpected help from old friend and racing financier Harry Earl, proprietor of the Walnut Gardens Speedway in Mooresville, Indiana, twelve miles southwest of downtown Indianapolis. Earl again offered to rent his speedway to the Gold and Glory organizers for one dollar in exchange for his standard percentage of the gate receipts.

The Elks Club was holding its thirty-fourth annual convention in Indianapolis that year. The group agreed to be the sponsor of the Negro racing spectacle, which was dubbed the Elks Gasoline Derby. Twenty-six drivers entered their speedsters for the event. Governor Paul V. McNutt was on hand to greet both members of the national Elks organization and members of the National Association for the Advancement of Colored People.

Charlie Wiggins captured black auto racing's top prize for the third consecutive year, edging out his own brother, Lawrence, who placed second, and Cleveland driver Homer Cloud, who earned third-place honors. Charlie started the race in last place, having arrived late and missed the primary qualification heats. In the race, Charlie received a five-lap penalty for inadvertently ignoring a yellow caution flag. Remarkably, he made up his five-lap deficit to capture the championship prize.

Entrant	City	Car (Type)
Barney Anderson	Detroit, MI	Frontenac
Hugo Barnes	Chicago, IL	Fronty Ford
Bill Blackman	Chicago, IL	Nickels Special
Bill Buckner	Windsor, Canada	Fronty Ford
George Cilek	Chicago, IL	Ford
Homer Cloud	Cleveland, OH	Fronty Ford
Gill Cunningham	Chicago, IL	Rajo Special
Paul Davis	Chicago, IL	Ford-Miller Special
Spencer Freeman	Detroit, MI	Freeman Special
Wilbur Gaines	Chicago, IL	H-2 Special
Malcolm Hannon	New York City, NY	Graham Special
Clifford Jackson	Chicago, IL	Jackson Special
Bill James	Indianapolis, IN	*unknown*
Bill Jeffries	Chicago, IL	Fronty Ford
Rufus Jones, Jr.	Cleveland, OH	Chevrolet Special
Walter Jones	Cleveland, OH	*unknown*
Johnnie Jordan	Fort Wayne, IN	*unknown*
Robert LaSallica	Chicago, IL	McBride Special
Sumner "Red" Oliver	Dayton, OH	Fronty Ford
Jack "Long Shot" Sargent	St. Louis, MO	Fronty Ford
Bobby Wallace	Indianapolis, IN	Chevrolet
William Walthall	Chicago, IL	Walthall Special
"Toots" Washington	Pittsburgh, PA	*unknown*
Charlie Wiggins	Indianapolis, IN	Wiggins Special
Lawrence Wiggins	Indianapolis, IN	Model A Ford
Fred Wilson	Detroit, MI	Ford

July 4, 1935—Indiana State Fairgrounds, Indianapolis, Indiana

The Gold and Glory Sweepstakes was not held in 1934. In 1935, a promotional team from Dayton, Ohio, took over its organization. They trumpeted aerial stunt shows, fireworks, and an all-day band concert surrounding the race, which again was to be held on July 4. The race was never held, however. According to many reports, the promoters slipped out of town during the air show, taking with them thousands of dollars in gate receipts. There was no purse for the drivers. Most of the competitors refused to go ahead with the race, choosing not to risk their lives without the opportunity to win prize money.

Some eyewitness accounts noted that members of the crowd "passed the hat" to collect a small purse to offer the winner, if the drivers chose to race. Some witnesses remembered an abbreviated racing event being run that day. There is no record of a race being held, or any documentation of a winner.

Entrant	City	Car (Type)
Roy L. Artist	Indianapolis, IN	Chevrolet
Don Bailey	*unknown*	Triumph 4
Bill Blackman	Chicago, IL	Blackman Special
S. A. Buford	Coal City, IL	Ford Special
Homer Cloud	Cleveland, OH	Riely Special
William Cutshaw	*unknown*	Schofield Special
Paul Davis	Chicago, IL	Devil Special
Hollis Ford	Indianapolis, IN	Frontenac Special
Wilbur Gaines	Chicago, IL	Riely Special
Curt Gilbreath	Chicago, IL	Boyle Valve Special
Sam Jones	Indianapolis, IN	Graham Special
Charles Meredith	Tulsa, OK	Tulsa Special
"Squeaky" Mills	Indianapolis, IN	M & M Special
Andy Pryor	Indianapolis, IN	Hal Special
Paul Richmond	Indianapolis, IN	Rajo Special
Charles Stewart	Indianapolis, IN	Miller Schofield
John Tanner	Indianapolis, IN	Green Streak
Bill Valentine	*unknown*	Roof Special
Bobby Wallace	Indianapolis, IN	Fronty Ford
William Walthall	Chicago, IL	Ansted Special
Louis Weaver	Indianapolis, IN	Washington Special
Charlie Wiggins	Indianapolis, IN	Wiggins Special
Lawrence Wiggins	Indianapolis, IN	Fronty Ford

September 20, 1936—Indiana State Fairgrounds, Indianapolis, Indiana

A thirteen-car pileup marred the 1936 running of the Gold and Glory Sweepstakes, injuring several drivers and threatening the life of racing great Charlie Wiggins. The accident occurred on the fourth turn of the second lap of the race. The event, scheduled for a hundred miles, had been shortened to fifty, due to a delay caused by a controversy over the admission of a midget car into the field, as well as another to allow paramedics to rescue drivers wounded at the crash scene. Chicago's Bill Carson, aboard a Boyle Valve Special, won the abbreviated event at an average speed of 57.69 miles per hour. Sumner "Red" Oliver was awarded second-place honors.

Entrant	City	Car (Type)
Hudson Andrews	Indianapolis, IN	R & R V-8 Special
Garland Brooks	Terre Haute, IN	Black Tom Special
Percy Brown	Indianapolis, IN	Fronty Ford Special
Bill Carson	Chicago, IL	Boyle Valve Special
Hollis Ford	Indianapolis, IN	Dreyer Special
Spencer Freeman	Detroit, MI	Freeman Special
Wilbur Gaines	Chicago, IL	Ford Special
Ed Hill	Kokomo, IN	Fountain Cooney Special
Bill James	Indianapolis, IN	Stewart Radio Special
Robert LaSallica	Cleveland, OH	Barr Special
Sumner "Red" Oliver	Dayton, OH	Studebaker Special
Leonard Powell	Chicago, IL	Schropp Special
Andy Pryor	Indianapolis, IN	Ob Special
Paul Richmond	Indianapolis, IN	Rajo Special
Henry Rogers	Indianapolis, IN	R & W Special
Charles Stewart	Indianapolis, IN	Schofield Special
Frank Toy	Cleveland, OH	Hal Special
Fred Toy	Paoma, OH	Hal Special
"Klondike" Tucker	Chicago, IL	*unknown*
Bobby Wallace	Indianapolis, IN	Dreyer Special
Johnny Wand	Indianapolis, IN	Fronty Ford
Leon "Al" Warren	Indianapolis, IN	DeSoto 6 Special
Nolan Webb	Indianapolis, IN	Fronty Ford Special
Charlie Wiggins	Indianapolis, IN	Roof Wiggins Special
Fred Wilson	Detroit, MI	Hal Special
Herb Woods	Detroit, MI	Miller Schofield Special

Notes

1. The Adventurer

1. Frank A. Young, "Fay Says," *Chicago Defender,* July 5, 1924, p. 11.

2. Emma Lou Thornbrough, *Indiana Blacks in the Twentieth Century* (Bloomington: Indiana University Press, 2000), p. 7.

3. Ibid., p. 3.

4. Quoted from "Lyles Station," a televised documentary segment featured on *Across Indiana,* WFYI-TV, Indianapolis, Ind., February 1996, written and produced by Todd Gould.

5. Ronald L. Baker, *Homeless, Friendless, and Penniless: The WPA Interviews with Former Slaves Living in Indiana* (Bloomington: Indiana University Press, 2000), pp. 60–64.

6. John E. Iglehart, *History of Indiana from Its Exploration to 1922,* vol. 3: *An Account of Vanderburgh County from Its Organization* (Dayton, Ohio: Dayton Historical Publishing Company, 1923), p. 542.

7. Boniface Hardin, "The Gold and Glory Sweepstakes," *The Afro-American Journal* 3, no. 3 (May–June 1975), p. 3.

8. Ibid.

9. Ibid., p. 4.

10. Darrel E. Bigham, *We Ask Only a Fair Trial: A History of the Black Community of Evansville, Indiana* (Bloomington: Indiana University Press, 1987), p. 111.

11. Ibid., pp. 120–121.

12. Ibid., p. 122.

13. "Full House at Coliseum for Klan's Meeting," *The Evansville Courier,* June 10, 1922, p. 1.

14. James H. Madison, *The Indiana Way: A State History* (Bloomington: Indiana University Press, 1986), pp. 290–291.

15. M. William Lutholtz, *Grand Dragon: D. C. Stephenson and the Ku Klux Klan in Indiana* (West Lafayette, Ind.: Purdue University Press, 1991), p. 24.

2. The Dawn of a New Opportunity

1. "City of Progress," *Indianapolis Star,* February 7, 1999, Section D, p. 6.

2. "Commander Sullinger Returns from Tour of Midwest Cities," *New York Age,* September 12, 1936, p. 1.

3. "Entertainment Review," *Indianapolis Times,* January 30, 1926, p. 6.

4. Boniface Hardin, "The Gold and Glory Sweepstakes," *The Afro-American Journal* 3, no. 3 (May–June 1975), p. 4.

5. Richard Hough and Michael Frostick, *A History of the World's Racing Cars* (New York: Harper and Row, 1965), p. 51.

6. "Promoter Tells of Old Time Auto Race," *Indianapolis Recorder,* February 2, 1929, p. 2.

7. William F. Nolan, *Barney Oldfield: The Life and Times of America's Legendary Speed King* (New York: G. P. Putnam's Sons, 1961), p. 107.

8. Ibid., p. 109.

9. Ibid.

10. Frank A. Young, "Fay Says," *Chicago Defender,* July 5, 1924, p. 11.

11. Frank A. Young, "Colored Auto Races to Be Grand Affair," *Chicago Defender,* August 2, 1924, p. 10.

12. "Gold and Glory Drivers Await Checkered Flag," *Indianapolis Freeman,* August 2, 1924, p. 8.

13. Young, "Colored Auto Races to Be Grand Affair," p. 10.

14. Frank A. Young, "Chicago Driver in a Class by Himself," *Chicago Defender,* July 7, 1928, p. 8.

15. Dempsey J. Travis, *An Autobiography of Black Chicago* (Chicago: Urban Research Institute, 1981), p. 40.

16. Dempsey J. Travis, *An Autobiography of Black Jazz* (Chicago: Urban Research Institute, 1983), p. 30.

17. "Record Crowd to See First Derby Race at Hawthorne Race Track September 14," *Chicago Defender,* September 13, 1924, p. 11.

18. Frank A. Young, "Sidelights of the Big 100-Mile Derby," *Chicago Defender,* August 9, 1924, p. 11.

19. Ibid.

20. "Hannon Winner of Local Auto Race," *Indianapolis Freeman,* August 9, 1924, p. 8.

21. Young, "Sidelights of the Big 100-Mile Derby," p. 11.

22. Ibid.

3. 100% American

1. M. William Lutholtz, *Grand Dragon: D. C. Stephenson and the Ku Klux Klan in Indiana* (West Lafayette, Ind.: Purdue University Press, 1991), p. 18.

2. Ibid., p. 20.

3. Ibid., p. 41.

4. "Chicago to Have 100-Mile Auto Derby at Hawthorne," *Chicago Defender,* August 9, 1924, p. 11.

5. "Entries Received for 100-Mile Chicago Auto Derby," *Chicago Defender,* August 16, 1924, p. 12.

6. Ibid.

7. Frank A. Young, "Change 100-Mile Derby to 100 Miles of Auto Racing," *Chicago Defender,* August 30, 1924, p. 10.

8. Ibid.

9. "Record Crowd to See First Derby Race at Hawthorne Race Track September 14," *Chicago Defender,* September 13, 1924, p. 11.

10. "William Carson Wins National Negro Auto Race," *Chicago Defender,* September 20, 1924, p. 11.

11. Frank A. Young, "2 Killed in Chicago Auto Race," *Chicago Defender,* September 20, 1924, p. 1.

12. "Bury Heroic Cab Driver with Honors," *Chicago Defender,* September 20, 1924, part 2, p. 6.

13. Lutholtz, *Grand Dragon,* pp. 85–86.

14. Ibid., p. 80.

15. Emma Lou Thornbrough, "Segregation in Indiana during the Klan Era of the 1920s," *Mississippi Valley Historical Review* 47, no. 4 (1961), pp. 610–611.

16. Ibid., p. 598.

17. Ibid., p. 599.

18. Ibid., p. 597.

19. Elwood Knox and Freeman B. Ransom, "Some Primary Election Revelations and Discoveries," *Indianapolis Freeman,* May 17, 1924, p. 1.

20. Ibid.

21. Ibid.

22. Lutholtz, *Grand Dragon,* p. xi.

23. "K. K. Nightriders Threaten Man, Burn Fiery Cross," *Cleveland Call-Post,* January 21, 1924, p. 1.

24. "Klansmen Burn Girl," *Chicago Defender,* August 14, 1926, p. 1.

4. The Negro Speed King

1. Frank A. Young, "All-Colored Race Attracts Large Crowd," *Chicago Defender,* August 8, 1925, p. 10.

2. "Wallace First in All-Colored Race," *Indianapolis Recorder,* August 9, 1925, p. 8.

3. "Auto Pilots Await Starter's Bomb," *Chicago Defender,* August 7, 1926, p. 8.

4. Frank A. Young, "Wiggins Wins 100-Mile Auto Race," *Chicago Defender,* August 14, 1926, p. 6.

5. "Chas. Wiggins Wins Gold and Glory Race, Carter Runs Second," *Indianapolis Recorder,* August 14, 1926, p. 6.

6. Frank A. Young, "Fay Says," *Chicago Defender,* August 14, 1926, p. 6.

7. "Gold and Glory Auto Race," *Pittsburgh Courier,* August 21, 1926, p. 8.

8. Frank A. Young, "Wiggins Wins: Pilots Own Make of Car to Win Third Annual Gold and Glory Auto Sweepstakes," *Chicago Defender*, August 14, 1926, sec. 2, p. 4.

9. "Wiggins Cops Detroit Race Title," *Chicago Whip,* September 11, 1926, p. 6.

10. Sol Butler, "Wiggins Speed Demon on Dirt Track," *Chicago Bee,* October 8, 1927, p. 10.

11. Emma Lou Thornbrough, "Segregation in Indiana during the Klan Era of the 1920s," *Mississippi Valley Historical Review* 47, no. 4 (1961), p. 611.

12. Richard B. Pierce II, "Beneath the Surface: African-American Community Life in Indianapolis, 1954–1970" (Ph.D. dissertation, Department of History, Indiana University, 1996), p. 26.

5. Charlie's Gang

1. Terry Reed, "Joie Ray," *Open Wheel* 16, no. 7 (July 1996), p. 27.

2. Boniface Hardin, "The Gold and Glory Sweepstakes," *The Afro-American Journal* 3, no. 3 (May–June 1975), p. 4.

3. Ibid., p. 5.

4. Ibid., p. 4.

5. Mark L. Dees, *The Miller Dynasty: A Technical History of the Work of Harry A. Miller, His Associates, and His Successors* (Moorpark, Calif.: The Hippodrome Publishing Company, 1994), pp. 218–219.

6. Art Petacque, "No Corrupt Union Boss Can Top 'Umbrella Mike,'" *Chicago Sun-Times*, April 30, 1990, p. 52.

7. Ibid.

8. "Mike Boyle Long a Storm Center in City's Unions," *Chicago Tribune*, January 23, 1937, p. 2.

9. Ibid.

10. "Klan Makes Last Stand in Politics," *Indianapolis Recorder*, October 14, 1926, p. 1.

6. "A Darn Good Move on Us"

1. "Wiggins Enters 100-Mile Auto Race at Indianapolis," *Chicago Defender*, June 21, 1930, p. 10.

2. "Over Twenty Cars Have Entered Century Auto Grind; New Records Expected Here," *Indianapolis Recorder*, June 29, 1929, p. 6.

3. "Wiggins Enters 100-Mile Auto Race," p. 10.

4. Frank A. Young, "Jeffries, Gaines, Carson, and Buckner in 100-Mile Auto Derby on July 4," *Chicago Defender*, June 29, 1929, p. 10.

5. "$2,500 Prize Spurs Drivers for Record," *Indianapolis Recorder*, July 4, 1929, p. 6.

6. Advertisement, *Indianapolis Recorder*, July 4, 1929, p. 5.

7. "Anderson Cops Negro Speed Title," *Indianapolis News*, July 5, 1929, p. 8.

8. "Thousands Cheer As Winner Gets Race Victory," *Indianapolis Recorder*, July 13, 1929, p. 6.

9. Ibid.

10. "Barney Anderson First in 100-Mile Indianapolis Derby; Wiggins, Carson Finish 2nd, 3rd," *Chicago Defender*, July 13, 1929, p. 10.

11. "Grice Speed Victim," *Indianapolis Recorder*, July 13, 1929, p. 1.

12. Frank A. Young, "Sidelights of the Big 100-Mile Derby," *Chicago Defender*, August 9, 1924, p. 10.

13. Boniface Hardin, "The Gold and Glory Sweepstakes," *The Afro-American Journal* 3, no. 3 (May–June 1975), p. 4.

14. "Auto Races Change with the Years," *Indianapolis Recorder*, May 26, 1928, p. 6.

15. Advertisement, *Indianapolis Recorder*, June 21, 1930, p. 10.

16. "Wiggins in Walnut Gardens Auto Race," *Indianapolis Recorder*, July 19, 1930, p. 12.

17. Quoted from "Marion," a televised documentary segment featured on *Across Indiana*, WFYI-TV, Indianapolis, Ind., November 1998, written and produced by Todd Gould.

18. "Indiana Mob Lynches Two Boys While Police Look On," *Chicago Defender*, August 9, 1930, p. 1.

19. Eugene N. Burdette, "Poor Indiana," *Chicago Defender*, August 16, 1930, p. 9.

20. "Marion," WFYI-TV, November 1998.

21. Burdette, "Poor Indiana," p. 9.

22. Emma Lou Thornbrough, *Indiana Blacks in the Twentieth Century* (Bloomington: Indiana University Press, 2000), p. 76.

23. Ibid., p. 78.

24. Ibid., p. 80.

25. Articles of Incorporation, Colored Race Drivers Club, January 12, 1928, State of Indiana.

7. A Bad Premonition

1. "Wiggins, Wallace among Pilots to Race at State Fair Grounds as Part of Gala Celebration," *Indianapolis Recorder,* June 29, 1935, p. 2.

2. "Drivers, Fans Eagerly Await Thrilling Race," *Indianapolis Recorder,* September 19, 1936, p. 1.

3. "Two Bands to Play Gold and Glory Dance," *Indianapolis Recorder,* September 19, 1936, p. 13.

4. Lee A. Johnson, "Shooting the Works," *Indianapolis Recorder,* August 29, 1936, p. 6.

5. "Gold and Glory Sweepstakes," *Chicago Defender,* September 26, 1936, p. 11.

6. "Race Pilots to Take Speed Test for Posts in Gold and Glory Sweepstakes," *Indianapolis Recorder,* September 19, 1936, p. 16.

7. "Local Pilot Will Drive Fast Mount during Gold and Glory Races," *Indianapolis Recorder,* September 12, 1936, p. 12.

8. "Highlights of the Big Race," *Indianapolis Recorder,* September 26, 1936, p. 11.

9. Fritz Frommeyer, "The Gold and Glory Sweepstakes," *Racing Cars,* spring 1980 (Speedway, Ind.: Carl Hungness Publishing), p. 41.

Epilogue

1. Reginald Bishop, "Black Mechanic Recalls Racing," *Indianapolis News,* March 21, 1975, p. 18.

2. Boniface Hardin, "The Gold and Glory Sweepstakes," *The Afro-American Journal* 3, no. 3 (May–June 1975), pp. 1, 3–4, 10–11.

3. Frank A. Young, "Fay Says," *Chicago Defender,* July 31, 1926, p. 10.

Index

Todd Gould is a ten-time Emmy Award–winning writer and television producer living in Indianapolis. His works have been featured on PBS, the Learning Channel, and the BBC. Todd has been honored by many organizations, including the National Academy of Television Arts and Sciences, the Corporation for Public Broadcasting, the National Black Programming Consortium, the American Legion, and the Indiana Film Society.

BOOK AND JACKET DESIGNER   Sharon L. Sklar

COPYEDITOR   Shoshanna Green

COMPOSITOR   Tony Brewer

TYPEFACES   Blackoak & Adobe Caslon

BOOK AND JACKET PRINTER   Friesens